Off-Shoring the Middle Class

Managing white-collar job migration to Asia

By Steve Mushero

"Off-Shoring the Middle Class: Managing White-Collar Job Migration to Asia," by Steve Mushero. ISBN 1-58939-913-7.

Published 2006 by Virtualbookworm.com Publishing Inc., P.O. Box 9949, College Station, TX 77842, US.

Manufactured in the United States of America.

Acknowledgements

Writing this book has been an interesting experience over the last three years, starting with a conversation with Sharon Barrington in a Palo Alto Starbucks in the summer of 2003. We met to discuss her book and after a while I mentioned I also wanted to write a book on global economics, but was unsure of the precise topic. As I talked passionately about the effects of globalization on the white-collar workforce, she asked the simple question, "Why don't you write about that?" The end result is in your hands now and I am very grateful for her initial direction.

Books are of course never the fruits of just one person's labor and many have helped get this one from my head to your hands. Thanks first to Noam Cohen and Tess Hand-Bender for helping me get the basic ideas on paper, which for them entailed sitting through hours and hours of discussions of all the major points.

Thanks especially to my personal reviewers, especially my good friends Derinda Gaumond, Dan Trimble, Julie Kuznetsov, and Julie Hersum. Other very helpful reviewers included Paul Cohen and Peter Young. Sara Agee was very helpful in hunting down and formatting the endnotes.

Thanks to my copy editor Chris Holland and the folks at Virtual Book Worm.

Thank you also all my friends for their support during this process.

And finally thanks to my wonderful parents, to whom this book is dedicated.

Table of Contents

Chapter 1.

Introduction

"The world has arrived at a rare strategic inflection point where nearly half its population -- living in China, India, Russia -- have been integrated into the global market economy, many of them highly educated workers, who can do just about any job in the world. We're talking about three billion people. The U.S. has a very simple choice to make. We have to decide if we're going to be competitive with these markets."

Craig Barrett, CEO of Intel[1]

The dawn of the 21st century finds America where it was at the dawn of the 20th, with globalization driving jobs, economics, politics, and potentially even war. The international exchange of money, goods, services, jobs, and people will be one of the most important social forces in the twenty-first century. Just as the world's economic engine crossed the Atlantic Ocean early in the 20th century, it may well cross the Pacific early in the 21st.

Globalization and the recent addition of three billion new global workers is already causing under-appreciated shifts in the economies of America and the West, as a wide range of jobs and markets migrate towards developing countries. So strong is this shift, that an entirely new word has been born, "off-shoring," to describe the movement of jobs overseas. And, as more and more white-collar jobs move to China, India, and beyond, insecurity, apprehension, and protectionism are being left behind in their wake.

Yet, trade has always been critical to the American economy's success, and never far from politicians' minds, even in the early days of industrialization. For example, early 20th century Americans experienced a variety of ups and downs in international trade, ranging from various tariffs and protectionist acts to President Wilson's Fourteen Points for World Peace. Delivered in 1918, those points focused on "The removal, so far as possible, of all economic barriers and the establishment of an equality of trade conditions among all the nations consenting to the peace and associating themselves for its maintenance."[2] Little did he appreciate that nearly a hundred years later, such open trade would allow almost any job to be done almost anywhere.

Of course trade has never been without challenges, displacement, winners and losers, and angst about the future. Just as with technological progress, there are many who would like things to remain the same, but history has shown that they never do; time, progress, and globalization always march on.

Trade-driven changes have been evident all through history, in the British Empire's trade with its colonies, the globalization of agriculture, and the textile migrations of the 20th century. The U.S. itself has been through similar displacement processes, including the Rust Belt's blue-collar employees suddenly competing with Japan and the Asian Tigers (Hong Kong , South Korea, Singapore, and Taiwan) in the 1980s .

While it's easy to dismiss today's white-collar job shift as an evolution of the same job migration, in reality it impacts a much larger section of American and European populations, as job movements start to encompass middle-class white collar workers. Programmers, engineers, scientists, lawyers, doctors, architects... the list of jobs beginning to move overseas goes on and on.

As a result, just when Mr. and Ms. Middle Class have finished school, gotten good jobs, bought their house, and had their kids, they find their jobs exported to China. Unsurprisingly, they are not excited about this outcome. And when the middle class becomes disillusioned and angry, they inevitably stir up their politicians, generating ill-advised and often protectionist legislation or tariffs that may even exacerbate the problem. Without well-thought-out action on many fronts, the Western world may face millions of disenchanted citizens and the potential for serious political upheaval.

Seeds of these challenges can already be seen in Europe, with frequent demonstrations, targeted work stoppages, and other evidence of unhappiness about the erosion in job opportunities, the loss of social safety nets, and jobs moving abroad. It's possible that the EU's economic engines will continue their decline as their jobs flow steadily eastward, to the old Eastern Block, and all the way to the Far East. As such, the European situation may be a harbinger of where America may find itself in only a few years, with 10-20% unemployment and no real growth in sight.

As a result, the 21st century path to prosperity is no longer as obvious nor as straight as it once was, as global labor competition becomes a reality at all levels. Given that everyone now needs to compete with everyone else all the time, it is time for governments, companies, and individuals to finally come to grips with how to compete at every level of the economy, from clerical workers to rocket scientists.

While heavily criticized from many vantage points (from the Left and far Right), off-shoring is potentially valuable, even lucrative for the West. Like all economic restructuring processes before it, this one will be tumultuous, but it could lead to higher productivity, improved standards of living, and increased economic output.

Just as shifts from agriculture to mass production or from horses to rail to automobiles drove economic and middle-class expansion in past centuries, today's shift will also bring about unforeseen changes and interesting opportunities. These will require significant changes at every level – within and among governments, corporations, and most importantly, individuals. And despite this phenomenon's similarity to prior job shifts, the stakes are now much higher, requiring a delicate coordination of government policies, corporate activities, and individual preparation to allow everyone to succeed.

Governments (and politicians) must accept the notion that the world is indeed flat, that competition is everywhere, and one of government's most important roles is to prepare individuals to compete. Further, governments and corporations must ensure they are structured for economic success, including facilitating a level playing field for everyone.

In particular, individuals must come to grips with being globally competitive across numerous disciplines; they must rapidly transition between numerous jobs and careers in their lifetimes. Continuous innovation, learning, and preparation on a global scale are rapidly becoming a pre-requisite for success in the 21st century. America and the West must prepare for significant changes as nearly every job, every citizen, and every company, no matter how talented, is forced to compete globally, every day.

Globalization affects every person on Earth, causing economic restructuring at the bottom, middle, and top of all the world's economies. There is a lot of heated pro vs. con discussion, but it is beside the point, as the world is integrating at a breathtaking pace. The real challenges are how to leverage the opportunities, manage the downsides, and help protect the displaced while ensuring maximum benefit for everyone.

Fortunately, even in this uncertain world, dynamic Western economies and their remarkable entrepreneurs should not be underestimated. Large and sophisticated markets, relatively mobile workforces (in the U.S.), and a strong knowledge base, coupled to massive capital and innovation-driven markets allow multi-trillion-dollar economies to rapidly adapt in unexpected ways. A few stumbles in the Far East and some well-managed transitions in the West, and the global economy of 2020 could look much like the one of 1995, with America and its developed siblings dominating the global economic stage while the new economies stumble, their gains eroded. Or not.

This book is about the off-shoring white-collar service jobs, taking an in-depth look at all its aspects, including the current situation and an analysis of potential solutions. It will then critically examine various options, from doing nothing and letting nature run its course, to various protectionist options, and finally to an aggressively managed job transition.

While this analysis is bottom-up in focus, examining the situation from several job and economic classifications, it also looks at the broader impact and public policy changes required to succeed in the coming century. This is not a book about how to save a hundred computer jobs here or there, but about managing the transition of 25 million workers in every part of the economy.

These analyses and recommendations are written for both employees and their government's policy makers, though each group operates at opposite ends of the economic continuum. Employees are at the bottom and every single job loss affects a real, live person and his or her family. For them, this is an acute issue that takes a very personal dimension. As such, individuals rarely have the luxury to consider the big picture, evolving economies, and their place in the complex and dynamic economic engine called the economy.

On the other hand, policy makers and corporate managers work in aggregate, thinking macro-economically about thousands or millions of jobs, about economies domestic and global, and (ideally) about the coming decades of competition and innovation. Unfortunately, these very high-level views often cause people to lose sight of those actually doing the work, inventing the technology, and running the companies that drive the economy.

This book seeks to bring these two often-opposing groups together, with argument, discussion, and a policy framework that is sensitive to individual needs while ensuring the continued march forward in innovation, trade, and growth that benefits everyone.

While many globalization books focus on specific jobs, such as computer programming or call centers, or geographic areas such as Mexico and NAFTA, the discussion here is broader. Many books justify or vilify globalization by describing its relative merits and challenges, typically providing little insight into managing it effectively. By contrast, this book subscribes to the world view that

Globalization is here to stay and accelerating, therefore it has to be managed in a manner most advantageous to all involved.

Early chapters will argue that off-shoring is not only unstoppable, but also underestimated as a mostly positive force in today's world, altering the underlying dynamics of every economy. White-collar off-shoring will be emphasized as a trend that sweeps far wider and deeper than most people are generally aware. Recently confined to computer and clerical jobs, the phenomenon is rapidly expanding to engineering, medical, legal, and many other careers once considered safe from globalization.

Serious discussion will also be given to the possible reactions by the ex-workers and their politicians, especially as the real challenges become apparent to all. Protectionism and nationalistic reactions will be outlined, especially the dangers of the latter, which largely drove the world to war in the last century and could again lead to isolation, feuding, and depression.

The second half of the book looks specifically at policy choices and recommendations for various players on the global stage. Modern economies are dynamic interplays of labor, capital, and trade at many levels, and from many directions. As such, it is not surprising that most viable solutions involve numerous players, each working to improve their piece of a very large and dynamic pie.

While this book focuses largely on the American situation and contains recommendations based on the American experience, virtually everything contained within applies equally well to Europe and Japan. In fact, America is probably the best positioned to take advantage of the opportunities created by 21st century globalization and trade effects, while the rest of the G-7 may be more in need of these recommendations, given their lag in productivity and innovation in the face of the relentless onslaught of less expensive talent from Eastern Europe and the Far East.

Finally, in the old days (i.e. 10 years ago) there was relative harmony in the world of trade. Roughly speaking, there was a skills-and-jobs pyramid, with the third world at the bottom performing agriculture and natural resource activities, second-world countries in the middle with inexpensive manufacturing, and first-world nations doing the high-end design, engineering, research, and medical work.

Today, the global skills–and-jobs pyramid is fattening at each level with numerous countries moving up the value chain. The question is where are those at the top supposed to go as they get squeezed into the little tip of the pyramid—where exactly do the nearly 1 billion citizens of the developed countries go from here? That is the question this book attempts to answer.

Chapter 2.

21st Century Situation

"There is no job that is America's God-given right anymore. We have to compete for jobs."

Carly Fiorina, Hewlett-Packard CEO[3]

The dawn of the 21st century finds modern economies at an historic crossroads. Western powers have assisted the developing world for decades, trying to improve their economies, free their people, and economically plug them into the world. This effort has been wildly successful, with the Asian Tigers as well as the rapidly developing countries of India, China, and Eastern Europe. In fact, since WWII, 127 countries have moved to or towards democratic government, paving the way for additional economic integration all across the world.[4]

At the same time, numerous forces have converged to make the world smaller. This is especially true of the Internet, but also includes global air travel, shipping, and far-flung commerce networks. As a result, today's business world is characterized by instantaneous global communications combined with rapid travel and shipping, resulting in the world being truly a small place.

Coupling the economic and educational progress of the developing world with technological advances, the day is rapidly arriving when nearly any job can be done nearly anywhere. As a result, significant portions of every economy will be exposed to global competition, at the country, company, and especially individual levels.

Mix that with a substantial shift from manufactured goods to services and knowledge work, and the developed Western world now finds that nearly all of its jobs can be moved nearly anywhere. Unlike the old days, employees need no longer be located where they actually deliver a service. While location flexibility may be old hat to catalog companies and call centers, many other services can now be located in far more places, and usually far away.

These factors and their underlying savings are driving a major job shift from developed to developing countries. While such shifts are nothing new in manufacturing, this white-collar version is startling in its breadth and speed, so much so that it's a hot topic of discussion among employers, employees, politicians, and the media.

Thus, today's white-collar workforce is increasingly seeing its jobs, careers, and future drain away to a foreign land. Needless to say, this is causing considerable apprehension, especially among the first waves of positions to go, in call centers and information technology (IT).

To get a handle on the magnitude of the challenges that lie ahead, Cynthia Kroll, an economist at the University of California, Berkeley estimated that over 10% of the workforce, or as many as 14 million U.S. jobs, are at risk of being sent offshore over the next few years.[5] While 10% may not sound significant, these are all white-collar positions. Further, given that each good job helps support other businesses and often a family, the rather sudden loss of such a large portion of the economy could be quite painful indeed.

On the political side, U.S. Senator Charles Schumer and Paul Craig Roberts said in a recent New York Times op-ed piece, "We are concerned that the United States may be entering a new economic era in which American workers will face direct global competition at almost every job level."[6] The reality is that this era is already here.

All of this uncertainty translates into understandable anxiety among workers. According to a new Gallup Poll, 58% of Americans say that outsourcing will be "very important" when they decide their votes for president, and 61% are concerned that they, a friend or a relative might lose a job because their employer is moving work to a foreign country.[7]

Future of Western Work

For decades, the U.S. economy has been shifting from agricultural activities to manufacturing to services, not only keeping people employed, but also continuously moving them up the value chain, doing more difficult and thus more valuable work. This process included farm girls going to Lowell, MA factories nearly 200 years ago, though worker migration really began in earnest in Henry Ford's era of mass production nearly 100 years ago. Manufacturing was the dominant force in America from WWII until the Japanese and Asian Tigers arrived late in the 1970s.

When manufacturing jobs started declining in the 1980s, factory workers moved on to the service industries, where the lower-end white-collar folks already were doing clerical, customer service, repair, and other work. These jobs were seen as far more secure; after all, no one imagined how a service job like answering the telephone or designing a bridge could be exported.

Those are precisely the jobs now being sent abroad, but with the transition from agriculture to manufacturing to services essentially complete, it is difficult to see where the affected workforce can go next. To a large extent, there is no next rung in that upward mobility ladder, forcing everyone on the ladder to re-examine their current rung, their career, their ambitions, and where their climb is leading.

The famous business strategist Tom Peters argues that the off-shoring of service jobs poses a challenge ten times greater than that of moving manufacturing jobs abroad. Further, he says, "Americans' 'unearned wage advantage' (being born in the U.S.A.) could be erased ... permanently. WE WILL NEVER AGAIN BE AS DOMINANT AS WE ARE TODAY."[8]

Needless to say, for America to lose its dominance in any area is very troubling to politicians and to a populace that appears to believe dominating the world is its birthright. This loss of dominance alone is enough to cause heartache among all involved, as realistically globalization will significantly level the playing field among free nations over time, just as it did with Europe, America, and Japan in prior centuries.

Some would argue this global job trend breaks the general "educational and social contract" that drives every modern society. For instance, most Americans expect that getting a good education, working hard, and gaining good experience will lead to success. Even if overnight success can't be expected, a stable, bill-paying job has always seemed reasonable; however, this may no longer be true if substantial portions of professional work move abroad. A recent World Affairs panel asked what could be the major question of the day, "If advanced degrees, years of experience, and a good job history can't assure a job, then what have we done?"[9]

Education, experience, and hard work have always driven success, but breaking this chain does not bode well for any society or economy. For instance, blue-collar or the uneducated presumably understand the limits of their upward mobility, given that their backgrounds don't often allow them to have high aspirations or expectations. To a large extent, they take what they get, though unions are often able to secure artificially good wages and other benefits they would be unable to get on their own.

The professional or educated classes presumably have precisely the opposite perspective. Middle and upper-class citizens go to school, get good jobs, and presumably believe they are entitled to a larger slice of the pie, as are their children, and their children's children. As Alan Tonelson, author and research fellow at the U.S. Business & Industrial Council Educational Foundation, a Washington research organization, explains, "In the 1990s, we were all promised, 'If you would only retool yourself as a software engineer you'd be fine.' Now, lo and behold, those jobs are going, too. As they go, the remaining non-superstar tech jobs will become lower and lower paid as the threat of off-shoring cows workers."[10]

Now large numbers of these people, with their good educations and comfortable life-styles, risk ending up unemployed. Imagine these people's surprise to be out of work, having lost their job to a young Chinese girl earning 25% of their salary. Suddenly they are told that their education and their long service in seemingly stable industries are no longer useful. As a consolation, they are often told to retrain for new industries, but ones that may or may not still exist by the time they are prepared. Unsurprisingly, they are typically not pleased with this turn of events.

In addition, talented high school and college students no longer know what direction their lives should take. Majoring in English or the arts in college may no longer be sufficient, and even those that take seemingly more practical paths like engineering or medicine can't be sure they'll find a stable job in today's market. The traditional high-end job market certainly looks challenging to today's college graduate, since entry-level jobs are difficult to find and those that remain could be swallowed up any day; no one can be sure what career path is safe to take.

And, as one Wall Street Journal writer asked, "Much of the American anxiety about outsourcing to India and China can be boiled down to this simple question: Will there be good jobs left for our kids?"[11]

Hollow Jobless Recovery

The American economy has always traded and shed jobs as various industries and trading patterns have evolved over the decades. The current fundamental concern is that insufficient new jobs are being created to make up for the losses. In addition, even though employment numbers in 2004 improved, the crucial challenge is the mix of jobs created, as positions in burger flipping are hardly helpful to ex-computer programmers. And in an interesting twist, even fast-food jobs are being sent abroad, so the person taking the drive-through order and sending it to the kitchen might actually be in China.[12]

In particular, Bureau of Labor Statistics(BLS) data show a split both in the new jobs created and in income growth. Numerous jobs are being created at the bottom, though they are mostly taken by relatively poor immigrants.[13] In addition, there is good income growth at the top, but job and income improvement in the middle is nearly non-existent-- some would cite this as direct evidence of hollowing out of the middle class, an effect that will only get worse, though it may be temporarily masked by the growing economy. As one pundit put it, "We've lost track of the 35- to 40-year-old white-collar person who needs to broaden his or her skill set. They've become the forgotten middle, and they need some help."[14]

Regardless of its effects, this job shift is unmistakably underway, as companies close domestic call and IT development-centers while hiring new staff or contracting out to shops in India or China. Forrester Research projects the transfer of 3.4 million American jobs and $151 billion in payroll in the next ten years, in jobs such as office work, IT, architecture, legal, and the life sciences.[15] And while it is important to keep this in perspective in relation to the millions of jobs created and lost each year, the middle class is already getting squeezed by this phenomenon.

Looking at some of the job losses and subsequent re-employment illustrates this middle-class wage erosion. Bureau of Labor Statistics data indicate that 5.3 million workers were laid off in 2001-2003 from jobs they had held for at least 3 years. One- third of these were in managerial, professional, or related jobs and presumably all were middle class. Roughly 57% of the long-tenured workers (including manufacturing) who found new jobs ended up with lower earnings. About 30% of these lost at least 20% of their prior income. In addition, those working in service sector jobs had the lowest reemployment rates.[16]

Further, there has been a recent rise in middle-class bankruptcies, a situation that presumably cannot improve if there is wage erosion and fewer available high-paying positions. The Wall Street Journal reports that "(In 2003), there were more than 1.6 million filings, compared with 875,000 a decade earlier. Some experts say much of the increase is being driven by older people, many of whom have decades of work experience in white-collar jobs. The so-called sandwich generation often bears financial responsibility for both their children and their parents."[17] Being financially squeezed by children, parents, health care, reduced pensions, and now eroding wages certainly does not bode well for the economic future of many Americans.

One can imagine the fear and concern among typical middle-class workers, say a 45-year-old accounting manager making $60,000 per year with a large firm in Kansas. His job may well go to a 25-year-old Chinese accountant in Qingdao, a place he's never heard of and cannot even pronounce.

Others worry directly about how losing jobs abroad is affecting middle-class workers today: "Sending many of the country's best paying and highest skilled jobs overseas is a dire economic threat to employees and their families," says former IBM employee Lee Conrad. "It jeopardizes the financial well-being of middle-class professionals."[18]

Further, an Economic Policy Institute review of unemployment statistics found that, starting in 2002, the number of unemployed college graduates exceeded that of high school dropouts for the first time.[19] While there are three times as many college graduates as high-school dropouts, this does illustrate the bifurcating process, creating jobs at only the low and high ends of the spectrum, leaving regular graduates in the troubled middle.

In addition, and for the first time, the so-called boomerang effect is quite noticeable, where college graduates return to live at home after graduating. The U.S. Census Bureau estimates that 40 % of young adults are returning to live with their parents after leaving home. This figure is up from the 20% 50 years ago. In fact, nearly one-third of men aged 18-34 were living with their parents in 2004.[20]

A final and longer-term challenge is that once this cycle begins in earnest, people will not only lose the jobs they already had, but they will lose any potential for growth as well. Many college graduates face the old paradox - you need experience to get a job but you need a job to get experience - but this will only become a harsher reality as the entry-level jobs migrate away, leaving no stepping-stone jobs for the inexperienced. So, even if truly high-level jobs stay in the U.S., it's possible no one will be qualified to do them once current professionals retire (already a serious problem at technical institutions like Boeing and NASA).

Hollowing Out

Beyond the fundamental issues of losing one's job or what course of study to pursue are the serious macroeconomic effects of widespread job loss. The obvious question is, "If everyone works only at Wal-Mart, who can afford to purchase the things sold there, let alone higher-end products from Macy's or Harley-Davidson?"

Given that economies are highly internally interdependent, draining away major wage sources can have a rather unpleasant trickle-down effect. In addition, given the market's reliance on group psychology effects, even the threat of such a drain or job uncertainty can have substantial macroeconomic effects, especially dampened growth brought about by falling consumer confidence.

For instance, Detroit and other rust-belt regions in the U.S. or Eastern Europe clearly illustrate the dismal effects of job loss. Unfortunately, it's not clear that the magnitude of these challenges is well understood. Thea Lee, assistant director of the AFL-CIO's international economics department, says U.S. policy makers don't understand the economic implications of this trend yet. "The logical extension is that you will see massive erosion of living standards of a big chunk of the U.S. middle class," Lee says.[21]

Boom in Asia

At the same time, these are boom times in large portions of Asia, particularly in India and China. These economies are large and growing by 8% and 9.5%, respectively, in large part due to business from, and exports to, the Western world.[22] India has so far dominated the off-shoring business, especially in IT, while China has become the world's manufacturing center for everything from toys to advanced computer chips.

Wandering around India's boom cities, one can find numerous gleaming office parks, often with thousands of employees each and relatively indistinguishable from Silicon Valley. In China, where the economy is booming from Beijing to Guangzhou, Shanghai is especially blossoming as it undergoes a construction boom to rapidly reclaim its nearly century-old reputation as the New York of Asia.

Indeed, most white-collar workers employed by foreign companies in Asia work in environments similar to those found in the West, as the Indian or Chinese offices of companies like Intel, Dell, or Microsoft are usually indistinguishable from their American counterparts. For instance, their Shanghai workers live in modern housing or high-rises, just as their peers do in Silicon Valley, Seattle, or Frankfurt. Realistically, these foreign facilities, especially in India, are often little American bubbles of time, culture, food, TV, and even American accents (needed for call-center work).

Asian countries have been undergoing Westernization for decades, but these off-shore facilities are often hotspots of American culture, where foreigners eat American food, dress like Americans, and consume American media (the only thing on at 3am), especially in India. Call centers in Manila report their employees even dying their hair lighter and wearing baggy clothing in order to advertise their status as American employees.[23] In essence, their daily work routine is little different than workers in the U.S., as they go to the office at 9am, American time, work all day with American computers in cubicles, interact with Americans or their paperwork, and go home at 5pm, American time.

And while historically China and India have focused on commodity manufacturing, back office processing, and IT outsourcing, these countries are rapidly moving up the value chain. India is rapidly expanding its high-end technology universities, (especially the Indian Institute of Technology, often called the MIT of India), its medical and biotech research facilities, and its global consulting and services businesses. At the same time, China is moving to higher-end manufacturing such as electronics and chips, building university-based biotech research centers, and expanding its educational and technology-oriented activities.

Media Portrayal

Foreign competition and the perceived job shifts have translated into a stream of gloomy headlines in the American press, each griping about the numbers of jobs being lost overseas, the hollowing out of America, and the potential need for government action. The numbers being presented are certainly impressive, with thousands of jobs at a time going here, there, and everywhere. Many of these articles also express the general unrest caused by white-collar jobs moving overseas. In 2004, most articles focused on IT and call center jobs predominately shifting to India (while manufacturing employment moved to China).

Wired, Businessweek, the Wall Street Journal, CNET, the New York Times, and many other publications have featured cover stories or prominent articles on off-shoring and its challenges. As noted, most pieces focus on Indian IT, though they are starting to examine the larger picture in engineering, architecture, some areas of medical and legal work, and even research and development.

Given such stories and projections, IT workers are understandably unhappy about such prospects, and some have found convenient outlets via the media and of course the Internet. Others have even formed anti-off-shoring groups to help fight for what they perceive as their rights as Americans to keep good jobs. These include groups with nationalistic names such as “Hire American Citizens” and “American Labor First.”

Unfortunately, rarely do the media focus on the benefits of these changes, either to the developing countries involved or the U.S. economy in general; it’s a fairly one-sided gloomy view. There seem to be few publicized off-shoring success stories or profiles of jobs saved by off-shoring. Just as there are no stories of planes landing safely or the electricity staying on all day, success in off-shoring results in good services delivered at competitive prices and is therefore not newsworthy. Columnists such as the New York Times' Thomas Friedman have done positive reporting in this area, in his case touring Indian service campuses and illuminating the benefits to both sides, but most media are unsurprisingly doom-oriented.

Further, politicians and ratings-seekers, such as Senator John Kerry and Lou Dobbs, work hard to make headlines with phrases such as "Benedict Arnold Companies," while other anti-globalization and anti-off-shoring books continue to be published.

Public Perception

People have reacted to politics and media portrayal of off-shoring with fear and worry. Workers are becoming increasingly anxious about globalization and its effect on their own futures. A recent poll by the Program on International Policy Attitudes (PIPA) reported that in 1999, 53% of people thought globalization was more positive, but only 40% perceived it as positive in 2003.[24]

It is easy to see why people have become less supportive of off-shoring, as they read more headlines about the loss of American jobs, and hear local and national politicians railing against it at every opportunity. Suggesting that globalization and the need to actually compete for jobs are beneficial is becoming a dangerous idea, especially since it is so poorly understood by those most affected, not to mention their elected decision makers. So much so that when Gregory Mankiw, one of President Bush's economic advisors, mentioned that off-shoring was natural and useful, the resulting deafening criticism forced him to recant his statements.

In any event, for people employed in the industries making the headlines, the fear is tangible and at their door, sometimes even in their cubicles, where they are often forced to train their foreign replacements. The Wall Street Journal quoted a programmer referring to off-shoring as an "epidemic," which in essence it surely is. Slashdot.com, a popular website frequented by programmers and IT people, is filled with negative opinions of off-shoring and globalization. Given these challenges, job insecurity caused by the fear of foreign competition and global markets is perhaps the new anxiety of the early 21st century.

For instance, Forbes readers overwhelmingly chose "white-collar outsourcing" as the most significant trend of 2003,[25] and the 2003 Davos World Economic Forum of the world's brightest and most influential minds focused on this very issue. Nonetheless, most of the more well-off citizens are still able to take a "that won't happen to me" attitude. Engineers, accountants, attorneys, doctors, and others can react to reports of job losses by saying, "that's sad, too bad for IT and call-center people, but it won't happen to me."

It may not help that many people probably have an image of computer programmers as overpaid Silicon Valley kids who ride scooters to work and spend their paychecks on sushi, expensive wine, and Porsches. As a result, those in the heartland presumably don't fret too much over the loss of Silicon Valley technology jobs. Unfortunately, few people think about the thousands of IT and other jobs at risk at larger firms, in companies far away from Silicon Valley, in industries far from high technology. These jobs are outlined in the next chapters.

In addition to a rising tide of anxiety about outsourcing, the public also worries about the current U.S. economy and a slow to modest recovery. People are worried about losing their jobs to a recession or foreigners, but unfortunately they aren't necessarily worried about being personally globally competitive. They have general anxiety and are beginning to see globalization as a negative force, but often don't have a good handle on what the core problem is or what they can do about it. The numbers in the newspaper sure sound scary, but many feel all they can do is cross their fingers and keep hoping it's other people's jobs.

What's Really Going On

While the media hypes the problem and the masses fear the future, both miss the larger economic and job shift underway in the professional ranks. They also miss both the challenges and opportunities such a shift presents. Unfortunately, the headlines for once are not over-exaggerated, as the depth of the challenges to come is still under-appreciated. Things may actually be worse than they seem, especially as the currently improving economy is likely hiding longer-term negative trends such as a looming reversal in the trade surplus in services and job re-structuring in many sectors.

Numerous processes are underway, as companies and industries adjust their staffing, services, and global operational plans. For instance, several large companies are reported to be moving more jobs overseas. IBM moved 5,000 jobs to India and China in 2004, then bought the #3 off-shoring provider to help other companies move yet more positions, and is now selling its entire PC business to a Chinese company. Other firms as diverse as Citibank, Oracle, Intel, Ernst and Young, EMC, and Accenture have hired thousands of Indian workers, some of whom returned from working in the U.S., essentially exporting their own jobs back to India.

The reality is that this phenomenon is not limited to outsourcing; it isn't just IT and call center jobs that are moving, and it isn't just to India where the jobs are moving. It is actually more fundamental and will over time change the way in which all economies operate, East, West, and South (the developing countries). In the end, essentially any job that does not require direct physical contact can and perhaps will be moved, and sooner rather than later.

To put this in perspective, look at the tall office buildings in any city; many of the jobs in those buildings will probably move abroad over the next decade. Likewise, suburban office parks, especially those supporting larger organizations, may well be drained of jobs during the same period. By any measure, such losses will affect a significant portion of the workforce.

Why will these jobs move? The simple answer is because they can, and because there are strong wage and other cost saving economic incentives to do so. Those office towers in every city are filled with tens or hundreds of thousands of clerical, professional, and other jobs that will simply transition to a computer or another country, much as automation and trade displaced factory jobs in prior decades.

Generally speaking, everything a worker does uses technology located on their desk. This technology is portable, the desk is portable, and now the job is, too. If a warm body can be found that speaks English and has appropriate education and/or training, they too can sit at the same desk and have the same American job, just not in America. And to top it off, the new workers are often cheaper, better educated, and more motivated to produce better results.

At the same time, overseas markets are booming as developing countries build their middle classes and modernize their economies. They need to buy large quantities of the products and services offered by American companies, from generators to computers to engineering, legal, and consulting services.

And while it would be nice to supply all of this from American shores with American jobs, that is neither realistic nor even desirable; after all, what group of Americans can provide training in Shanghainese (one of China's many dialects) about IBM servers running Chinese accounting systems? Or, why should Microsoft add special features for the Thai language using workers in Seattle? And where is Boeing going to find Americans to service its planes in Bombay? These sorts of questions will drive IBM & Accenture to add 9,000 jobs in India by the end of 2005.[26]

Further, as Dell CEO Kevin Rollins observes, "The technical competence of many of the organizations that we use outside the U.S. is either superior or equal to what we have in the U.S. You can't be a global company, and you can't operate in a trade environment and say, 'But all of the jobs are going to stay in our country.' You can't. They won't let you in, and therefore we can't sell our goods to them."[27]

The world is not standing still, as developing countries aggressively try to move up the value chain. In the 20th century, many countries struggled to stay afloat, often on International Monetary Fund (IMF) loans and other handouts while dealing with the myriad of challenges that confront low-income countries the world over. In the 21st century, smart countries have figured out what Western countries sometimes forget, that economic development and growth drives and enables everything else. In fact, the IMF reports that developing countries now account for one-third of global trade and that "integration into the world economy has proven a powerful means for countries to promote economic growth, development, and poverty reduction."[28]

While countries are spread out all along the economic development curve, they are all investing in what they see as the future, namely education, infrastructure, market economics, technology, and efficiency. Membership in previously elite organizations such as the World Trade Organization is becoming mandatory, even though it often imposes painful rules and market liberations.

As a result, many countries are walking and even running headlong into the future, churning out hordes of educated women and men focused on all sorts of white-collar jobs. Countries and companies are building office parks, installing fiber optics, and teaching English at a furious pace. Fortunately, much of this building involves American technology and know-how, as the new office parks often use American computers and software, American air conditioning equipment, and get electricity from power plants running on American generators.

In the end, all of these countries have done exactly as the West has asked, and to some extent they are now resented for it. "For a long time now, I've felt that what we're really facing is not a clash of civilizations, but a clash of generations," argued David Rothkopf, a former Acting U.S. Under Secretary of Commerce. "You have an aging developed world, particularly Europe, that is trying to protect its jobs, and you have a young, job-seeking, job-needing emerging world, particularly the Muslim world, that will go anywhere and do anything to either seize the job opportunities or express their frustration with not having opportunities."[29]

More than IT & Call Centers

Job movements are most visible in the IT and call center industries, though these are a small part of what will be a much larger trend. Losses in IT and call centers may total only 400-500,000 jobs so far, but the next million jobs lost will affect nearly every segment of the white-collar economy.[30]

In addition, growth in some industries is masking underlying job movement, as jobs are still added in the U.S. even as more "move" abroad – for instance, if a U.S. office hires five new employees each month, that looks good, but the same company may be hiring 100 per month in India. This may not seem like a loss to off-shoring, but it certainly is as long as those 100 new Indian jobs would have previously been added domestically.

For example, many large Silicon Valley companies such as Intel still add new employees in the Bay Area, but the bulk of their new employment is overseas.[31] It's also important to keep in mind that while some of these jobs move to lower cost, others are created overseas because those markets are rapidly growing and local expertise is required to properly design and sell specific products. As such, the real impact is difficult to discern, either in IT or other areas. Regardless, reduced job creation can be a serious challenge in a U.S. economy that needs over 100,000 new jobs every month to just keep up with population growth.

IT and call centers are just the beginning, with accountants, lawyers, and engineers not far behind. And this trend is already expanding to cover scientific research and even medical work. For instance, many hospitals, such as Massachusetts General in Boston, send nighttime x-rays to India to be read in real-time, as the patient waits. Radiologists, in a highly paid and very skilled profession, can provide high-quality health care from an entirely different country.

Though such high-end job trends are in their infancy, they will only increase as other nations continue to produce more educated workers and technology continues to make the world an ever-smaller place.

Scope & Scale

In addition to the plethora of job categories moving abroad, the size of the organizations and job movements involved are rapidly expanding. Indian IT companies such as WiPRO and Infosys used to be small consulting houses, but they are now billion dollar companies, with multiple campuses of several thousand people each. In addition, global players like IBM, EDS, and Accenture are becoming involved, hiring the bulk of their new employment abroad.

As some have observed, "It used to be a niche market -- you had some Indian companies like TCS and Infosys and then some American companies like iGate and Cognizant doing this. Now it's EDS (a very large American consulting firm)."[32]

In addition, operations where the foreign employees actually work for American firms are growing. General Electric led the way with nearly 17,000 Indian employees (although this business was recently sold to take advantage of the hot market and prospects of such operations). Intel, Oracle, Microsoft, and many others are also following the path laid down over decades by global manufacturers such as Proctor & Gamble, which have continually moved their operations around the globe in search of lower production and labor costs and expanding markets.

Not Just to India Anymore

Despite the fact that nearly every headline covering the current white-collar job shift focuses on India, other countries are also displacing American workers. Constant focus on India often misses the bigger picture, especially as the off-shoring trend is not terribly country-specific. Given that smart developing countries such as the West African nation of Ghana see middle-class job growth as their key to prosperity, many lesser-known destinations are also working to become more enticing off-shoring destinations.

Over time, the process will undoubtedly evolve to mirror Nike's experience over the last three decades. As an aggressive early user of off-shore manufacturing, Nike hopped from country to country, ever in search of lower costs, moving from Taiwan and Korea to China and Vietnam.[33] Off-shoring will likely follow a similar course, as some countries exploit their natural skill or cultural advantages while others focus on staying ahead of the cost curve. Just as every country is different, every off-shoring contract and industry likewise differs.

These days, any nation with English speakers and Internet access can supply employees and services to American companies and effectively take away American jobs. At the moment, most white-collar jobs lost to off-shoring are going to Asia and to some extent Eastern Europe, but over time will branch out to other poor Asian countries, then the Middle-East, and eventually Africa. Even now Ghana is a growing player in Business Process Outsourcing (BPO), handling insurance claims and other clerical processing for American companies).

Back in Asia, where India is strong at the moment, China is laying the groundwork to transcend its current low-wage industries and move into the middle and upper levels of off-shore work. With a large and diverse economy and citizenry, China can also be home to many different industries, perhaps eventually resembling America's diverse markets.

In fact, China is the only country that has ever managed to work at all three levels of global business: at the low end with manufacturing of toys and simple items, in the middle with services such as IT and more advanced chip or equipment manufacturing, and at the high-end with biotech and other advanced research and development. China really is developing into a one-stop-shop for nearly everything every other developing or developed country does. This obviously has interesting geopolitical and economic implications; after all,

Japan was originally going to take over the economic world in the 1980s, but China has ten times the population and will eventually be a big player at every economic level.

Finally, in addition to China, India, and Ghana, jobs are headed to a myriad of other locales, from Vietnam to Moscow and other Eastern European capitals to New Zealand to Latin America and beyond.

Technology & Off-shoring Together

To further imperil job growth, technology is rapidly transforming many service industries. Just as voice mail and email have reduced the need for secretaries and telephone operators, the Internet and other back-office automation technology are supplanting various service jobs, especially at the low end.

For example, the self-check-in kiosks at airports have forever reduced the need for highly paid counter agents at airports. Further, airlines are driving all possible bookings to the Internet, further reducing their headcount; for instance, Southwest Airlines has closed one-third of its call centers as more than 50% of their customers book online.[34] And many travel agents have lost considerable business to the same forces.

While this book is focused on off-shoring instead of automation, these two forces often combine to further erode service employment. In addition, when technology such as kiosks or the Internet directly eliminate jobs, it increases worker anxiety and adds fuel to the fires of personal economic uncertainty.

There is also an interesting distinction in most people's minds between technology-driven job losses and those lost to off-shoring. Automation is eliminating scores of jobs, probably far more than off-shoring ever will. But, no one is really complaining about it, because in many people's mind, if an airport kiosk replaces ten people, that's just progress. However, if those same jobs move to India, it's treason.

On a related note, there are clearly nationalistic challenges based on where a lost job moves. It's okay if jobs move from Chicago to Charlotte, but not to Chengdu, even though the difference in real economic terms is difficult to discern. Misperceptions regarding off-shoring drive much of the fear and political hand wringing in response to off-shoring versus other types of job losses.

Additional Challenges

In the end, this is largely about competitiveness - of countries, companies, and individuals. And while America currently retains many advantages and is still the place to create companies and make a future, numerous challenges loom on the horizon. These include a workforce with limited knowledge about the rest of the world, a poor education and worker training system, a very high and ever-rising bill for health-care, a focus on the war on terror, and an increasingly anti-immigrant attitude.

These are all long-term challenges beyond the scope of this book, but their incessant drag on prosperity requires an even greater effort to succeed by managing the challenges and leveraging the opportunities presented by off-shoring.

Remaining Advantages

It's very easy to get depressed about off-shoring's challenges, to conclude there is no future, or to say that everyone will end up with a dozen McDonald's or Wal-Mart uniforms in his or her closet. While this danger is real and increasingly palatable, the reality is that America retains numerous advantages, not the least of which is a huge head start and a variety of structural advantages that if properly managed will be very helpful in the long run. The American economy is still the strongest and most productive in the world. Not only is it the world's largest, but also the most dynamic, creating millions of new businesses and jobs each year; almost as importantly, it also rapidly destroys numerous companies and jobs to free up critical resources to be deployed in the next round of creation.

The American economy is also extremely innovative, with a massive homogeneous market, an ultra-efficient economy, fast and powerful sources of capital, a decent physical and communications infrastructure, and deep reserves of historically flexible talent on many different levels. There really is some black magic deep inside such a dynamic economy and culture, and care must be taken not to derail progress with misguided nationalistic protectionism.

Further, in something called "in-sourcing," foreign corporations employ 5.4 million Americans in a variety of well-paying positions.[35] While many blue- and white-collar jobs are fleeing the shores, others are making their way over the beaches to the heartland. Thousands of foreign companies invest in America every year to have access to the market, technology, money, and workers that only America can provide. After all, the U.S. was the largest recipient of foreign direct investment (FDI) up until 2004 (when China took over the top spot).[36] Such massive investment continues to illustrate the value of the American economy to the rest of the world.

America and the West are at a crossroads here at the beginning of the 21st century. The global economy is booming and developing countries are finally climbing up the value chain and delivering real prosperity to their citizens. Unfortunately, this prosperity is neither uniformly distributed nor without problems, especially among the developed world's workforce. Nonetheless, global dynamics are re-allocating middle-class service jobs in a leveling process that inevitably leads to wealth transfer and even standard-of-living reductions.

Chapter 3.

Fundamental Forces at Work

Off-shoring is not a new phenomenon. In fact, historians such as Alvin Rabushka of the Hoover Institution have argued that America exists because the British Empire had an explicit mandate to off-shore various parts of its economy to the colonies. The British even privatized and outsourced much of its vaulted navy, in the form of privateers and paid merchant marine ships.[37] The British Empire was nothing if not a global trading empire, seeking the right materials, products, and services from the right places for centuries.

Historically, though, the range of jobs that could be sent abroad was largely limited to the industries making physical goods, agriculture, or raw materials. This limitation persisted up through the 20th century, even though ocean freight containerization and manufacturing globalization spurred enormous trade growth over the past half-century. Today, better education, open economies, and telecommunications are finally enabling significant trade in services, allowing developing countries to capture work historically performed in the developed world.

Important Cost Advantages

For many companies, saving money is undoubtedly a primary goal, as the savings are often dramatic. Though wages are rising in some portions of the off-shoring industry, the cost differentials are still enticing, as Indian off-shoring consultants still cite 40-50% cost savings; some companies, regions, and industries save even more.

Insurance companies, for example, pay Ghanaian workers in West Africa $5-$10 a day for data entry. This is obviously substantially less than an American wage, but it is five to ten times the minimum wage or average salary in Ghana, and the workers often receive health insurance, meals, and subsidized transport.

In fact, Affiliated Computer Services, a Texas-based off-shoring firm, is Ghana's largest private employer, potentially paving the way for real economic development and movement into the middle class.[38] Even though today's off-shoring focus is on Asia, as long as education and technology are available, Africa too can be home to American work.

As another example of the savings potential, General Electric employs nearly 17,000 back-office workers in India, saving an estimated $340 million in administrative and operational costs per year.[39] And Proctor & Gamble says it has saved $1 billion over the last five years by sending back-office work abroad.[40]

Global Companies

For a larger multi-national organization, the picture is more complicated. Such companies compete globally against market players who utilize a variety of labor and geographic structures. For instance, Western companies often have competitors whose entire workforce is in low-wage regions. That point alone often forces large American companies to diversify their employees across regions, to stay price competitive.

For them, there is a marked difference between off-shoring and expanding overseas. The former involves moving American jobs abroad, as General Electric has done for back-office services and Wall Street for equity research, where an

Indian job simply replaces an American one. For example, while Intel has maintained roughly 60% of its employees in the United States, it has added 1,000 software engineers during the last year in China and India. These new employees are working on projects that might have been done previously in America. As CEO Craig Barrett notes, "To be competitive, we have to move up the skill chain overseas."[41]

Overseas expansion, on the other hand, occurs as companies grow their international businesses and have to serve foreign customers. As the foreign customer or manufacturing base grows, companies generally feel they need more employees closer to both their factories and customers. After all, it makes no sense for Motorola to retain all of its employees in the U.S. when it sells the bulk of its products in Asia.

As a result of this trend, any firm with a growing Asian customer base (i.e. nearly all large firms) needs to think about having facilities in the region, if only to understand and connect with the customer.

For a specific example, China is Oracle's fastest-growing market, increasing at 50% in the last year alone.[42] As such, Oracle is investing heavily to understand and serve that market, including a new Beijing development center, and an R&D office opened last year in Shenzhen with 100 software engineers.

Other companies with large foreign markets, in industries such as electronics, find that having engineering teams or factories in the same country and time zones adds value as local language, regulations, and relationships come into play.

In this sense, even if companies had to pay foreign employees on par with their American staff, many would still move jobs overseas to be closer to their customers. After all, many foreign firms are hiring expensive employees in the U.S. for the very same reasons.

These foreign beachheads often pave the way for true off-shoring from the U.S. Once these foreign offices are in place and integrated into the company, they become a perfect base for moving the firm’s low-level work off-shore. In this sense, Oracle and Microsoft are using their Asian technology centers to leverage the less-expensive local talent for use on a global basis.

Even a seemingly American firm like Proctor and Gamble is actually a global company with over 50% of its sales coming from outside of North America. As such, they have 22 R&D centers spread across a dozen countries.[43] P&G's newest global research center is in Beijing, and though it probably focuses largely on its new Chinese markets, it will undoubtedly be tempted to move routine research work in that direction to save money. This, in turn, will really blur the lines of who does what, where, and what really comprises off-shoring.

Finally, some countries are simply better environments than America for some technologies. For example, Hewlett-Packard (HP) is opening a research center in Korea to work on the "digital home" because Korea is so far ahead of the U.S. in telecommunications infrastructure.[44] Similarly, Japan is far ahead of the rest of the world in the areas of cellular phone and gaming advances.

Leveraging Expensive American Talent

Doing work abroad not only costs less and is closer to potential markets, but has other dynamics as well. For instance, second-shift workers in Asia help improve productivity for expensive American employees. Such a multi-shift approach to leveraging valuable assets has long been common in manufacturing, maximizing utilization of very expensive equipment.

This practice is only now taking hold in service industries, where the expensive assets are costly U.S. staff and time on the calendar, so finding innovative ways to leverage expensive talent and work around the clock provides considerable advantage in some industries. In the simplest approach, the time difference allows two different shifts to work on a project, allowing for round-the-clock work without paying overtime. This is particularly helpful in software and chip design, where tight deadlines require a break-neck pace of development.

Many American software firms write code or do design work during the U.S. daytime, while their Indian counterparts review and test at night. The result is that every morning the

American team can come to work with a precise list of what they need to fix, allowing them to focus directly on what they need to do. For example, workers in 15 countries recently completed a computer system-on-a-chip design in only 70 days, far faster than normal.[45]

In addition, even if companies don't have their employees work such a specific shift cycle, foreign workers provide ample opportunity for companies to cut the busywork out of their American employees' workday. American workers are still better paid and typically more skilled than their foreign counterparts (though this balance is changing). Therefore, firms move mundane tasks off-shore as a cost-savings and productivity measure that, while losing some local low-level jobs, allows them to retain their most highly-paid staff in their most productive mode. For example, software companies often send documentation, testing, and simple programming work to India, freeing up expensive programmers to focus on the key challenges of a new system.

As a result, these hybrid approaches allow companies to be more productive, more efficient, and more competitive. This, in turn, lets them prosper, perhaps creating more and better jobs than were sent abroad in the first place.

Enabling New Business Models

Other new and interesting business models become possible by effective use of off-shoring. These often occur when it has historically been so expensive to perform certain types of work that companies ignored lost opportunities. Now, with inexpensive yet talented expertise available, tasks previously too onerous or expensive become viable and create new sources of revenue or information.

For instance, airlines and hotels rarely have the time or staff to fully review older tickets and other billing items for errors. They typically only review the most expensive invoices, potentially leaving uncollected revenue buried in small bills. But some airlines moved this time-consuming work to India, where they performed a 100% review and ended up finding millions of dollars in previously lost revenue.[46]

In another example, Wall Street financial firms generally cannot afford to manually review nearly as many companies and reports as they'd like, as labor is too expensive, especially in New York. As a result, they review only key items, but can often miss important issues. By leveraging inexpensive labor in India, 100% of the reports can be reviewed, efficiently staying on top of things in a way they could never afford to in the past. The same goes for patent searches and many types of research, where the application of high levels of inexpensive efforts can dramatically improve results. Further, while everyone benefits, these processes don't cost American jobs, as the work couldn't have been done in the U.S. anyway.

Foreign Labor Supply

A key driving force in the whole process is the rapidly increasing supply of talented and educated people in the developing world. Three billion new people are currently integrating themselves into the global workforce as a result of democracy, technology, education, and free trade; if even a few percent of them have skills on par with Americans, it means tens of millions of new workers to compete with.

As another measure of emerging new talent, while the U.S. graduates about 60,000 engineers per year, India and China together are turning out roughly 250,000.[47] Many of these are needed for their domestic infrastructure and basic industrial work, but tens of thousands are available to do American work or think up the next big innovation.

Working Harder & Smarter

Sending jobs off-shore often results in an American worker's efforts being traded for someone else's. This "someone else" is normally cheaper and often less productive, at least at the outset, though not always. In some cases, that person is better educated, more motivated, and thus can do a better job.

For instance, while call-center workers in the U.S. rarely have college degrees, most in India do.[48] As with many developing countries, there are often more educated citizens, especially women, than there are good jobs for them. This results in highly qualified employees, though it may also drive future turnover as the economy evolves.

While some would dispute the notion that foreigners work harder, part of this is the motivation of the up-and-comer and the poor worker in developing countries. America is a country of immigrants and there is certainly a stereotype of immigrants working harder than natives; likewise foreign workers tasting good work and success for the first time also tend to work very hard. The Asian Tigers and Japan have certainly borne that out, working harder and often smarter in recent decades.

While many factors are involved, from culture to economic necessity, these workers are often motivated by intense social pressures to perform, and see being employed by an American company as a valuable opportunity for personal growth and success. These jobs are often their first in a professional industry, and like all newcomers, they want to impress their bosses, do a good job, and propel their families solidly into the middle class.

Further, workers in key developing countries such as India and China are often younger, having the enthusiasm of youth while being able to take risks and invest in their future in ways that are more difficult for middle-aged or older Americans.

Plus, long-serving employees in any industry tend to become bored and complacent over time, especially when unions, civil service, or other sclerotic factors are present. It often takes young newcomers to shake things up in any work place, as shown by the effects the Japanese had on American industry in recent decades.

Relative job security has led to complacency among American service workers, especially in the low and middle-level white-collar jobs (these distinctions are outlined in a later chapter). As in the manufacturing industries, after decades of being on the top, Americans are simply less hungry than their foreign counterparts. They are less likely to work hard because traditionally they haven't had to. Such differences are evident to anyone who has spent time in Asian offices or factories, where workers are focused and work hard. As a result, the productivity differential between an eager newcomer overseas and a domestic old-timer can be quite dramatic, especially once language, cultural, and training barriers are overcome.

In addition to hard work, off-shoring operations often produce better work as some companies cite superior quality, faster turn-around time, and lower turnover. All of these translate to lower costs, but also better services and additional customer satisfaction. For example, for his report, "Went for Cost, Stayed for Quality," Stanford's Rafiq Dossani interviewed hundreds of companies sending work to India, where many companies have enjoyed unexpected benefits beyond simple cost savings.[49]

Studying the automotive industry, A.T. Kearney looked at sending engineering, IT, and finance abroad and found that 90% of the U.S. companies said quality was as good or better than when they used all U.S. workers.[50]

In some cases, being off-shore forces companies to provide superior service and quality levels just to be considered in the first place. For example, many Indian firms lead the world in software development capabilities. In that industry, high-end software engineering capabilities are measured by something called the Capability Maturity Model (CMM), which was developed at Carnegie Mellon University and has five certification levels. Most American companies are level 1 or 2, with some running at level 3. There are very, very few American companies at level 5, no more than a handful, as it's expensive and often difficult to convince domestic firms of the necessity to improve to that level.

India, on the other hand, has many IT firms certified at CMM levels 4 and 5, just to show their commitment to quality and doing things right. This makes them demonstrably better than virtually all Western firms, at any price.

In addition, focusing on specific tasks and doing it well can improve quality in many areas, such as radiology, where the quality of breast cancer screening via mammograms is directly proportional to how many images a radiologist reads each month.[51] While doctors in New York see very large numbers of these X-rays, those in rural Utah may not. In the latter case, sending the images to India not only saves money, but also ensures that they get seen by a radiologist who sees hundreds or even thousands per month, delivering a better diagnosis at lower cost.

Finally, in addition to the cost savings, many foreign firms have lower turnover, allowing them to build institutional knowledge and really focus on projects over the long term. For example, low turnover has kept some Korean animators working on The Simpson's TV show since its 1989 beginning, something very rare in the more tumultuous American market and a prime example of non-cost advantages provided by off-shoring.

Productivity Growth

Productivity growth is another key driving force behind job realignment in the early 21st Century. Job losses due to off-shoring become even more difficult to manage when combined with general productivity growth. Such growth, often driven by technology advances and process improvements, has allowed many companies to eliminate the busy work done by actual workers.

In fact, some would argue the number of employees displaced by off-shoring pales in comparison to those being lost to automation and productivity enhancements. This is in a country that has had roughly 4% productivity growth in the last few years, eliminating millions of jobs under the label of "progress" and productivity. Such growth is probably a significant contributor to the creation and destruction of over 1 million jobs each week in the U.S. economy.[52]

Such productivity growth stems from many places, though the Internet probably leads the way in displacing jobs. And, like all technology, it's a double-edged sword, driving workforce reduction while simultaneously creating a myriad of jobs higher up the value chain. These new jobs include engineering and technology design, along with selling, manufacturing, and servicing the computers involved.

Educational Globalization

A bigger force eroding the United States' education supremacy is simply that an excellent education can now be found elsewhere. Countries are not only improving their economies, but also their education systems, often with educational facilities rivaling those anywhere in the world. In fact, many American universities are building satellite campuses in these countries, creating an educational export that brings in much-needed revenue.

As foreign universities improve, more foreign scientists are able to work in their home country. They wonder why they should travel halfway around the world to a place they are sometimes not wanted, when great alternatives exist at home.

Further, as noted on the more technical side, Indian and Chinese universities are turning out far more engineers and other advanced degree holders than American schools do. And the schools are often top-notch; the Indian Institute of Technology (IIT) accepts only 2% of its 200,000 annual applicants. IIT is also creating whole new campuses to graduate even more talented professionals each year.[53]

In addition to regular college graduates, professional training is also changing to meet globalization's demands. One of the more difficult aspects of doing sophisticated work from afar is understanding the culture and laws of the country in question. This is an obvious challenge for Indian or Chinese recruits trying to do American legal or accounting work without ever having lived or worked in the U.S.

Fortunately, foreigners can get such training in the U.S., or increasingly, in their home countries. In fact, many foreign-born lawyers who attended top American schools and passed the Bar have returned to Asia where they perform American legal work as well as anyone living in California performs.

Further, some American schools focus on training Chinese or Indian accountants and other professionals, even helping them pass the CPA and other exams.[54] Alternatively, large firms in audit, tax, and accounting simply train their foreign employees as necessary. Their final work is approved by licensed professionals before delivery to the customer.

Regardless of how the training happens, there are interesting entrepreneurial opportunities for Americans to train, support, and provide materials for these hordes of foreigners who are "working" in the American economy, though they are just not doing it in America.

Realistically, though, there are still strong forces bringing students to America: the top tier universities; academic and personal freedom; top scientific work; and the ability to start companies and reap the fruits of one's labor. The challenge will be to keep these students coming and to retain them after graduation, lest they return home to build innovative product and companies outside the U.S.

And while many of the world's best students are still coming to the U.S., the globalization of the scientific community has already caused the U.S. to lose its leadership position in many areas, as evidenced by recent shifts in scientific paper publication and country of origin for patent filings. The U.S. now produces only 52% of the patents issued by the Patent Office, and the American percentage of published papers continues to decline, while Asian sources of both papers and patents are rapidly increasing.[55]

Losing U.S. leadership in scientific circles has a far broader impact than purely providing intellectual bragging rights. The most important research and development for new products in industries such as biotech and nanotech occur in university settings, not within companies. Therefore, the more scientists America loses, the less innovation happens on American soil. As the U.S. loses its grip on the scientific world, its ability to produce quality research and develop cutting edge technologies will gradually erode. This will in turn make it more difficult for America to innovate its way out of the job displacement crisis.

American Disadvantages

Closely related to the positive factors pushing work off-shore, there are some distinct disadvantages to having large American workforces. These generally mirror the benefits of going off-shore, but deserve particular attention because any re-balancing of the job loss situation will likely require attention to each of these challenges.

Americans are Overpaid

An obvious fundamental challenge is that lots of Americans are highly compensated for jobs that can be done less expensively elsewhere by equally skilled people. The skill or productivity differentiation simply can no longer justify the significant difference in compensation for a wide range of jobs.

That leads to the natural conclusion that many Americans are overpaid when their skills are compared on a global basis. In most cases, foreign workers simply cost less than American ones for the same work. For instance, a senior IT manager recently mentioned at a conference that he was able to hire experienced technology managers in Malaysia to oversee work in Colorado for much less than an American would cost, and the Malaysians did a better job.

It's also easy to get qualified entry-level software programmers in India for $20-$25/hour, which is 40-50% of the going American rate. As a result, it's quite difficult for the expensive Americans to justify their worth, especially when their price is based solely on being geographically or culturally closer (i.e. it has nothing to do with their skills).

As a result, while a 45-year-old senior accountant genuinely believes he merits $75,000 a year, a nice house, two cars, and a stay-at-home spouse, this is fairly difficult to justify on a global basis, not when his job can be done by a 30-year-old woman in China with an American CPA , for $10,000 a year.

This implies that in the end, few Western service employees are adding value to the world commensurate with their compensation. This is especially true in the lower-level service industries, where the skills are minimal – as the question naturally arises "does an American worker really deserve ten times the Ghanaian wage for typing the same insurance claims into the same computer?" The answer is perhaps self-evident.

This is a difficult idea for American workers to accept, especially given the high cost of living throughout much of the U.S. However, from a global perspective, domestic American workers are often simply not productive enough to command their wages. Unfortunately, most Americans feel entitled to their jobs and their high wages; many even feel underpaid and thus perhaps are not working as hard as they should or could, a sure route to a pink slip in the coming decade.

What is not yet evident to them is that they may have peaked and are probably headed into earnings or at least professional decline. At the end of the day, many American workers are simply not adding sufficient value to the world, especially not when their jobs can be done better by someone one-half their age for one-half the price in a country one-half a world away.

Unions

Another challenge related to wages, productivity, and motivation is unionization. At the moment, unions such as the Communications Workers of America (CWA) are fairly rare in the white-collar world, typically limited to the lower-level clerical work. Larger mid-level white-collar unions are also generally confined to civil servants, perhaps with the exception of Boeing engineers and Microsoft contractors.

Regardless, some laid-off or vulnerable workers are talking about forming unions to combat the off-shoring trend. This is perhaps strongest amongst IBM's staff, though it's not clear if any of these efforts is gaining traction, as the white-collar ranks are much more difficult to organize than their blue-collar siblings.

As with nearly all unionized workforces, wages and benefits tend to creep up while flexibility and productivity growth declines, often to the point of imperiling the company. (e.g. the air travel and steel industries, where unions and poor management combined to destroy whole industries, not to mention the pensions of those responsible). As such, any unionization efforts are likely to only accelerate jobs movement, as that can easily be the deciding factor when companies are planning their off-shore strategies.

Unfortunately, there are some sectors where employers can't so easily send unionizing jobs abroad, especially in government. For instance, fear of off-shoring was a key issue that helped the CWA organize 250 engineers and architects working for the city of San Jose, California.[56] Unfortunately, like all civil service union efforts, this will raise governments' costs and the taxes necessary to pay for them. These taxes, in turn, add friction to the economy in general, thwarting economic growth efforts and thus imperiling job growth for everyone.

Off-shoring Enablers

In addition to the various forces at work, such as cost savings and proximity, other factors have come together to enable the off-shoring process to work. Many of these are technology-related, while others include improvements in foreign governance, the realization that jobs are the best form of foreign aid, and other ongoing changes in American business structure and practices.

Technology's Role

The current technology boom has its roots in decades of computerization. This process began in earnest in the 1970s and culminated in the '90s, by which time nearly every firm moved their business processes to computers. Even entry-level white-collar employees now routinely have computers, at their workstation and usually at home.

This has resulted in large numbers of employees working at desks that consisted of only a computer and perhaps a pile of paper and/or a telephone. For decades, the (mostly) women at these desks handled much of the daily work underlying American business. They sat in cubicles and executed simple, repetitive processes that were the backbone of the companies for which they worked. Now, since these computers are connected to a global web of information and communication moving at extremely high speeds, that desk can be nearly anywhere on the planet.

Communication improvements are not the only technological advance driving off-shoring. Other key elements include global call routing for call centers, high-speed scanning machines for payment and claims processing, and advanced corporate IT systems that more easily support global and partner operations.

Modular businesses

Automation efforts not only funneled everything through the computer, they also forced the standardization and modularization of the business processes themselves. This, in turn, has allowed individual functions and departments to be moved around, from floor to floor, town to town, country to country.

For example, travel expense processing is a back-office function that is almost completely separated from the rest of any business. Expense forms and receipts arrive, get typed into a computer, then are filed, approved, and finally paid. Any office in the world can do this, so it's not surprising that these types of functions are often centralized, outsourced and/or moved off-shore.

And this is not just for big businesses, as small companies are increasing their outsourcing, though usually to domestic companies. Cutting Edge Information Inc. studied outsourcing and found that 90% of all U.S. businesses now outsource some work (presumably things like accounting), though undoubtedly much of that is done locally.[57] Still, once a given task moves outside a given firm, it can then be pushed off-shore when the timing and costs are right.

In addition to companies creating modular processes, they also have become part of a modularized value chain, where any given firm provides only part of the effort to create a final product or service, such as an automobile, software, or tax return. This is especially true in the vast American market, as individual firms often specialize on a specific set of tasks. This value chain essentially consists of a single company at the top and a whole series of sub-contractors or outsourcing providers below. Such an arrangement, long common in manufacturing, can lead directly to off-shoring of the standard components and functions in the value chain.

Many other industries, from law to architecture to Hollywood routinely outsource portions of their work to other domestic firms. As a result, an architecture firm sending structural drawings to St. Louis for engineering calculations can just as easily send them to Shanghai.

America's creative arts industries have long modularized and outsourced various portions of their work--the popular television show "The Simpsons" provides a good example of the future of American work. The creative part of the show, the writing, voices, storyboarding, etc. is done in Los Angeles and involves nearly 300 (largely part-time) people. However, the animation is done in Korea by a team of 13 highly skilled artists paid one-third the going rate in Hollywood.[58]

Host Country Developments

In addition to technology and modularity, other factors are in play in the host countries themselves. Developing nations (and sometimes developed ones, too) have learned that a strong economy and jobs are the keys to long-term success. Foreign aid is helpful, but buying products and services from third world nations is perhaps the best foreign aid ever devised, simultaneously adding value to first, second, and third world economies.

As such, many countries are getting their houses in order to accept work from the western world. This includes working on legal and contractual frameworks, joining the World Trade Organization, fixing intellectual property laws and enforcement, installing better telecommunications infrastructure, improving education and worker safety, and building better roads, container terminals, and airports.

Youth & Culture

Not only are various countries changing, but so is their citizenry. While there is much press about youths dominating Muslim countries, many regions involved in off-shoring are themselves awash in young people, many of whom grew up assimilating portions of American culture into their own.

They often embrace portions of Western culture and much of what goes with that, including money to spend, the latest gadgets and clothes, free time, and often freedom from the watchful eye of mom and dad. They are ready for their slice of the American dream, but unlike generations of youth before them, they don't need to go to America to succeed.

These countries are churning out millions of well-educated, English-speaking, motivated workers who are no longer content to sit at home or take bureaucratic jobs in the aging state apparatus. Many are entrepreneurs and risk-takers, out to change the world, move their societies into the 21st century, and make a buck, yuan, or rupee along the way.

Outsourcing vs. Captive Operations

A final driving factor is a trend towards more captive off-shoring operations, especially among larger firms who have historically done a lot of outsourcing. Unfortunately, the media and most discussions on this topic confuse these two different approaches to getting work done abroad. As such, it is important to differentiate between outsourcing and off-shoring, as both models are in play and intertwined in the U.S. and abroad.

A company outsources when it hires another company to do some of its work, but these companies remain separate entities. This is fairly common in a variety of industries and is just a form of subcontracting – it's called outsourcing because the work being subcontracted would normally be done by employees in the normal course of operations, such as IT or accounting. Outsourced work is sometimes still done on the company's premises and even with the same personnel (as is common for IT.) Small companies sending their accounting work to their local CPA demonstrate another example of very common outsourcing.

On the other hand, off-shoring is sending jobs to a different country. Often this work is be done by a different company in the foreign country, which is outsourcing combined with off-shoring. This is the classic case where a company such as Chevron hires WiPro in India to build a computer application for them, using personnel in India.

Or, a company can hire its own foreign workers in another country. This is the case when Oracle's Chinese team builds a product instead of the California team doing so. This is an example of captive off-shoring, and has often been a favored route for global manufacturing companies (who have built their own foreign factories).

While outsourcing gets all of the press, captive off-shoring probably provides larger long-term threats and opportunities; they are typically the preferred arrangement for larger companies, as it gives a business more control and lower cost. Captive off-shoring greatly simplifies the interface between the foreign operation and the U.S. company, as everyone works for the same boss. Workers and managers can also be more motivated, as they work directly for the Western company paying the bills, not a third-party contracting house.

As a result, captive arrangements are likely to grow significantly in the future, so much so that some firms specialize in creating these under build-operate-transfer (BOT) arrangements. In that model, a group starts and operates as an outsourced service center run by a third party, but the entire operation is eventually transferred to the real customer, such as General Electric. Since another company sets up the operation, this reduces the startup risk and eventually cements control over the operation.

In the end, there are a myriad of forces at work, globalizing every one of the world's economies as countries, economies, citizenry, companies, and the very nature of work shift in new and interesting ways.

Challenges lie all along this transformative path, from sorting out the appropriate political and economic response, to individually determining one's own trajectory along the path.

Chapter 4.

Is Your Job Moving?

"We are now competing for low-skilled and higher-skilled work, both in IT and elsewhere, and we will need to replace both with high-skilled, high-wage opportunities to raise our standard of living. No jobs are 'safe,' and our success or failure will turn on our ability to create and retain new jobs, new industries and new processes, goods and services – to innovate,"

Bruce Mehlman, U.S. Assistant
Secretary of Commerce
for Technology Policy[59]

Someone's job is disappearing every minute, in IT, call centers, and beyond. Many categories of American jobs are candidates for off-shoring, so even positions traditionally considered "safe," such as hands-on medicine, Wall Street equity research, or proprietary product engineering, are no longer secure. Every layer in the economy, from blue-collar to the highest level white-collar, is at risk in a surprising range of industries. Plus, additional hiring which might have happened domestically will likely occur overseas, robbing workers of jobs that never were.

In order to understand how to keep Americans employed, it's first necessary to characterize the jobs at risk. White-collar jobs (i.e. those not involving manual labor) are most vulnerable to the job shift. This does not mean that blue-collar jobs are not experiencing shifts, but the loss of manufacturing and labor workers has been ongoing for decades and has already been well-explored elsewhere, especially in relation to NAFTA.

America is now facing an entirely new challenge, the loss of millions of white-collar jobs at all levels, jobs that were considered safe from globalization forces. This chapter takes an analytical look at the at-risk jobs to identify and forecast which job categories are at risk, and conversely, which have relatively 'safe' futures for Americans, at least for now.

White-Collar Job Classes

While white-collar work can be complex and organized in a number of ways, here it is divided into three classes: customer service & clerical, accounting & design, and professional & research.

Customer Service & Clerical

The first layer of interest contains low-end white-collar service jobs, which includes almost anything clerical or customer-oriented, as well as back-office processing jobs. People with jobs in this category fill most city office towers and suburban office parks, constituting a significant portion of the workforce. A recent report estimates over 11 million jobs in this group are at risk of being outsourced.[60]

These jobs typically involve executing repetitive processes by phone or computer, and always working under a supervisor. Workers generally have limited input and follow pre-designed protocols that can be learned fairly quickly on the job or with modest training. These positions tend to experience significant turnover and are designed to allow new employees to replace departed ones with relative ease.

People often work these jobs on a temporary basis, and even permanent employees move in and out over time. So it's unsurprising that it's easy to simply hire a new employee in India rather than Iowa. These jobs form the core of the

Business Process Outsourcing (BPO) movement and very few of them are safe in the 21st century.

It should be noted, however, that many employees stay in the same job for decades, for diverse reasons ranging from love of the job to all too often having few prospects for finding significantly better positions. This is particularly true at larger companies with good benefits and a seniority system, where it's not uncommon to see a 50-year-old clerical employee who's been there 20+ years.

One significant macroeconomic challenge of customer-service or clerical jobs is that they often employ the wives of blue-collar men.[61] For instance, being a claims processing clerk or customer service representative is roughly equivalent to being a factory or semi-skilled construction worker, as they often draw from the same education and cultural pools.

This combination can cause a double blow to many American households, as husbands watched their blue-collar jobs go overseas in the 1980s or '90s, and now their wives may experience the same phenomenon with clerical jobs. This forces both of a family's breadwinners to make a difficult middle-age transition to new careers, frequently at lower wages.

In a further intertwining of entry-level economics, low-end white- and blue-collar workers are often in the same position when faced with being laid-off. Their jobs tend to involve rote, repetitive work that does not educate them in any way or develop their skills. Nor do most of these workers typically have much education beyond high school or even significant additional training from their employers. This is a serious challenge, as it impedes their ability to learn quickly or move to new, more innovative or intellectual careers.

While these jobs are found at the low end of the American economy, they are a step up for the majority of Indians or Chinese. People take these jobs in Asia for the same reasons they do in the U.S.; they need work, they are often (but not always) relatively uneducated, and can do these jobs with relative ease. In Ghana women will be quite happy doing these jobs for $5 per day, given their other choices of either unemployment or work in dirty factories for much less money.

Call Centers

A key segment of the customer service or clerical white-collar job class is the call center. These are perhaps the most well-known of the jobs being sent abroad, both because they are in the news and because many citizens have recently found themselves talking to an Indian person on the other end of the phone.

While there has been some well-publicized retrenchment in this area, this effort is proceeding fairly rapidly. So much so that there is even the threat of legislation to force call center representatives to identify their physical location, in a bid to pressure companies to bring jobs "back home."

There are also call center and other service-oriented jobs such as sophisticated technical support and other higher functions that are not included in this low-level white-collar class. Such roles are still being sent abroad, but have a different dynamic; these are the jobs that Dell recently returned to the U.S. because it was too difficult to get them up and running quickly in India, especially with sufficient customer satisfaction. Dell is sure to return to that effort, however, once they revise their training programs.

Further, call centers and other clerical activities are under technological attack everywhere because of the Internet and other self-service forms of interaction.

For example, Southwest Airlines is eliminating 33% of its reservation centers as customers increasingly buy tickets online.

In the long run, it's difficult to separate these automation effects from jobs eliminated via off-shoring, since both result in fewer jobs in the economic recovery.

This twin squeeze of technology and off-shoring further erodes job stability as the clerical classes struggle to stay employed - the computers take over everything that's easy and the inexpensive foreigners dominate the remainder. This is the fundamental conundrum of this class.

BPO

Business Process Outsourcing (BPO) is one of the latest buzzwords in off-shoring, though the term rarely makes it into the popular press. BPO essentially entails sending abroad one or more modular business processes, such as accounting, claims processing, or check entry. BPO is what the Ghanaian claims processing companies do, as are handling credit card payments in China, or GE's accounting in India, usually with the assistance of high-speed scanning equipment to avoid moving the actual paper around the globe.

This industry is booming because technology makes the move easy to accomplish and unlike call centers, the employees never speak to the public. One Indian consulting group estimates that up to 1 million Indians will be employed in BPO industries by 2008, up from 171,500 in early 2003.[62] That's 45% growth per year and can only mean a significant drain on American clerical employment.

Further, some would argue the practice of moving business processes is still in its infancy, as there are still plenty of tall buildings and office parks full of people pushing paper. As such, numerous consulting firms have created or expanded their practices to help study, modularize, and move these jobs abroad.

Finally, the dynamics for low-end service work are much like those of the 1950s & '60s – everything was changing and automation was a scary thing, potentially draining away all the entry-level jobs. President Kennedy even created an office of Automation and Manpower in 1961 to "maintain full employment at a time when automation, of course, is replacing man"; and President Johnson in 1965 created a National Commission on Technology, Automation, and Economic Progress.[63] Neither of these really went anywhere or had any effect, but they reflected the concerns of the times, just as similar political efforts do now.

Accounting & Design

Mid-level jobs involve professional work, including financial and accounting, engineering, and computer software positions. There are also numerous smaller specialties included in this group, such as paralegals, laboratory technicians, statisticians and analysts, and middle management of all types.

These are generally positions requiring a college education, specialized training, and varying degrees of independence, but the work is almost completely computer-based, with some collaboration, and often limited customer contact.

Currently, while there is significant off-shoring action is at this level, the real job movements are probably yet to come, despite the fact that these jobs require more expertise and training than low-level jobs. A major driving force is supply and demand, since these jobs are relatively highly compensated in the West, but low-wage countries have the necessary skills to do them. Such an imbalance between American wages and foreign talent cannot continue without movement of jobs, wages, or both.

And while these jobs are good for Americans, they are outstanding in the Far East, where universities are churning out hundreds of thousands of new graduates each year in precisely these fields. These newly budded professionals are under a fair amount of cultural pressure to find good jobs to support their families and do better than their parents, not unlike the American Dream of yesteryear. Globally, Asians, Americans, and Europeans with sufficient training and education all seek out these same mid-level jobs, as they are the stepping-stone to the middle class the world-over.

Many employees at this level perhaps also believe they are the best in the world at what they do. They think they are at the top of their game and have a solid future in an ever-growing market. This feeling of superiority and security is especially pervasive in engineering and IT, where workers tend to believe that they are irreplaceable, artisans at creating technology, or harnessing the world for the betterment of mankind. This can be seen on Slashdot.com, a popular IT and computer discussion site, where numerous workers who are bitter about the off-shoring phenomenon post their missives.[64]

These messages also appear constantly on nationalistic anti-offshoring websites, such as that of Hire American Citizens, which ". . . does hereby dedicate itself to the protection and promotion of the American Citizen professional, the best, the brightest, and the most innovative workers in the world."[65] Such attitudes help feed significant backlash when a middle-class worker gets displaced; they are furious that their version of the American dream is slipping away from them.

Regardless of their feelings of perceived loss, employees in this group are rightly concerned about where to go next, as their education and skills are rapidly becoming global commodities, making them uncompetitive personally. For instance, by 2015 Forrester Research estimates that 39,000 life science, 79,000 legal, and 191,000 architecture jobs will have moved abroad.[66] The latter statistic means the loss of nearly 200,000 architects, a job long considered highly desirable, but never mentioned when discussing off-shoring.

As a result of such potential losses, mid-tier employees are the core of the anti-globalization and anti-off-shoring groups, fighting for state-level legislation to prevent jobs from leaving, thinking about unionization, and generally taking a protectionist line. They are the middle class, they feel they deserve better, and they are angry about their American Dream being usurped by foreigners.

Another challenge for employees at this level is how to gain the experience necessary to obtain high-end and well-paying jobs as senior engineers or lab technicians. Historically there has always been a ladder supporting upward mobility, where fresh grads started as junior engineers and worked their way up to lead engineers, managers, and beyond. But if all the junior work goes overseas, the bottom half of the ladder may no longer have any rungs.

Summarizing this challenge is an observation from an engineer at CollabNet, a Bay Area startup that has sent many jobs to India to save itself: "A 21-year-old who just got out of school here with $100,000 in debt, what did he get for that debt? What does he have to look forward to now? We don't hire those people anymore. We only hire senior engineers."[67]

Finance

Finance and accounting cover all types of financial work, including corporate accounting departments, auditing, analysis, and tax preparation for both corporate and personal clients. While there are some high-end functions in this group, most day-to-day financial work is little changed from decades or even a century ago. As such, there is no shortage of qualified numbers men and women around the world ready, willing, and able to count all the beans.

As such, accounting and tax processing have already begun to move off-shore and the volume is surely going to rise as the infrastructure and regulatory approvals are put in place. Much of this simple financial work is just that, simple, and can be done by anyone, anywhere.

Outside of accounting and tax, a wide variety of financial service functions are ripe for off-shoring, for everything from basic back-office processing to high-end equity research and everything in between. Firms are so strongly incented to use foreign staffers that some companies fly their employees to the U.S. or Hong Kong to take securities exams.[68]

One concern is the regulatory and legal environment in which many financial professionals operate, especially for audit and tax work. To help address this issue, the American Institute of Certified Public Accountants (AICPA), which governs U.S.-based Certified Public Accountants (CPAs), has recently approved the practice of processing returns overseas, even though some domestic practitioners are concerned about quality and privacy.[69]

Regardless, this is sure to open the floodgates for the big firms such as H&R Block, Ernst & Young, and others to move this work, especially as these companies often have very cyclical work, clustered around the year's end and April 15th. Off-shoring may allow them to avoid the seasonal variations in employment and related costs to pay expensive American contract accountants every spring.

Looking at the possible savings in the financial services market, Deloitte & Touche observed: "Indeed, it offers a once-in-a generation opportunity to reduce significantly the operating costs of the majority of financial institutions. We estimate that $356 billion of cost for the global financial-services industry will be relocated offshore within the next five years (Exhibit 1)." Further, 15%, or 2 million of the 13 million people employed in financial services, will move abroad.[70] That's nearly over a quarter TRILLION dollars of savings in the next five years - that's serious money and these are actual jobs that will be directly transferred abroad out of Western economies.

As with all mid-tier workers, the psychological factors at work in this sector could be significant. While clerical workers in finance may not be overly surprised to lose their jobs to foreigners, the accounting manager or financial analyst surely is. He generally considers himself to have made it, to be at the top of his game, and finally compensated for his two decades of hard work.

Engineering & Information Technology (IT)

Technology-driven jobs such as engineering and IT are also not only at risk, but are already bearing the brunt of the current job displacement process. Engineering jobs include traditionally outsourced roles in civil and mechanical engineering, plus in-house product design, and even leading-edge technology positions at Intel or Microsoft. Information technology and computer programming jobs encompass nearly everyone who works with computers.

Engineering is an area already moving abroad, as Indian and Chinese universities churn out hundreds of thousands of new engineers qualified to do every-day American design work. Design and engineering jobs are shifting in a variety of industries, from automobiles to packaged goods and especially electronics. Intel, AMD, Flextronics, and other manufacturers are building or expanding design centers in India and China.

Taking advantage of low-cost yet well-educated engineers, these centers employ hundreds or even thousands of engineers, in jobs that will never return to the U.S.

The same is true for electronics engineering, where collaboration and outsourcing has long been the norm; unlike architectural or other engineering segments, electronics has long been a global effort, with outsourcing and collaboration routinely reaching deep to Asia. For instance, Dell's computer engineers routinely work between Austin, Texas and their design partners in Taiwan and factories in China. Moving jobs among such global partners, including small companies, is increasingly routine.

This process has even moved into the most sacred of fast-moving and innovative entities, the Silicon Valley startup company. Most such companies now have an off-shoring component to their business plan to conserve their precious investment capital.

The jury is still out on whether off-shoring software for startups really makes sense, but the venture capitalists funding the whole process are certainly on board and often demanding that work be sent abroad right from the beginning. This, in turn, is forcing companies on both sides of the Pacific to build new business and managerial processes that can manage a global workforce when the company only has 10-20 employees. Such techniques and related technologies will then undoubtedly support accelerated job migration for larger companies all across the economic spectrum.

The effects of all this movement are slowly becoming apparent, as employment in some engineering and science specialties in the U.S. is already declining. For example, the American Chemical Society concluded in 2003 that "times are becoming very tough for the chemical profession," with unemployment rates at an all-time high. With fewer jobs available, new Ph.D. chemists taking postdoctoral positions rose by 10 percent in 2003.[71]

Finally, it's not only high-tech engineering and design work that's being displaced. Even low-tech electrical utilities are getting involved, such as when California-based utility PG&E outsources some of its routine power engineering work to an American firm that has, in turn, been doing the work in its Bangkok office.[72]

Other Specialties

Mid-level work at risk is hardly limited to IT, BPO, and finance, though those probably represent the big movements of hundreds or thousands of jobs at once. On a far broader level, there are many jobs that are similar to engineering in that they involve smaller companies, more modular businesses, and smaller movements at a time.

These positions include analysts of various types, paralegal work, mathematical and statistical or actuarial work, electronics technicians, quality control of various types, and laboratory workers.

Professional & Research

High-end white-collar jobs are not immune from the incessant pressure driving jobs abroad. Such roles are the cream of the crop and include the traditional licensed professions, such as medicine and law, as well as advanced scientific and development work. These jobs are at the top of any developed economy and require advanced degrees, years of specialized training, and often professional certification. Such positions tend to involve high levels of customer contact along with complex interactions of business, technology, and/or finance. They also often require ongoing education and the need to stay plugged into the community, business, and environment in which they operate.

Given such barriers, these high-end jobs are often perceived to be the most protected jobs of all, especially since occupations such as law and medicine make it notoriously difficult to enter the field. They are essentially exclusive clubs, but outsiders are already looking working to get their piece of this high-value market.

The reality is that at least some of these jobs are already starting to emigrate. Many of the above-mentioned barriers are only an illusory speed bump, as the bulk of those actually employed in these professions need not always jump through all the hoops that the old guard have set out for them.

Given their backgrounds, these workers are understandably irate when they lose their 'safe' jobs to foreigners even though the numbers of jobs moving are smaller. This group is normally used to a very high income and the lifestyle that goes with it. While this will be maintained for a majority of practitioners, some will be in for surprise and frustration, when a decade of schooling and training finds them working for a guy in Delhi.

Legal

In the case of law, there are many U.S.-trained and U.S.-bar admitted attorneys practicing in Asia, often for local companies. Many of these went to good U.S. schools and have returned to their homelands for a variety of reasons, including the U.S. making it difficult to get visas and green cards. More and more of these lawyers have also returned home to work for U.S. companies or firms with branches overseas, like the Indian engineers essentially exporting their own jobs.

Regardless of their training, the reality is that much of the typical work done in an American law office can be done overseas. This is especially the case with routine, but expensive Initial Public Offering (IPO) or real estate transactions that can be done in Bangkok; just as routine tax preparation can be done in Hyderabad. Forrester Research predicts that by 2015, more than 489,000 U.S. lawyer jobs, nearly 8% of the field, will shift abroad.

As long as lawyers don't need to set foot in a court room, and few lawyers do, they don't need to be U.S.-based, especially if a domestic firm manages the client and process. Further, they don't even need to pass a U.S. Bar exam, as long as their work is properly reviewed. This is especially useful in specialized areas such as patent law, where much of the action is international anyway and routine work is easily transferable.

For example, the prestigious English law firm of Allen and Overy has outsourced significant portions of its legal document production to India. [73] "There are lots of opportunities to use {foreign} lawyers in place of outside counsel or other lawyers at a lower cost structure," says Suzanne Hawkins, senior counsel at (American) General Electric Company.[74] GE began adding lawyers and paralegals in India several years ago, saving millions of dollars on routine agreements and contracts.[75]

It's also not just large conglomerates like GE that use foreign lawyers. Small companies such as the Andrew Corporation in Illinois, a telecom equipment maker, send patent work to a law firm in Wellington, New Zealand.[76] This also demonstrates how globalization has spread some work around to very diverse places, where subject matter experts living in high-wage countries can still get customers from anywhere; later chapters will cover this very important aspect of globalization, as highly-paid western entrepreneurs perform work for many other parts of the world, developed or not.

Health Care

Jobs in medicine are also slowly beginning to transition overseas. Though doctors seem to be the most obvious example of a profession that needs hands-on interaction and can't move abroad, even this is slowly changing. Mid- and low-level workers in hospitals and doctors offices can be moved, as there is no reason that a person filing charts, analyzing labs, or reading X-rays needs to be in the same geographic location as the patient. Even extremely high-level, specialized doctors with decades of training will soon be able to work remotely as medical technology improves to the point that surgery itself can be done from India.

Sometimes, it's not single jobs that are moving, but the delivery of an entire service such as in-patient surgery. Indian hospitals are increasingly performing routine operations for a fraction of the cost of an American operation. In this case, the customer is taking themselves to the foreign specialist, personally off-shoring the highest-end medical work, such as heart operations and all the supporting infrastructure and employment that goes with them.

For example, Apollo Hospital in Madras, India has become a major provider of inpatient care for the entire globe. A recent Wall Street Journal article[77] told the story of a Canadian man who couldn't stand the year-long wait for free care, so he traveled to India, where a partial hip replacement operation cost just 25% of what it would in the U.S.

Apollo has long provided insurance processing and billing services for U.S. hospitals, but now it threatens to take American patients and jobs, too. The cost of a plane ticket in many instances can be far less than the cost of a hospital stay in the U.S., especially for the un- or under-insured.

This industry is much larger than most people realize, with players such as Thailand and Malaysia attracting 600,000 medical 'tourists' back in 2003.[78] In fact, global strategy firm McKinsey & Co. projects that this "medical tourism" could become a $2 billion-a-year business in India alone by 2012. Those jobs will be directly drained from the western world, but in an example of the complexity of the issue, virtually all of the equipment used in those new facilities will be made in the U.S., Europe, or Japan, creating more high-end jobs in the West.

Eventually, even surgeons will be able to work remotely via high-speed Internet links and advanced robotics. The U.S. military is funding numerous efforts to make this a reality for the battlefield, but the same technology allows a doctor in China to perform surgery in Chicago, or even tiny Chippewa Falls, Wisconsin, where advanced surgical techniques or expertise may not be available.

Research & Development

Other high-end professions, such as corporate and university research, are also moving abroad. This should not be surprising, given that many top researchers in the U.S. are foreign-born and some countries, especially China, are keen to get them back to bolster domestic R&D.

Examples abound of work moving abroad or never coming ashore in the first place, as companies build and expand their global research and development operations. For instance, nearly 400 western companies have set up research centers in India and/or China in the last few years.[79] These range from tiny beachhead offices to General Electric, which spent $80 million in India to build its first and largest R&D center outside the U.S., with 1,800 scientists and engineers, 25% of which have PhDs, and 40% with global experience. In fact, GE's Indian facility specifically recruits Indians in the U.S. who want to return home, essentially taking their job with them.

Other large companies involved range from Pfizer, which spent $12 million setting up 100 scientists in its ever-expanding Indian R&D facility, to Texas Instruments, with 900 chip engineers in India who have already created hundreds of patents. Some of these companies are moving engineering jobs, but many involve serious research and design - 75% of all R&D in the U.S. is manufacturing related, so any movement of large design centers necessarily impacts employment in these sectors.

Of particular interest on the high-end of scientific work is pharmaceutical research, where clinical trials in China and India are growing in number and sophistication. According to the FDA, the number of foreign clinical investigators that conducted drug research for trials increased from 271 in 1990 to 4,458 in 1999. And between 1995 and 1999, up to 35% of the trials that were conducted for new drugs included foreign sites.[80]

Part of this trend is Stanford Research Institute (SRI), a Silicon Valley-based world-class R&D organization that recently scouted China for research partnerships. They didn't have to look far, as they quickly found world-class research labs in places such as Shanghai, staffed with Ph.D. and post-doctorate subject experts, and new Western equipment. Such facilities and staff will likely be at the forefront of new global biotech and research in the coming years, creating innovations and companies far from U.S. shores.

While it's becoming easier to run straightforward clinical trials in India and China, additional value-added functions are also beginning to be done there, such as trial and protocol management, statistical analysis, and related work. As the groups involved become increasingly successful, it's only a matter of time before these health centers grow in prominence and begin doing world-class research in the new sciences of biotech, stem cells, and gene therapy.

For example, while still lagging far behind their western counterparts, Indian drug companies have recently tripled their research spending, with firms such as Dr. Reddy's leading the way. A leading integrated health firm, Dr. Reddy's has 300 drug discovery researchers, a New York Stock Exchange listing, a new drug licensed to Novartis, and a focus on bringing their own biotech molecules to market – they embody the 21st century Asian pharmaceutical and health care industry.

In other cases, they are undertaking world-class research, both for local and global issues. Work in this area includes an AIDS vaccine that may start human trials in 2005. It was developed by India's national laboratories using advanced genetic engineering techniques.

In addition, some countries, such as China, are offering various incentives for companies, and even individual researchers, to move. Incentives for companies are nothing new and while there is debate on how effective they are, they point to a global market with serious players intent on pulling advanced companies, technology, and employment in their direction.

Finally, there are apparently no limits to some types of jobs moving abroad, as even religion is being outsourced. Indian priests routinely perform "mass intentions," which are requests for giving thanks or forgiving sins. Rather than being a cost savings measure, these 'tasks' are sent abroad due to shortages in local priests. These priests often earn about six dollars for each intention "processed."[81]

Why Some Jobs Won't Go Abroad

While there are many classes of jobs in danger of heading overseas in the near-term, there remain a wide variety of positions that will stay put, depending on the companies involved, the work itself, embedded knowledge, or just the difficultly in changing employment and services.

The most obvious jobs that will stay in the U.S. are those that simply have to stay, based on the nature of their hands-on work. People who sell things, install technology, do on-site repair, teach classes in person, or investigate insurance claims will certainly retain their positions. And, if a job requires staff to routinely leave their desks and interact with people face to face in ways that cannot be done over the phone or through email, it is likely to be safe, at least for now.

In addition, jobs in government or those with security implications will presumably remain, although outsourcing is increasing in these areas; so even these historically safe jobs are slowly becoming vulnerable.

Many jobs that could move abroad will not, because they are difficult to transport or advantageous for Americans to perform. These types of jobs are where future job growth lies. These include much of the non-drug medical field, consulting of almost all types, and jobs tied to long-term customers or communities. Much legal work, especially anything not routine, will remain in the U.S., along with nearly any culturally-sensitive work, such as public relations, marketing, publishing, movie and television creative work, almost anything with content. These jobs could be moved, but doing so wouldn't benefit anyone. The work done in these fields is less modular, and training foreign employees is far more costly, if it's even possible (e.g. don't look for Beijing ad agencies creating U.S. Army commercials any time soon).

Beyond those jobs that must and probably will stay, there are many jobs that could move, but really shouldn't. These are roles that are both desirable for the U.S. and are difficult to move effectively. This includes high-end activities in nearly every field, including finance, IT, and engineering. Irrespective of the quality issue and overpaid nature of rank-and-file work, American often still has the most talented and productive workers in these fields, and companies that move these jobs overseas often only end up disappointed and bringing them back (at least for now).

Further, jobs that require interfacing multiple specialties or reaching across the aforementioned modular business units will stay. These will likely be the coveted mid-level jobs of the future.

Most small and many medium-sized businesses simply will not be moving their core jobs any time soon given their lack of modularity, inability to manage geographically dispersed teams, and other factors as described in the driving forces section. Given that these firms employ the bulk of the workforce, there is no fundamental danger that 50% of the economy will suddenly migrate to the Far East.

Information & Knowledge Flow Characteristics

While individual talented employees can retain their jobs, the movement of a company or industry's jobs en masse is modulated by the jobs' information and knowledge flow. Many jobs are information-driven, especially the BPO and claims processing environments. This information comes in as paper forms or phone calls and goes into computers. There is not much knowledge involved, just relatively simple processes to move things along.

On the other end of the spectrum are high-knowledge jobs such as legal and medical work, where a wide variety of decisions are continuously made based on a vast sea of knowledge gained over the years.

Some industries, such as manufacturing and finance, are a mix of the two, where many tasks are pure process and information-driven, while others are highly-skilled knowledge jobs. Further, some types of companies, such as high-tech startups, are highly knowledge-driven, and have few, if any, processes in place that can be easily modularized and sent abroad.

One of off-shoring's challenges is moving information and/or knowledge over long distances. With today's telecommunications technologies, the cost and difficulty in transmitting information does not rise with distance, i.e. it's just as easy to send phone calls and computer screens to India as Indianapolis, but the cost and difficultly in transmitting or transferring knowledge rises sharply with distance. For instance, just splitting up a ten-person team and sending half of them to a different building makes interaction more difficult. Sending them to Atlanta is worse, and moving to New Delhi yet more difficult.

This problem is particularly acute when "sticky knowledge" is involved. This type of knowledge requires context to have meaning and often involves considerable uncertainty and frequent change. Such knowledge is often best transmitted in person, the difficulty of which obviously rises with distance and additional time zones.

As such, Western service economies and their jobs will likely evolve towards activity that cannot be easily moved across long distances. As such, it certainly behooves workers to identify and develop their talents in these areas.

Why Some People Will Always Succeed

Not only are there certain job classes that won't be going abroad, so are there types of individuals who are well matched for advancement in the 21st century economy. While almost no particular job is safe, individuals who can move among jobs, rapidly acquire skills, and differentiate themselves from their lower cost foreign competitors will find numerous lucrative opportunities.

Talent vs. Commodity

Remaining employed will depend on numerous factors, but the real trick will be for each person to clearly understand the structure of their sector, particularly the difference between being talent and being a commodity. In the end, talent will always have opportunities, but commodities are continually exposed to global price competition and the subsequent risks of wage deflation.

Talent is just that, someone with more-or-less unique skills that cannot be easily found in a typical worker. Usually attributed to star performers in the arts, sales, or management, everyone knows true talent when they come upon it. But talent also shows up in everyday businesses, as everyone knows who the key players are in every department or organization, whether secretarial, managerial, or technical. They are a cut above the rest and create real value in and for the organization.

Commodities are also just what one would expect, easily replaceable components whose market price follows the laws of supply and demand. As the global supply of commodity service workers rapidly increases, the price undoubtedly will decline.

The challenge, of course, is to be talent and not a commodity. This requires differentiation, usually through education, training, skills, and attitude, which can be as simple as being able to do something better than anyone else or, being able to do multiple things, or being able to bridge many types of things. Commodities, like iron, copper, or gold, tend to be focused on, or useful for, only one thing, but talent crosses lines, specialties, and cultures.

It's rare for a single individual to span these different worlds, but being able to understand and connect different parts of the pie allows individuals to work magic by understanding and coordinating the disparate parts of complex 21st century organizations and systems. This concept works in nearly any industry, whether two portions are technical and business, finance and sales, medical and insurance, or America and India - these connectors will be the real talent in the 21st century.

Talent in the Movie Industry

The movie industry provides a good microcosm of the various levels at work, the talent vs. commodity curve, and the propensity to move certain work in search of lower costs. The industry is nearly 100 years old and generates billions in revenue, as well as a huge trade surplus for the U.S. When a film is made, thousands of people are employed at every conceivable skill level in a very diverse array of industries, often spread across the globe. And since this industry is very financially driven, it has generally found optimal processes for every portion of its work.

For instance, movie work requiring massive resources, especially the actual shooting, is often done in low cost areas, often overseas or in Canada. This part of the process of movie making employs hundreds of commodity-like carpenters and other tradesmen who are globally plentiful; in fact many countries develop these skills specifically to attract lucrative film projects.

The mid-level work, such as pre- and post-production work, is done by specialized firms that employ a mix of strategies, including farming out work to overseas partners when they can. For instance, much of a film's standard computer animation or graphics work can be sent to companies overseas, while high-end imagery and editing that requires heavy interaction is usually done in California.

High-level work in this value chain involves the creative forces behind the film. The producers, writers, directors, and actors are nearly always loosely based in Hollywood, but are highly mobile and can travel to all the other locations a film requires. Even the slow globalization of movie talent still revolves around key high-level interactions involving the same Hollywood-oriented people, even though interestingly enough the new talent often involves Indian and Chinese actors.

A Wide-Spread Phenomenon

Looking at the above job classifications ripe for export, it is apparent that large swaths of the American economy are potentially vulnerable. Again, the tall towers of nearly any city and the broad complexes of any suburban office park could essentially be drained away to identical buildings 10,000 miles distant.

Even if 10% or so of these positions disappear, that leaves millions of people angry at being out of work. Future chapters discuss some of the dangers this poses and potential solutions to both minimize the damage and prepare displaced individuals for employment in the future.

Every industry will have some jobs that have to stay, some that ought to stay, and some that really ought to leave. The most obvious jobs to move are those that involve little training or skill and which operate via paper, computers, or telephones. These jobs can easily be shipped off, and as other chapters will illustrate, they probably ought to be.

Mid-level jobs will be split between going and staying, while high-end jobs will tend to stay, at least for now. Large companies will lead the way, while small firms will proceed at a more measured pace as the savings and competition become too large to ignore any longer.

Chapter 5.

What if We Do Nothing?

"Too many Americans lack the training, education or opportunity to shift their focus mid- life and mid-career, from the jobs that are going global to the jobs we will be creating here at home."

Bruce Mehlman,
Assistant Secretary for Technology Policy,
United States Department of Commerce [82]

Millions of jobs lost. Wages falling. Long lines at soup kitchens. Personal bankruptcies.

Headlines from the Depression Era? Or, as some anti-off-shoring critics see it, America's future? While most of these fatalist scenarios lose sight of the resiliency and dynamic nature of the American economy, if they are even half right it will mean hard times for the Western world.

The only way to survive these challenges is to become globally competitive, both individually and collectively. As one might imagine, this is no easy task, especially for those not used to further education, training, and plain old hard work. To succeed in this century, nearly all Americans have to make several interrelated changes in both their attitudes and working style. They will need to go one step at a time, for a long time, perhaps even thinking back to when their families were immigrants and how hard they had to work to succeed.

Unfortunately, Americans and their politicians tend to focus on simplistic solutions that fit within sound bites. These quick fixes only address, at best, one facet of the problem at a time and generally do nothing for the overall situation.

Without action on the part of many parties, serious challenges almost certainly lie ahead for Western economies. While relatively unrelated to off-shoring (for now), Europe's current economic situation portends some of the depths of the problem should this get out of hand, with 10%+ unemployment, an aging workforce, and declining social state, followed by increasing tax burdens and renewed nationalism. These factors are also self-reinforcing, as Europe realizes how their higher taxes and social costs are increasing job flight.

Rising Unemployment

Without action, increasing waves of high school and even college graduates will simply have fewer and fewer job opportunities available to them as entry- or mid-level white-collar jobs evaporate. This has far reaching implications, as un- and under-employed workers, especially young men, challenge society on many levels, from crime to an inability to provide for their families and children.

At the same time, most of these lower level job seekers rarely did well in school and are probably not up for years of additional training to take a $25,000 per year position in a temporary or fleeting job, only to have to repeat the process a few years later.

It's not inconceivable to see 15-20% unemployment over time, concentrated in the lower or middle ranks of previously well-employed citizens – this is already a reality in Europe where 2003 unemployment for 15-24-year-old men is nearly 25% in Italy and almost 20% in France. And over 50% of the unemployed in Italy and Germany have been looking for work for over a year.[83]

Some people take solace in recent job creation statistics, showing a few hundred thousand new jobs created each month; however, they forget the workforce is also growing at or above that rate. With 120 million people in the workforce, it takes

100,000+ new jobs every month just to keep up with the 1-2 million new workers added each year. Plus, any shortfall in sufficient new jobs in one month has to be made up in the future, as all of the numbers are cumulative.

The negative effects of unemployment on the economy and society at large are obvious. More and more people will become a burden on the government, and fewer and fewer people will be able to participate in the market economy, pay taxes, add value, etc.

Demographics such as an aging and shrinking workforce may mitigate some of these effects, but will exacerbate others. Smaller workforces obviously require fewer jobs and can lead to lower unemployment, but aging populations create additional Social Security, pension, and Medicare recipients. This in turn dramatically raises the cost to support them, especially on a shrinking base of workers. Fewer workers also reduces overall economic output and growth while reducing tax revenue. In addition, while the U.S. needs more risk takers and worker flexibility, aging workforces tend to be headed in the opposite direction.

Permanent European-style double-digit unemployment would be bad enough, but things could become even more challenging, as official unemployment figures miss three key aspects of the true employment picture: non-job seekers, the under-employed, and the self-employed.

Non-seekers, which include "discouraged workers" or those who have given up looking, have long been an issue in the numbers, though they are perhaps historically limited to under 1%.[84] This number could rise in a true job recession, especially as new graduates move back in with their parents, others simply give up, or families try to get by on a single income.

Non-seekers also include homemakers, retirees, and others who may be drawn back into the workforce as support from their spouse's job or pension declines. Many of these returnees can be seen saying "hello" at a local Wal-Mart.

Then there are the under-employed, working below their prior or potential income level, often part-time or in temporary positions. The extent of these workers is difficult to gauge, but most economists believe it's getting worse, though there are complicating factors like new moms and the semi-retired taking part-time jobs by choice.

Vast armies of temporary workers may not show up as unemployed, but their modest wages coupled with tenuous job stability means they are earning money but are not really fully-employed. Further, many low-end white collar workers may be drifting downward to Wal-Mart and similar full-time jobs, further eroding their standard of living. And, many if not most temporary jobs have no health insurance, further burdening existing health programs and raising costs for everyone.

Finally, and probably on a positive note, the ranks of the self-employed have swelled in recent years, enough to cause significant disparity between official unemployment numbers and household income surveys, which differ by millions of workers. While this is heartening on one front, as it lowers actual unemployment, many self-employed workers are really only riding out tough economic times and may never work full-time again. This was clearly evident in the post-dot-com period in Silicon Valley, where scores of people became consultants and did odd jobs at 1/3 their previous salaries, often with no way to ever again be employed at their previous, albeit inflated, income level.

Psychological Effects

Off-shoring's most devastating effect may well be on the mental life of the nation, which in turn feeds back into its economic and political well being. This is not just about losing someone's job, but losing a whole set of jobs and perhaps a career. Suddenly, everything a person has worked towards for years or decades disappears, taking with it their job, economic security, and slice of the American dream.

For workers, this means rude awakenings about their true global market value (or the lack thereof), and pessimistic expectations about falling wages for themselves and their children. For consumers, this means anxiety about their employment future and reduced consumerism all the way around.

Americans in general, and white-collar workers in particular, tend to harbor the misconception that they are the most vital component of their companies' and the nation's economic success. White-collar workers perhaps think that only blue-collar guys have to worry about job migration, since they do "unimportant" manual labor and often get laid off, but that educated people are immune to globalization. As they are rapidly finding out, this simply isn't true.

Further, Americans feel entitled to the jobs they have; in fact, they feel entitled to even better jobs or higher salaries. This sense of entitlement makes it particularly difficult to accept the notion that they are not guaranteed a job and now must compete with a third-world foreigner just to hold onto what they've got.

Great personal and political turmoil could easily arise when the white middle class finally realizes just how easily they can be replaced and how quickly their secure suburban lives can change for the worse. They will wonder what they did wrong and why the American Dream has apparently slipped away from them. They will blame their former employer first, their government second, and the foreign country or replacement employee third.

Rarely will they look at their own lack of preparation, their lack of global perspective, or their inability to move up to the next plane of success along life's path. It's never them, but someone else's mistakes and fault that they cannot compete. But if they are not careful they will spend the next several years complaining while their competition increases its capabilities and thus its lead, leaving them in the dust.

Displaced workers face a number of psychological challenges, only the first of which is realizing their rather small value in the global economic picture. Many will eventually realize or be told how under-trained and poorly educated they actually are, given rapid new technological and global developments in nearly every field. For college graduates, suddenly a liberal arts education won't seem so useful; nor will their years or decades of seniority or experience in what has become for them a dead-end occupation.

Once they accept that they may need to get retrained and develop new skills, they are still unlikely to find a job in a new sector or industry that pays anywhere near the amount they made previously. This will all suddenly hit home for the 45-year-old accounting manager in Iowa. He will be particularly unhappy about his prospects, having done all the right things, gone to school, gotten his CPA, worked for two decades at good companies, etc., only to find himself unemployed and perhaps unemployable as his job migrates half-way around the world.

Still, worker backlash will only be the first wave in a flood of negative psychological effects. Such a negative view of where things might be going is perhaps the most serious challenge of this entire job movement. When people perceive they have few job prospects, whether because the media tells them that or because they've been laid off, their confidence will wane and then they won't be buying new cars or putting down payments on houses any time soon. Unfortunately, this is precisely the behavior that leads to the root of economic slowdowns and recessions.

Consumer confidence is often the single most important barometer of economic activity in the economy and history shows that economic downturns and subsequent upswings are heavily dependant on what consumers think. This is why Wall Street, the Federal Reserve, and the media continually look to consumer confidence indexes to gauge the economy's future.

While some look at this in terms of raw consumerism (i.e. buying more clothes and TV's) and say it doesn't matter because those things are imported, they miss the bigger picture of economic mainstays such as homes, automobiles, computers, and a vast array of services.

Once confidence erodes, there is almost no way to prop up an economy, which can slide into permanent recession. And when the world's largest economy goes down, it drags the entire world into a recessionary spiral.

Wage Deflation

Wage deflation is another concern as rising unemployment sharply increases the available workforce, especially in the most vulnerable sectors. This is already apparent when laid-off white-collar workers end up selling electronics at the local mall, where they typically earn little more than minimum wage.

In addition to losing money when switching to the Wal-Mart economy, workers can lose compensation within the same industry or even the same job, as both direct off-shore pressure and numerous local job applicants keep wages down. Also, rising health care costs are increasingly being passed on to workers, further depressing real wages.

In the end, even with low to modest inflation and limited layoffs, such wage deflation directly leads to real income stagnation or erosion, which in turn leads to reduced confidence, reduced expectations, and a generally depressing view of the future.

The end result could be the loss of only a few million jobs, but the accompanying wage and confidence deflation may push the entire economy into stagnation as the global economic center of gravity moves permanently to the Far East.

Many jobs will remain in government and health care, but no one will be able to afford them. This is especially true in government, where taxes are the only way to pay for things; the destructive burden of these taxes will only accelerate an economic downturn, as it already has in Europe. Cutting taxes, government wages, and benefits is of course extremely difficult, as seen in Paris or other European capitals; the end result could be permanent economic stagnation. For instance, the EU projects 2005 Euro Zone GDP growth to be an anemic 2%.[85] By contrast, U.S. growth is roughly double that rate, while India and China are growing at 7-10%.[86]

Long-term Challenges

There are other long-term concerns as real wages fall and confidence wanes. When every penny of a family's reduced pay checks go to afford the basics or pay off debts, their ability to invest in the future or drive the economy wanes considerably as they essentially become the working poor.

Further, income distribution will become more polarized, with the rich only getting relatively richer and the poor only getting poorer, a phenomenon some would argue is already well underway. The Economic Policy Institute estimates real median family incomes fell nearly 1% per year from 2000 to 2003. The middle class also actually shrank by 8% from 1979 to 2002. They also estimate that globalization is responsibility for 1/3 of the total growth in wage inequity in recent years.[87]

One of the challenges of reduced wages is an eroding tax base, as the government will be forced to take larger and larger portions of increasingly meager wages. As the government gets poorer, its ability to maintain infrastructure, entitlements and public commitments will go away, again a process some would argue has already begun. California has become the poster child for such income dependency, with too much spending largess on too narrow a tax base; it's no coincidence that California's European-style, tax-and-spend government is in deep trouble, with no clear solution in sight, other than painful service cuts and/or economy-killing tax hikes.

At the moment, many pundits are unwilling to accept these possible views of the future; as one Business Week editorial put it, the wrenching adjustment is only "short-run friction." Unfortunately, this change is actually structural and will likely last far longer than the "short run". Countries such as India and China have enormous populations and increasingly educated workforces. While upward wage pressure will undoubtedly erode their advantages vis-à-vis America (though the Asian Tigers still have such advantages decades after they started down that road), numerous countries wait in the wings, especially Vietnam, Iran, and perhaps Pakistan and various African nations.

American companies will continue to leverage these nearly inexhaustible labor bases, never needing to turn back to domestic workers. And they will never need to pay better wages, as there will always be other foreign workers that will work for less, much as one sees today as country-hopping manufacturers continually move along to new low-wage locales. American wages potentially could fall faster than Asian wages will rise, a scenario in which American workers face decades of job loss and wage reduction.

Additional long-term challenges include New Deal-style pension and Social Security plans that have significant long-term funding problems. This could return the elderly to poverty with no easy solution, especially for Europe and Japan, which are aging faster and whose governments and people may not be able to grow or innovate their way out of the problem. Plus, in addition to governmental programs, the U.S. has bloated and decaying pension programs that continue to damage large companies that granted such benefits; the airline and auto industries are illustrative of this challenge, one that will reduce benefits and burden taxpayers as plans fail.

Europe: A Frightening Future

Many of these processes are already underway in Europe, where the unemployment rate is stubbornly stuck over 10% (over 12% in some industrialized areas of western Germany).[88] This is due, in part, to both economic stagnation from over-taxation and over-regulation, and the increasing availability of intra-EU job migration after the addition of lower-wage Eastern EU states. Further privatization of state-owned companies and reducing their subsidies will exacerbate the problem, especially as newly-added expansion countries continue to supply inexpensive labor and consume EU-wide development subsidies.

Eventually, the addition of large, poor, and inexpensive countries such as Turkey will severely strain the system on economic, agricultural, and social levels, as companies will easily be able to "off-shore" inside the EU, removing much of the need to employ anyone in the northwestern EU (though language proficiency will initially limit this process in customer services and BPO).

In many cases, solutions already attempted by the Europeans mirror suggested strategies in America. Unfortunately, they generally tend to be counter-productive, such as the French and German government buying stakes in domestic 'champions,' shortening the workweek, or proposing only tiny reductions in their socialist states.

New American Ghost Towns

Before long, the tall office towers that peak over every city's skyline could be emptied, and the only warm bodies left in suburban office parks will be in the executive offices. Like the empty mining towns of the American West, these office towers and parks could become the new American ghost towns.

The 21st century American city could become a computerized ghost town, where everyone turns on his or her computers to book tickets, buy products, manage bank accounts, and communicate with their families. When something breaks they will call India, and when a new toy comes in the mail it will be from China. The American worker will become an anomaly, an old world idea that subsists only because technology hasn't totally eliminated it yet.

As one unemployed information specialist in the Bay Area put it, "If we're not careful, we're going to end up with a few CEOs here and no one else."[89] Certain older manufacturing industries have certainly gone this route, with everything except sales having long since migrated overseas.

For example, if Forrester's job loss projections come to be, those 3.4 million jobs will free up roughly 500 million square feet of office space, equal to all the buildings in New York City.[90] And, if U.C. Berkeley's projections of 14 million jobs are accurate, that's the loss of over a billion feet of office space. Not all of these jobs are in traditional offices, but considering the national office space market is only about 3.3 billion feet (17% vacant in mid-2003), anything approaching this is quite a loss, with cascade effects on construction jobs (which are among the few job classes to remain firmly in America) and real estate values.[91]

San Francisco and Silicon Valley also provide a good example of the hollowing out of the value chain; no average person can afford to live there since the gap between the cost of living and the average wage have widened to an un-spannable gulf. Lots of people work in such areas, but live an hour or more away in a place they can afford.

No Big Deal?

Some argue that this whole job shift is no big deal, and that Americans can innovate their way out of the problem. They claim that the economy is extremely dynamic and flexible and can compensate as needed. Innovation and entrepreneurship will save the day, they opine, so there is no need for anything to be done, certainly not the mercantilist policies advocated to combat the Asian Tigers in the 1980s.

Some politicians even point to the U.S.'s current low unemployment rate as the envy of the world and assure everyone that this is proof that there is no need to worry. A few media outlets, such as Business 2.0, have even run cover stories that talk about the coming worker shortage and why everything will work out, through they ignore obvious demographic shifts in progress. Some also talk about how America triumphed over the Japanese in the last decade and remain poised to win any economic battle.

Each of these arguments ignores several of the realities of the situation. This jobs shift, while certainly outwardly similar to the manufacturing job shift of the '80s and '90s, is a new kind of battle, with new players, issues, and driving forces. Things will not be as easy this time, as the job shift resolutely marches up the job chain, leaving little room at the top for anyone.

A key aspect of the change is that the American economy has already shifted to a service focus, leaving no "new" place for employees to go on a mass scale; the tens of millions of good jobs needed in the coming decades don't yet and may never exist.

New economy jobs in nanotech, software, biotech, and medical devices, etc. are certainly promising, though they too can largely be developed elsewhere and are unfortunately out of the reach of most service employees. And with top foreign students ceasing to come to American shores, their innovations will be developed in their home countries and their companies built and staffed with their countrymen, from whom Americans will license their technology.

In addition, jobs with real value will require flexibility and education, and while the former is a strong American attribute, the latter is weak and declining in comparison to other countries. Many American white-collar jobs could become antiquated, unnecessary components of an archaic system, like manufacturing and agriculture workers before them. This time there will be nowhere left for the economy to shift to, and the entire American system may well be left to stagnate and deflate until the land of plenty isn't so plentiful any more and the American Dream becomes the Asian Dream.

Chapter 6.

How Affected People Are Reacting

Nearly 60 % of those polled said companies that send work overseas should be punished by the federal government – a survey by the Employment Law Alliance (ELA).[92]

Intel's CEO, Craig Barrett, on whether Americans entering the workforce in coming years face a generation of lowered expectations: "It's tough to come to any other conclusion."[93]

A secure middle class is critical to maintaining political, social, and economic stability. Such importance would thus suggest that any significant disturbances to the American middle-class could negatively affect the citizenry, economy, and politics of the nation, and thus the world. While public policy experts and books on the topic tend to discuss economic theory and lofty academic goals, none of these are overly helpful to a middle-class worker losing her job to an Indian man making a quarter of her salary.

Job movements tend to generate heat and friction everywhere - among media, politicians, and even academics. Their reactions are all interesting, but the most important reactions belong to those who are actually laid-off. As might be expected, displaced workers are angry and their first natural reaction is to demand that the government fix the problem. Calling for bans or other protectionist policies to try to halt off-shoring is a typical worker response, especially when the worker poorly understands global economics or their (rather low) place in the global value chain. "I don't see any other options," said a 52 year-old who has joined a Seattle-based union trying to organize tech workers around the country. "There's no loyalty anymore. I feel my job was taken by corporate greed."[94]

Anti-Off-shoring Organizations

These types of positions can be seen in IT-oriented groups such as the Organization for the Rights of the American Workers (TORAW). These groups stage demonstrations outside IT conferences and petition their congressmen for ill-defined protectionist actions. Their general position is that off-shoring is a terrible and misguided hollowing out of the American expertise and economic base and should be prevented. Among these groups "globalization" is a dirty word, only uttered with contempt and bitterness.

A similar group, Hire American Citizens, "does hereby dedicate itself to the protection and promotion of the American Citizen professional, the best, the brightest, and the most innovative workers in the world."[95] This sort of national arrogance particularly annoys and dismays America's closest friends, though it's largely in line with common attitudes amongst citizens and politicians alike: America is great and deserves all the jobs the foreigners are trying to steal away.

On a more proactive, though misguided level, groups such as the American arm of the IEEE are calling for restrictions in both H1B (foreign temporary worker) visas and off-shoring in general to protect their membership. They are concerned less about immediate jobs than about the need to maintain a technological and innovative edge to provide future jobs for their members and the economy at large.

These reactions are understandable from an individual perspective, even if they make no macroeconomic sense, for it's difficult to imagine people sitting sit back while a growing number of companies whittle their employees down to only the most necessary and talented.

Political Implications

Angry white middle-class workers left in the wake of the job shift can only spell trouble for politicians in power. When citizens complain, politicians listen, especially if the complaints come from the middle class or unions, and both are agitating about off-shoring. As such, the opportunity for destructive political behavior seems inevitable. To some extent this has already begun, especially at the state level, with numerous protectionist bills passed or under consideration.

As is to be expected, displaced workers will have a rather one-sided view of the situation and thus only react with protectionist and sometimes nationalistic fervor. For instance, a recent Pew Research Center for People and the Press poll observed that 78% of respondents said "protecting the jobs of American workers" should have top priority in deciding U.S. policies about trading with other countries.[96]

Former presidential candidate John Kerry's call for taxes and other restrictions on "Benedict Arnold" companies is a good example of politicking without forethought. Without thinking about the global picture, economic realities, or numerous trade issues, Kerry tried to tap into the votes of the angry unemployed and gain union support. And statements crying "traitor!" are cropping up all over the place as politicians continue to jump on the anti-off-shoring bandwagon to sound patriotic and garner easy votes.

Anti-globalization statements from a few politicians running for national office are expected and may not seem overly harmful, but these sentiments are even stronger among state legislators. State-level politicians tend to misunderstand or care even less about economics and world trade than Congress, and are more sensitive to the opinions of the citizenry. They also can move faster to create their own economic havoc.

Several states have already passed laws requiring that state work be done in America. This effort started with a recent New Jersey case where some state call center business was moving to India. The 12 jobs involved were eventually brought back at a cost of nearly $1 million to New Jersey taxpayers (even though they would have had no problem with the work done in Puerto Rico or Alaska, with about the same economic benefit to New Jersey.)

In another example, Indiana Governor Joe Kernan canceled a $15.2-million contract to the Indian software firm Tata and gave it to an American firm, a move that will cost the state $8.1 million, or about $150,000 per job temporarily saved. Imagine how that money could have been put to better use, especially since the winning bidders were not even located in Indiana.[97] The larger issue is whether or not the taxpayer is going to be pleased with cuts in services (a real issue in California) to afford these very expensive out-of-state jobs.

It's also interesting that many people complain about call center jobs going off-shore, but are very happy with the new telemarketing "do-not-call registry" which the industry claims will eliminate 2-3 million U.S. jobs. Thus, saving 10 or 100 jobs at a time is okay and worth increasing taxes for, but saving a million is apparently not important if dinner is interrupted.

Along the same vein, it's interesting how reactions vary depending on whether the jobs move to Delhi or Des Moines - either way the same employee is losing his or her job, but somehow it's okay if another worthy American gets the job, but not so if it goes to some foreigner in a far away land. This key distinction is a good window into some of the xenophobic or nationalist sentiments underlying many of these reactions, even if the economics of such a position doesn't add up.

Protectionism

The natural reaction to all of this is a call for protectionism, as it has been for centuries the world over. Protectionism by itself has probably never worked and can be expected to lead to declining and non-competitive industries. Further, in today's markets, it often serves only to antagonize trading partners and ends up with a net job loss, as witnessed by the recent steel tariff debacle of 2002-03.

Regardless of its efficacy, and given that many people are loudly clamoring for more protectionist measures, it is unsurprising that politicians are moving in this direction. After all, few politicians gain votes by thinking long-term or worrying about diffuse benefits to everyone when there is acute pain to be assuaged, especially in their individual districts.

Politicians are constantly inventing new ways to misunderstand trade and the dangers of protectionism. Comments in this area include the following message from Senator Hollings (D-SC) in a Washington Post op-ed piece entitled "Protectionism Happens to Be Congress's Job:" "To really level the playing field in trade would require lowering our living standard, which is not going to happen. We value our clean air and water, our safe factories and machinery, and our rights and benefits. Both Republicans and Democrats overwhelmingly support this living standard and many are prepared to raise it. The only course possible, then, is to protect the standard."[98]

That comment has no reflection in reality, as Congress surely has no way to prevent a lowering of living standards via wage erosion, and the environmental and safety issues are largely irrelevant to service industries. Senator Hollings goes on to say, "Our trouble is that we have treated trade as aid."

The reality is that trade is precisely the best aid, but more on that later. But then, Senator Holling's home state of South Carolina has never ceased to try to distort free trade realities by protecting textiles and destroying the economies of African and other developing countries, although the WTO is finally forcing them to level the playing field.

This sort of protectionism is not an exclusively American game. German Chancellor Gerhard Schröder described moving jobs off-shore to save money as "unpatriotic."[99] Increasingly protectionist politicians are alarming for many reasons, but three challenges stand out:

First, protectionism is bad economic policy that damages the outlook for all workers and increases costs for consumers, governments, and the economy at large. It's essentially a tax and thus a drag on all economy activity. Not only is off-shoring unstoppable, but also it has numerous advantages both geo-politically and locally, though not without some pain along the way. Sticking a few fingers in the dike will hardly stem the torrent of economic change underway, though it can do a lot of damage on its own in the meantime. There will be more on this issue later in the chapter.

Second, such protectionism overflows into other non-employment-related areas such as farm subsidies, WTO rulings, tariffs, and free trade agreements. It does not take much of an effort to throw monkey wrenches into the works of free trade, as seen in the 1930s with legislation like the protectionist Smoot-Hartley Act and subsequent global retaliation, which many argue helped bring about the Depression and subsequently WWII. A general protectionist sentiment or even modest backtracking on steel tariffs or agriculture subsidies can reverse decades of progress in general world trade and especially in the vast improvements it has brought about in developing countries. The WTO needs support and additional free-trade momentum, not new barriers and protectionism.

And third, it helps build xenophobic sentiment by creating an us-versus-them mentality. Some of this can be seen in 19th century anti-immigrant conflicts, anti-French tirades during the Iraq war, and general anti-Latino feeling in recent times.

Unfortunately, it is so easy to demonize the "enemy"—witness attitudes towards the Japanese in the 1980s. Much care should be taken so this type of attitude is not directed against the Chinese again in this century (one hundred years after they were last targeted for discrimination). These attitudes become particularly dangerous in a world where nuclear-armed Communist China may have divergent military or political interests in Taiwan, North Korea, Tibet, or in oil in the East China Sea.

Protectionists

Protectionists generally fall into a variety of camps: They are concerned about the loss of jobs and falling wages in the U.S; they think international trade is unfair to Americans and their companies; they are concerned about the conditions of worker's in American companies overseas; they are afraid of globalization altogether; or they simply have nationalistic tendencies and dislike the rest of the world.

Protect Jobs

The most common protectionists are probably those prudently concerned about job losses or reduced wages in the U.S. To them and most protectionists before them, tariffs and other protections are needed to protect jobs and wages. Without such measures, foreigners will steal their jobs, their careers, their pensions, and their futures. Very focused on individual workers at individual sites, they work hard to combat natural economic forces and are hardly aware of macroeconomic forces or trade factors at all, as long as they keep every single job at home.

Unfortunately, these groups also miss or ignore any possible benefits to foreign competition or lower costs. To some extent, their arguments are similar to those opposing automation since that, too, kills individual jobs, though it creates more in the technology fields, just as off-shoring does in many fields.

Allowing jobs and companies to fail is critical as "Microeconomic failure is not macroeconomic failure. Quite the opposite, 'failure' is the way the macro economy transfers resources to where they belong. It is the paradox of progress: a society can't reap the rewards of economic progress without accepting the constant change in work that comes with it. Efforts to soften the blows, by devising policies or laws to preserve jobs or protect industries, will lead to stagnation and decline, the biggest threat to American workers."- Michael Cox and Richard Alms in New York Times Op-Ed.[100]

Tariffs and other barriers to free trade simply impose costly burdens broadly on society while reducing competitive pressure on domestic companies to improve. Further, they often do great damage to related industries.

The recent steel tariffs, for example, have raised steel prices while trying to help save the dinosaurs in the steel industry. General Motors has to pay hundreds of millions of extra dollars a year to save some steel jobs, hardly a good deal for their workers, customers, or investors, who are forced to pay more in order to save the steelworkers' jobs. The reality is that people subsequently buy fewer cars and then the car companies have to lay people off or idle plants, hardly a positive outcome. This sort of end result is effectively trading some jobs for others, but if policy makers are not careful, they leverage in the wrong direction.

This was sharply illustrated in this steel tariff case, where the Institute for International Economics estimates the tariff (temporarily) saved 3,500 jobs, but lost between 12,000 and 43,000 in the steel-consuming industries. Therefore the leverage was 10 to 1 in the wrong direction, hardly a good ratio, especially given the billions it cost the economy in the form of higher prices, unemployment, and lost taxes. All that money would probably have been better spent simply buying out the employment contracts of affected employees and sending them to Hawaii, as it would have incurred much less damage to the economy.

Along the same line of protectionist thought, computers should also be completely made in the U.S., raising their cost, lowering corporate computer spending, and thus slowing productivity growth (the engine that sustains economic growth). Another way to look at the challenges of such policies is fewer computers in companies means fewer $100,000 Intel or Oracle technical jobs, all to save some $10/hour assembly jobs. Again, negative leverage in action.

And, how does automation fit into such schemes? If a call center representative is replaced by a kiosk or an Internet program, that is okay, but if she is replaced by an Indian, that's not? What if the computer program is in the U.S., but written by an Indian? There is no end to the tangled possibilities, all of which have the same endpoint, an out-of-work representative, but more computers, software, and related services.

Along these same lines and regarding political interference, Jacob F. Kirkegaard of the Institute for International Economics argues "U.S. policymakers that limit U.S. businesses' use of cost-efficient foreign labor will likely not result in many U.S. jobs retained but rather a doubling of efforts by these businesses to automate tasks, ultimately perhaps resulting in at least the same number of job destructions."[101]

Even if there is political interference, at least on the services side, there are few effective methods to stop the growing trend of off-shoring anyway. Taxing companies for off-shoring simply won't work. Those companies that can afford to will either pay the taxes, which will probably never outweigh the benefits they get from such job movement, or find loopholes and other ways to avoid paying them, usually by subcontracting, buying subassemblies, bundling services with products, or just expanding their overseas operations, i.e. not making new hires domestically at all. Given the economic toxicity of taxes, even if this so-called solution somehow saved short-term jobs, it would be disastrous for the economy over time.

Capital and capitalism will always find a way to make a good return and it's nearly impossible to erect complete barriers to subcontracting and other types of economic activity involved. Even if government can erect temporary barriers, in the end the jobs will move away anyway, but away from a weakened economy that does no one any good.

Short End of the Trade Stick

Others think that without protectionist tariffs American companies stand to get the short end of the stick in international deals. Other countries often place explicit barriers on American products such as automobiles, as well as more subtle structural barriers like biased quality rules and labeling requirements. These are direct protectionist measures that certainly don't do the American economy any good.

Protectionists argue that these obstacles, along with countries artificially fixing their currency to low rates, make trading with these nations unfair to American companies and thus their employees. If the U.S. makes comparable tariffs and requirements on foreign imports, their argument goes, and then the playing field would be leveled. The fact that foreign companies aren't held to the same environmental and human rights standards as American firms also makes the idea of a more leveled fields all the more attractive for protectionists (although environmental issues can also be a smoke screen for blatant protectionism).

This level-the-playing-field argument is interesting, but in the wrong direction. If everyone keeps raising the barriers until everything is equal, then by extension, there is no trade. And zero trade is not a good way to promote strong economies, economic integration, and global development through economic growth.

Instead, barriers should be lowered by everyone, everywhere, all the time. This is essentially the theory and strategy behind the WTO (and its 50-year-old predecessor GATT, the General Agreement on Tariffs and Trade). Serious progress has been made on many fronts, and barriers are falling every day in India, China, and beyond. Adherence to the rules is not complete, even by America, but is certainly improving.

In addition, India will begin enforcing western patents in 2005 [102], helping create a huge market for western pharmaceutical companies, an area American firms dominate with tens of thousands of well-paying jobs.

At the same time, there are valid dumping cases that should be vigorously pursued, though they are difficult to see and prove, and they are often politically motivated rather than driven by facts in the field. This is a particularly thorny issue with respect to China and Vietnam. These nations are losing dumping cases based not on the facts, but because their non-market economy is automatically assumed to be guilty (on the assumption that the government must automatically be helping all firms in such an economy). The ongoing Vietnamese Catfish fight is a prime example of how such politics hurt consumers by allowing inefficient fish farms in the American

South to essentially block imports from their new, low-cost Southeast Asian competitors.

Currency issues also come into play when fairness is perceived to be a problem. China has recently been accused of maintaining a cheap currency to keep its prices low, and while many economists think the currency probably is too low, this is temporary however. And the demanded 20-30% adjustment will not realistically change the balance of trade since their costs are very low and both their investments and efficiencies are so high in numerous industries (especially textiles).

Further, a sloppy currency re-valuation could do real damage to the weak Chinese banking system, the failure of which would be catastrophic for every economy, not to mention possibly destabilizing to the region. And, it's somewhat hypocritical that Americans complain about Chinese currency policy while the U.S. government often works to keep the dollar weak for the very same trade-promotion reasons.

Regardless, fairness issues are usually temporary and need now to be worked out at the WTO in concert with related trading partners. These issues, which are important in certain industries and should be pursued vigorously, will abate over time and do not materially change the larger picture.

As with the Japanese in the 1980s, American firms should not worry so much about protectionism as much as how to be competitive in a global world, leveraging low-cost opportunities combined with participation in key new markets.

Concerns for Foreign Workers

People concerned about the safety and security of foreign workers have stereotypical pictures in their heads of children working long hours in sweatshops with unsafe working conditions. Many activists argue that foreign employment is just a haven for human rights violations. And while there are some legitimate concerns in these areas, they very rarely apply to white-collar service jobs.

The reality is that service jobs are just that, service, and poor working conditions are hardly conducive to customer satisfaction or directly competing against American service workers. Thus, foreign companies servicing the U.S. market certainly appear to be treating their workers very well, meeting or surpassing American standards in the relevant industries.

An employee of an American IT company in Bombay even described coming to work as, "total freedom," much higher praise than almost any American would give his or her workplace. After all, it's difficult to imagine a college-educated Indian answering phones for Dell while in a sweat shop, sitting on a wooden bench in stifling heat, with no breaks or food. Instead, they are in gleaming office parks with television, cafeterias, continual education, and conditions identical to or better than their American counterparts.

Further, it's critical to recall that safety nets and worker's rights don't cause wealth; they are an outcome of it. Just as America and Europe grew strong and then built big social safety nets, so will the developing world. These structures cannot be forced on developing countries up front or else they will never develop, forever miring their populations in poverty. It's obviously important to treat employees properly in any regard, but full Western-level policies are probably not the best route to prosperity. America does not use all of the European worker safety and environmental regulations and rights, so should Europe refuse imported American goods?

Anti-Globalists

There are also numerous anti-globalist forces at work, usually from the far-left groups, such as those protesting against the WTO in Seattle or the World Economic Forum in Davos. Such groups generally dislike commercialization and corporations in general, especially when it involves "weak" peoples or countries, since the American empire must be exploiting or taking advantage somehow, even when these developed countries are begging for the work and trade. Fortunately, these groups' power has waned considerably in recent years and their influence on the discussion is now nearly non-existent.

To some extent, it's unfortunate to see these groups' arguments go away, as they can add serious and interesting ideas to trade theory. Free traders obviously argue for more trade, for the market to rule, and for the chips to fall where they may. By contrast, the more thoughtful of these groups ask about the impact of American-style economics on the host countries, especially in such a short period of time. They worry about cultural destruction, military and government corruption, and many of the things that were seen in America centuries ago.

In many cases these are real concerns, though today's rapidly globalizing culture (driven by the Internet, Hollywood, and American culture in all its forms) arguably has a much stronger effect than trade or moving jobs. Regardless, it does make sense to be as sensitive to these issues as possible, incorporating these groups' ideas and concerns, in addition to bringing them on board with some of the efforts to build successful economies in the developing world.

Nationalists

The final group of protectionists are simply afraid of the world; this is the Pat Buchanan or Ralph Nader wing of the Republican and Democratic parties. They think that the U.S. economy should remain relatively isolationist to prosper and save the "American Way," whatever that is. These groups argue for nationalism, patriotism, and national security, and their voices have only gotten louder since 9/11, though they echo the 1920-30s' voices and are potentially just as dangerous now as in the past.

Most of these people are arguing from simple fear; fear that globalization will increase corruptive influences on the U.S., fear that they will lose the simple, dominant nation they imagine they have. Also, some groups appear to feel overrun by people of different colors, shapes, cultures, and religions that are somehow changing America.

Unfortunately for them, closing the borders and ceasing all interaction with foreign nations won't magically bring back a happier and more wholesome time that never existed anyway. Globalization is a reality, whether individuals are ready to accept it or not, and it's only a matter of how Americans plan to deal with this reality in the coming years.

The real challenge with nationalists is their plans for change are simply dangerous for the domestic and world economies, for instance keeping African farmers impoverished via the destructive effects of Western tariffs and agriculture subsidies.

In the end, protectionists threaten to destroy the very economy they seek to save. It is hard to know how much power protectionist forces will garner over the policy landscape in the coming years, but as more people become concerned and angry about the off-shoring phenomenon, the protectionist bandwagon will gain momentum and become easier to board. Once the great mass of the middle class has decided that nationalism and protectionism is what they want, it will be difficult for forward-thinking politicians to retard their efforts. This is already a problem in Europe, where the anti-immigrant backlash has already begun.

The protectionist groups miss the point that increasing trade improves global prosperity and thus global security. Given that trade and foreign direct investment (FDI) is the best foreign aid ever invented, countries should be fighting to improve trade, jobs, educational levels, and living standards among the countries or regions labeled as America's "enemies."

For example, the free trade agreement with Jordan embodies this exact spirit; it requires that Jordanian companies partner with Israeli firms to qualify for the reduced tariffs. In the end, it is increasingly difficult to hate the countries giving you the best jobs, wages, and benefits – if only this could be extended to Cuba, Iran, North Korea, and every other despotic region on the planet. This type of treaty, which provides incentives for geopolitical purposes, is the opposite of regulation and protectionism, but must be used sparingly, lest it cross the line into disruptive political interference in the markets.

Off-shoring is simply a reality, one that goes hand-in-hand with globalization and free trade. Protectionists react to the job flight by saying, "this can't be good for us; we're losing jobs;

let's make it illegal." But the forces behind the job shift are simply too strong, the technology is too developed, global education is too advanced, Americans are too overpaid, and foreign workers are too motivated.

No tariffs or legal obstacles that the U.S. government raises in front of businesses will stop these businesses from taking advantage of huge benefits to improve their bottom line. Hopes of stemming the tide of off-shoring are simply naïve. As President Bush has said, "We cannot expect to sell our goods and services, and create jobs, if America and our partners, trading partners, start raising barriers and closing off markets."[103]

Alan Greenspan weighs in on protectionism: "We can erect walls to foreign trade and even discourage job-displacing innovation. The pace of competition would surely slow, and tensions might appear to ease. But only for a short while. Our standard of living would soon begin to stagnate and perhaps even decline as a consequence."[104]

Corporate America's Nervous Reactions

Companies taking advantage of off-shoring are understandably nervous about the political fallout, fearing that their businesses will experience a backlash. These companies have to worry about hostile responses both within the ranks of their employees and in the socio-political environments in which they operate.

Within the company, off-shoring upsets remaining employees as they watch their coworkers be replaced; though some of them realize they get to keep their jobs because of the cost-cutting moves enabled by off-shoring. Outside the company are consumers and politicians, many of whom see companies that off-shore as traitors.

Fortunately, a visible backlash has not yet arisen, as a groundswell of either employee or consumer resentment, though not for lack of trying on the part of some in the anti-off-shoring groups or the media. For instance, some media players are attempting to drag the public at large into the fray, with folks like Lou Dobbs boosting ratings by maintaining a running list of all the "traitor" companies that send jobs off-shore.

Such lists are superficial and foolish on many levels. For one thing they completely miss the foreign subcontractors or suppliers of other large companies, which involve far more jobs and economic activity. After all, how does one distinguish between IBM deciding to buy a chip from Taiwan and IBM moving production for the same chip from New York to Taiwan? The end result is exactly the same and yet the latter is perceived as a horrible thing while the former is a normal business practice underlying nearly every product for sale in America.

In the same vein, how does one distinguish between IBM moving ten engineering jobs to Taiwan and simply hiring its next ten engineers in Taiwan? This is where the real job action is -- Microsoft recently announced it'll hire 7,000 new employees in 2005, with up to 3-4,000 in the Seattle area. Many of the rest are probably overseas, but because they are new hires and not "moved" positions, it's not considered classical off-shoring, even though the result is exactly the same. Many big companies are in this mode, with significant hiring overseas, but limited staffing increases at home. Sorting out who and what is going where in such an environment is truly a challenge (and a complex nuance beyond the simplistic analysis offered by protectionists or standard media.)

Corporate concern about reaction to these issues is palatable. Many companies now forbid their Indian suppliers from issuing "new customer" press releases or even publicizing customer names at all. And terms like "right sourcing" are now appearing on consulting literature, to move away from the stigma of "off-shoring."

White Collar Unions

Shortly after asking the government for help, some displaced workers try to form unions to protect what they perceive as their interests. Unions are fairly rare in the white-collar world, limited to the lower-level clerical work, e.g. with the Communication Workers of America (CWA). Large mid-level unions are generally confined to civil servants, with perhaps the exception of Boeing engineers (Society of Professional Engineering Employees in Aerospace or SPEEA).

There has been some talk of trying to create unions at various firms, notably IBM. The CWA Alliance at IBM has been leading this effort, so far unsuccessfully. Washtech/CWA is the other dominant white-collar union, though its efforts have also met with limited success outside of contract workers at Microsoft.

In addition, there are ongoing conflicts within the large unions, especially at the AFL-CIO, in terms of how to handle these issues. Some at the national level favor creating European-style sector unions, targeting an entire industry such as chip making, at once, while others bemoan the loss of their union's power. While this infighting is likely to distract them for some time, unionization efforts could still cause trouble at larger firms over time.

As with nearly all unionized workforces, wages and benefits tend to creep up while flexibility and productivity decline, often imperiling the company (the air travel and steel industries come to mind). Any unionization efforts are likely to only accelerate the move to automate jobs, as employee unrest can easily be the deciding factor when companies are forming their staffing and off-shoring strategies. Fears of such acceleration is a major reason that German companies are starting to win major concessions from unions with just the threat of moving jobs to eastern Europe. As a result, the possibilities of real union power arising in the private American white-collar workplace seems unlikely.

Worst Case Scenario - Potential Unrest

In the worst case the American middle-class will become increasingly angry and eventually regard the Chinese, Indians, and others as the scapegoat for their own lack of preparation and failure of their government's leadership.

With little economic growth and ever-rising unemployment, the Western world could again resemble Europe in the 1930s. When a population becomes disillusioned and desperate, political extremists can easily take hold of the nationalist ethos, especially when anger toward a marginalized group such as foreigners or Jews is already present.

The power of economics to create such a situation among the middle class cannot be over-emphasized. Fascism's rise in Europe was partly due to economic discontent, and the seeds of such a future are already being sown by the likes of Pat Buchanan on the right, and by the protectionist wings of the Democratic party on the left. If the government supports the protectionist or anti-foreigner fervor, as it did against France before the Iraq war or Japan in the 1980s, things would only get worse. Such challenging times and nationalistic fervor gave rise to Hitler and Mussolini and could theoretically repeat themselves in the coming decades.

Even without overtly nationalistic leaders, dismal economics and increasing trade pressures can start a trade war, with each part of the world retracting into a protectionist shell, as in 1935. Isolationism and nationalism could get out of hand, and the U.S. would likely find itself in a serious conflict with other world powers.

When all's said and done, off-shoring is happening but its negative effects can be managed. The trend will only grow, helping more companies and swallowing up more American jobs at the outset. Anyone who thinks that Americans are going to accept losing what they see as their right to a job is not being realistic. The West's future may well include political unrest in ways not recently seen, some of which is already apparent in Europe's anti-immigrant trends. Politicians and legislators can pander for votes by fanning the protectionist fire, or by trying to put it out with well-measured, constructive policies and leadership. Whichever happens, there is no fury like middle-class workers scorned, and any policy decision needs to remember (and probably counter) the reactions of the people for the interests of everyone involved.

Chapter 7.

Is There Any Good in This?

"Outsourcing is just a new way of doing international trade. More things are tradable than were tradable in the past, and that's a good thing."

Gregory Mankiw,
Chairman of the Bush White House
Council of Economic Advisers[105]

Can any good come of this off-shoring process? Losing jobs can't be good, can it? If a $100,000 a year accountant has to return to school to get a $50,000 job, how is everyone better off? What happens when every good job is moved abroad and Americans are reduced to "Would you like fries with that?" or "Welcome to Wal-Mart." Given that large swaths of journalists, white-collar workers, and politicians are all griping about job exports, is there any benefit to off-shoring at all?

As with all economic changes, the job shift will create economic advantages and disadvantages, creating disadvantaged and displaced workers alongside those benefiting from new opportunities. Unfortunately, one fairly significant challenge in balancing pros and cons in economics and trade is that the advantages tend to be fairly broad and diffuse, while the pain of things like losing a job is tangible and easy to see.

American Benefits

The benefits to developing countries are fairly clear, but what about the value to the U.S. of pushing jobs off-shore and throwing good, hard-working Americans out of work? While the benefits are far more diverse than the acute pain of a single job loss, they are no less real and will be much more important in the long run.

Direct Benefits

Global strategic advisors McKinsey & Company have tried to assess the benefits in purely economic terms, looking at cash and benefit flows of a single dollar sent abroad to buy an off-shored service. While not without controversy, they estimate that for every $1 sent abroad, about $1.12 returns to America, through a mix of purchased equipment and services, cost savings, re-deployed labor, and other benefits.[106]

Even if their assumptions are overly optimistic, they still render hollow the zero-sum claim of complete loss for the U.S. But how can this be, when, as some politicians put it, off-shoring is the latest of the "giant sucking sounds" draining away good jobs for honest, hard-working Americans? Where is this $1.12 coming from and do Americans really benefit?

Lower Costs

The most obvious direct benefit of off-shoring, lower costs, is the simplest, though its effects reach further than is generally appreciated. Everyone likes lower prices at places like Wal-Mart, but lower costs to the economy as a whole have far-reaching benefits that are often unrecognized by the critics.

First and fundamentally, lower costs of production or living automatically raise living standards, in much the same manner as enhanced productivity (which essentially lowers cost). Essentially, each consumer dollar goes further, buys more, and increases the ratio of income to what it can buy. Yes, losing jobs in a manner that lowers wages can lower living standards - the trick is to gain more than is lost; typically via the mechanism in which costs and salaries adjust in response.

For instance, if software development or claims processing costs are cut 50% by off-shoring, but domestic wages decline only 25%, then the economy wins, pure and simple. While good macro data are lacking, it's not even clear yet that wages are actually eroding, but the costs savings and benefits are quite evident to any Wal-Mart shopper or startup company.

Cost reductions also provide direct and very tangible benefits in many cases. Lower-cost medical devices or drugs allow the benefit to be spread more widely, as do technology and productivity enhancing systems in business. Cheaper microwave ovens and VCRs in the 1970s and '80s allowed every family to own one. The same can be said for less expensive computers - a powerful fully-featured computer now costs less than $500, allowing every family and business to own 21st century technology. Such ownership opens their world to the Internet, provides key tools to their children, and creates markets for other innovative technologies such as Voice-over-IP and blogging.

Lower costs also act as a powerful catalyst for economic activity, especially when they restrain that bugaboo of all modern economies, inflation. While the too-rapid fall of costs can trigger dangerous deflation (which wipe out asset values and create a recession), lower costs generally reduce inflation and thus raise living standards and eliminate the need to raise interest rates to brake the economy.

As such, sending a job to India lowers the pressure on companies to raise prices. This may not be a big factor in the preparation of a single tax form, but these savings directly lower inflation that would otherwise erode savings and pensions while reducing real wages.

It could even be argued that a key reason the economy grew strongly in the 1990s without triggering inflation was lower costs in many industries, due to imported materials or services. The next economic boom may well be initiated or sustained by off-shore-driven cost reductions.

This doesn't even take into account the marginal or economic leverage activities that are made possible by lower costs, greater efficiency, lower taxes, and lower transaction costs. The latter are extremely powerful, since many industries experience massive volume increases when transaction costs drop. Witness the strong price-lowering effects of volume increases as deregulation took hold in long distance and cellular phone rates, brokerage rates, trucking and air travel prices, etc. This is again leverage at work, where a modest price reduction can substantially raise volume. Creating more competition doesn't hurt, either.

Costs vs. Welfare

A few dollars saved here or there may seem inconsequential to most citizens, but such savings are critically important to those with limited means, especially those living on welfare or Social Security. Since both of these massive programs are tax funded, any reductions in the cost of living translates directly to lower taxes on workers across the board, which in turn allows money to be deployed in more productive sectors.

This is also true in health care, perhaps the most vexing public finance issue. It is certainly beneficial to reduce health care costs by exporting some of the work, as in the case of Indian doctors performing remote procedures or running trials for expensive new drugs. This is especially true when tax dollars are used to pay for such expenses, as it's far better to send a job abroad than to raise taxes to support one domestically.

Reduced Capital Needs

The importance of lower costs cannot be overestimated in relation to capital efficiency, or the cost it takes to start and run a business. Every day Silicon Valley startups are creating cutting-edge, next-generation technology using a mix of local and foreign talent. This use of off-shore expertise lowers costs and thus the amount of capital needed to get new products to market and get the company to profitability – this can make the difference between technologies and companies that succeed and those that don't. Since innovation, future industries, and increased employment are typically created this way, any mechanism that lowers costs spurs this crucial process and can only speed American job creation.

Along the same lines, lower R&D costs stretch research funds, allowing more and better science and products to be produced. This helps everyone as it creates more technology for more products, which then generates the next round of jobs for everybody.

Leveraging Low Costs to Save Jobs

Importing services and lowering costs can go a long way towards preserving jobs and companies that would otherwise disappear. As mentioned, globally competitive firms such as Intel or HP often off-shore a portion of their work, but retain the highest paying positions at home. This is also effective for small to mid-sized companies who provide the bulk of domestic employment, since they can leverage their local talent and still keep their heads above water. After all, small product or manufacturing companies have long since sourced components from overseas to maintain the viability of their domestic businesses.

Such split effects, long common in manufacturing where many suppliers are overseas, are often ignored in the winner-take-all or us-vs-them mentalities seen in the off-shoring economics debate. This idea of saving jobs by sacrificing others is not only an effective tactic for large companies such as Intel or Boeing, but is saving small companies every day.

For example, CollabNet is a San Francisco-based software firm that saved local jobs by sending some work off-shore, enabling it to extend its capital long enough to get its products to market. As Brian Behlendorf from CollabNet puts it – "We saved the jobs of the people who are employed in San Francisco by hiring people (in India). I don't know that we would be around as a company if we hadn't done that. What was the right thing to do, morally?"[107]

This is especially powerful in small and mid-sized companies, who cannot just move or expand their businesses overseas. The Germans call these the Middlestand, or the mid-sized companies responsible for much of German economic success in recent decades. Their American cousins' ability to leverage global sourcing and cut costs allows them to focus on what they do best, namely product innovation, customer services, and really understanding their markets. For many American firms, the cost-lowering benefit of being able to use foreign services provides additional advantage as they compete on the world stage.

Hiring abroad can also actually expand business at home. This is especially true in hi-tech industries, for companies such as IBM, Oracle, or even Boeing. When they hire 100 engineers in China and India to tailor products for local customers or to lower development costs, they increase sales of the company's major products in that market. This then provides more work for their well-paid American employees. After all, every million-dollar mainframe, software, or aircraft sale to Asia employs numerous manufacturing and programming jobs in places like New York and California.

Benefits to Investors

Further, even if massive numbers of jobs do go abroad with no new jobs domestically, there are still benefits to be had, namely to investors. While investors used to be limited to rich institutions and the wealthy, today more than 50% of Americans own stock, either directly or via mutual funds and pension plans. The oft-mentioned "little old lady on a pension" really does depend on corporate profits to provide her retirement income each month. As such, the well-being of companies like General Electric are very important and the $340 million they save by sending jobs to India flows directly into the pockets of little old ladies everywhere. It also provides additional capital to more Wall Street-oriented investors to invest in new companies, business models, and innovations.

Increased Exports

Another essential advantage to using off-shoring to grow developing economies is the resulting increase in American exports. Imports are at record levels, as is the trade deficit. Structurally, there is probably neither the mechanism nor desire to lower these import levels, as by definition it can only be done at higher cost to the economy.

The real underlying problem is one of global growth, or the lack thereof. In other words, other countries are not growing fast enough to purchase their "appropriate" level of American goods. Note this is also the area most sensitive to protectionism, so if the U.S. closes its markets, these foreign buyers will presumably dry up, too.

Given that America has the world's largest economy and is the world's largest exporter, any global growth helps the U.S. more than anyone. [108] Therefore, the question becomes how to sharply increase exports of all types. And not just a few billion here and there, but by tens of billions per month.

Fortunately, when a developing country grows and especially when its middle class expands, it starts importing high-value goods such as production machinery and technology, automobiles, telecommunications systems, and computers, as well as airplanes, power plants, and foodstuffs. Historically, these types of products have been made in the West and are generally at the top of the employment wage pyramid. This type of buying accounts for a significant portion of the McKinsey study's positive returns for every dollar sent overseas in off-shoring.

As a result, part of the underlying strategy has to include figuring out how to generate demand in Asia and Africa for things like 250 million new computers and 500 Boeing airplanes per year, i.e. everything on the list of America's top 25 exports. And every Asian child should visit Disney World to pour money into the American economy.

For instance, China is now the #2 market for personal computers, which provide substantial revenue and employment in the U.S., using Intel and Microsoft components, as well as hordes of commercial products from a wide variety of companies.[109] China is also the #1 market for cellular phones, further adding value to major American technology players and software systems of all kinds, including infrastructure and games.

Further, many large technology companies such as Oracle, Siebel, IBM, and HP get increasing amounts of their revenue from India and China, again employing increasing numbers of high-wage employees on both sides of the Pacific.

For example, IBM believes that its next big market for mainframes is China, which will lead directly to billions of dollars in American-made systems, supporting the jobs of thousands of engineers, managers, and factory workers. "China is a huge, huge opportunity," says Erich Clementi, who runs IBM's mainframe business. His group is adding nearly 60 new mainframe-related personnel in Beijing.[110] Note that IBM is also opening a mainframe laboratory in Beijing to train workers while finding ways to tailor the systems for that market. These are not off-shored jobs, but catalysts for even greater job growth at home. Those 60 new jobs are heavily Chinese-oriented and never would have been created at home, but they support many thousands of U.S. jobs in IBM’s mainframe and related business.

Further, IBM announced that it will be training 40,000 Chinese IT workers in writing Chinese software and using mainstream systems such as Java.[111] This can only sell more computers, benefiting IBM, Microsoft, Intel, and a slew of other American companies and their employees.

This is the essence of a global model at work, where toys bought at an American Wal-Mart help grow the Chinese economy so they need to buy IBM mainframes. That is the essential trade-off-- swap toy making for mainframe design and assembly.

This also raises the point that it’s much better for Oracle or IBM to begin to move some jobs, rather than allow an Indian competitor to arise to eat its lunch and force massive layoffs of American staffers. Boeing suffered exactly this fate at the hands of Airbus, and Cisco is finding this out now as the company competes with the giant Chinese electronics firm Huawei. No other American company wishes the same fate, so companies would be strategically smart to develop a global presence, using people and products in every market to protect their own market share at home.

A non-tech example of how important the foreign middle classes are, the Napa Valley Vintners Association has started making trips to China to begin pushing its wines in upscale restaurants. San Franciscan and other American architects design major building projects all across China. [112] Even American financiers are in the game, investing in Chinese and Indian companies, with the financial returns coming back to American pension funds, ironically to support retired and laid-off veterans of prior trade wars.

There are also softer benefits to buying or working American. Looking just at direct service and merchandise exports to China (~$35B) and India (~$10B), together they spent $45 billion on American products in 2003. Using an average of $200,000 per employee, that translates to 225,000 good-paying jobs, numbers that are only rising.[113]

Further, off-shored jobs also export good will -- a foreigner's increased wages allow him or her to afford domestic and American products, while those employed by U.S. companies also become more attuned to American culture and thereby become more likely to want American goods. Employees of call centers in Manila now listen to hip-hop and wear baggy jeans, all products from American companies, even if they are not made in the U.S.A. Their stable jobs with American companies have both culturally exposed them (sometimes to the chagrin of their elders) and perhaps given them a more positive picture of Americans as a whole.

This positive image of the U.S. helps Americans in a much more vital way than the increase of CD sales. The negative impact that foreign dislike or even hatred of Americans has wrought on the U.S. cannot be overemphasized. The image of America as an oppressive devil in the minds of poor, angry citizens across the globe has already bred too much violence and strife. Handouts and political grandstanding will not dislodge this hatred, but American businesses providing good jobs and political stability surely helps. It is difficult to think of Americans as the enemy when they provide you with a well-paying job with good benefits and help your country attain true democratic stability. The good will that comes from such interactions again cannot be overemphasized.

Other Benefits and Models

Another benefit of lower cost is more science and R&D, leading directly to more and better products for everyone. For instance, diesel engine maker Cummins used to introduce two new engine models per year. Now they do five or six annually by using their new Indian R&D facility, bringing ultra-efficient engines to market, reducing pollution, and conserving precious oil resources as truck and other heavy-engine users upgrade, all for the same R&D dollars.

As mentioned, lower costs can also create whole new business models and benefits that could not previously be afforded. The Delta Airlines billing analyses and Wall Street equity research examples illustrate how tasks that leverage foreign assistance can enable entirely new business processes that significantly enhance revenue and service.

Also, it's important to never underestimate the cost curve for innovation and high-end employment. For instance, foreign manufactured DVD players finally became cheap enough to allow every family to own one. Once that happened, the market for movie and TV show DVDs really took off, primarily supporting the American entertainment market. Further, DVD technology allows for added "bonus" content, requiring more writing, production, and editing jobs. So, using cheap foreign manufacturers spawned an entirely new multi-billion market for these products, creating jobs far better than assembling American-made DVD players every could have. This is the magic of an integrated global economy and the sum of the parts equaling far more than the whole.

This also points to how difficult it is to predict where and how individual advancements and importing deals will affect things macroscopically. Everything looks easy in hindsight, but it's very difficult beforehand to allow cheap DVD players, yet restrict the import of certain types of software. Often, the market really does need to sort it all out on its own, where less expensive items delivered at lower transactional costs can have a big impact in unexpected ways.

Creative Destruction

A more indirect, but possibly even larger benefit is creative destruction in the American economy. Through sending jobs abroad to lower cost to the economy, it also forces Americans to find better ways of doing things to stay competitive.

In a very real sense, this was the real reaction to the Japanese onslaught of the 1980s and early '90s. Old-line industries such as autos, steel, consumer electronics, and some high-tech sectors experienced very hard times. Some like autos and steel have still not recovered, although that's primarily a result of their failure to restructure (much like the airlines and other industries with old paradigms, particularly in labor and productivity).

The Japanese and the German Middlestand companies forced American firms and workers to really come to grips with their poor products and work practices. While substantial hardship ensued, the companies that emerged intact were much stronger and produced better products. Real competition forced them to do what some would argue Americans do best, innovate and change the way they do things. In just a decade the American economy went from a perception of straight decline and obsolescence to again leading the world in almost every area.

Japan offers a counter example, not coincidentally from the other side of America's dynamic success. After Americans started competing, and more importantly the world's economies changed, the Japanese could not change with it, resulting in a decade-long economic slide. This offers the lesson that the power of invention, flexibility, and driving change cannot be underestimated, especially for those economies not sufficiently dynamic to adjust to and take advantage of new opportunities as the world changes beneath their feet.

Taking an example from the automotive industry, it's easy to see how competitive pressures can alter long-standing processes, to everyone's benefit. As everyone knows, automobile exteriors are made from many large metal pieces. These pieces, used for the hood, trunk, roof, fenders, doors, etc., are made by stamping big pieces of metal into the proper shape between large specially shaped dies in a stamping press. These machines are the size of a small house and cost millions of dollars.

Given their cost, it's very important to keep them busy, so one machine usually makes many different parts, such as hoods, trunks, and doors. Each different piece requires a different die, but changing the heavy and complicated dies has historically taken a long time, as much as a full eight-hour shift. Therefore, companies usually made thousands of a single part, such as hoods, then changed dies to make thousands of doors, etc. Unfortunately, this builds up a large inventory of parts and if something is wrong with the machine or dies, a lot of pieces are ruined.

The Japanese had a different model for the very same process and same piece of equipment. They believed that inventory was evil, for money, space, and quality reasons, and to minimize that problem, they had to tackle the die-changing process that Americans had not improved for decades. While there are a myriad of details, in the end Toyota teams routinely changed dies in 20 minutes, versus several hours for American companies. That, in turn, allowed them to make only 50 or 100 of each item, enough for an hour or two, before changing to other parts.

When confronted with this reality and the major benefits it offered the factory, the American companies learned how to change the dies just as quickly, with the corresponding drop in inventory and storage space required.

The lesson is that, for no real additional investment, competitive pressure forced a company to learn and an industry to change for the better. This is precisely the type of efficiency improvement that global competition can bring about, helping everyone move to the next level of efficiency and productivity.[114]

So, while the blue-collar workers and firms bore the brunt of the change in the Japanese round, so will the white-collar workers in this Chinese and Indian round. The newly-at-risk must learn the same lessons from strong competitors, though as noted, this round is probably more difficult on many levels. The outcome will displace some, but leave the rest much stronger and better for the effort (even if it does not feel that way at the time). There is nowhere to run this time (e.g. from manufacturing to services), so companies and workers must stand and fight competition with innovation and improvement on every front.

This improvement will depend on one of America's core strengths - allowing for, and even encouraging risk, failure, and change. For instance, it's very quick and easy to start a company; hundreds of thousands are created each year, but many won't survive the first year and most won't make five years. An objective viewer might observe that these are terrible odds, but deep within them lies a key American strength – the ability to fail and then to pick oneself up, dust off, and try again. Unlike in some cultures, failure is not a career-ending move, but just a beginning, especially in Silicon Valley where it can be an emblem of lessons learned.

This sort of turnover and turmoil is the process by which the most competitive and deserving companies win out. Try as they might, societies cannot strive to keep people in ineffective, often pointless businesses – the telegraph business used to be a strong one, but is hardly worthy of investment or life-support today. It is painful, but far better to lose obsolete jobs and move on to better ones, or at least free up the money and people to work at value-creating activities. Tearing down obsolete structures that no longer work makes room for those that do.

Destruction is an accepted force in the economy. European nations (and the Japanese historically) have taken the opposite tack, choosing instead to prop up failing companies with tax breaks and funding in a feeble attempt to save businesses that are already going under.

In the end, propping up these companies only delays the Grim Reaper's visit, while squandering precious tax dollars and greater economic prosperity. The Japanese call these businesses "zombie companies," which are kept around for political reasons, but are quite literally the walking dead, falsely animated by tax dollars. This is the opposite of the American, or at least Silicon Valley, perspective, where failure is a learning experience and rapidly frees up resources to be put to better use.

One of the best examples was the dot-com bubble, which was widely derided as complete disaster, but in fact was an example of this process at work. As in the railroad, automobile, aircraft, and many other extremely successful American industries before it, a great deal of capital was deployed rapidly in a new sector to spur numerous innovations.

The sector drew scores of people, equipment, and facilities into a whirlwind of activity; and in the end, most enterprises failed, but that's the point – the companies that survived those battles are still here today as global leaders, and the technology they spawned still serves everyone well. Further, the economy destroyed the failed companies, redeploying the resources (including people) into other endeavors. Compared to the Japanese or European models, the American system recycles resources to their next best use very rapidly.

In-Sourcing

As a final benefit to off-shoring in America, there is in-sourcing, when foreign companies invest in America. According to the Organization for International Investment, U.S. subsidiaries of foreign corporations employ 6.4 million American workers, paying about $350 billion in payroll, largely for high-paying manufacturing, design, and marketing jobs. [115] That's fully 5% of all American jobs. If America becomes less hospitable to foreigners or fails to provide an attractive climate and free-trade support, many of these valuable jobs could evaporate, potentially taking with them more jobs than will ever be lost to off-shoring.

New Asian companies, like their European and Japanese counterparts before them, are becoming further enmeshed in the American business world. For example, one of the most innovative Chinese companies, appliance maker Haier, is building factories and design centers in America, both to better understand a critical market and to tap Western management and financial talent.

Such American integration exposes more of a foreign company's employees to American culture and business practices elements, including ethics, contracts, and the rule of law. Likewise, American workers and managers are increasingly melded into foreign operations, giving everyone a new and broader perspective that can only be good for global understand and stability.

Benefits to the other Countries

"Within four years, IT outsourcing will be a $57 billion annual industry - responsible for 7 % of India's GDP and employing some 4 million people."[116]

Most of the discussion surrounding off-shoring focuses on the challenges created for the American economy, but it's critical not to overlook the benefits (and challenges) to the countries supplying the workers.

New Middle Class

The most obvious off-shoring benefit is providing good jobs at good salaries, which builds a real middle class, typically leading to a democratic and stable country, with sufficient revenue to build homes, infrastructure, and a future for their children. Perhaps the most important result of this off-shoring process is the creation of a middle class, a force for political and social stability generated by a happy, hopeful, and well-employed citizenry.

Historically, a stable middle class has been elusive in developing nations, especially those nations at the bottom, at

$500-$5,000 GDP/person. The gap between rich and poor in these nations is extreme, with the majority of their citizenry falling on the very poor end of the scale – that's often tens or hundreds of millions of people. To put that in perspective, the World Bank reported recently that 50% of the world (over 3 billion people) live on less than $2 per day, with 1 billion living on $1/day.[117]

This sort of income disparity tends to lead to political instability and crime, with abusive governments and militant extremist groups, not to mention terrorists, fringe religious groups, and other nefarious entities. After all, it's difficult to be entrepreneurial or think about the future when just staying alive and fed is every day's priority. This is so important that the World Bank recently published a special report entitled "Eradicating Poverty for Stability and Peace."

As noted, there has been a dynamic shift in perspectives in recent years about how to best help developing nations attain economic and political security. World powers formerly assuaged their guilty consciences with handouts to lesser nations, often in the form of aid packages with plenty of strings attached. Unfortunately, donated money often ended up in the bank accounts of the most powerful citizens, and even if it did reach the poorest citizens, it only lasted so long, as people still want for ongoing income sources.

Now, first-world nations are beginning to see that such charitable donations do little to change these nation's situations. As the president of the World Bank said recently, "Countries don't need charity, they need opportunity."[118]

Money must be part of the solution, but not in the form of handouts. Trade is by far the most powerful form of foreign aid (Senator Hollings' comments about "Our trouble is that we have treated trade as aid" not withstanding). In fact, trade is so powerful that it's amazing more attention isn't paid to the ways in which domestic tariffs and subsidies are so destructive in the third world. Fortunately, this is changing via the WTO, both in recent trade decisions and the current Doha Round of negotiations, where developing countries are driving discussion on these issues.

At the same time, even small NGO-driven trade adjustments such as Fair Trade Coffee can lift entire groups out of poverty. Such efforts use marketing messages and branding to link the all-powerful consumer to the mechanisms that improve things among the most impoverished. And they do this rapidly, with private money and efficiently inspections, without regulation or government involvement.

Other on-the-ground efforts to use economics to improve the lives of the developing world, such as micro-lending, are also demonstrating that enabling economic activity is the only way the developing world has ever, or will ever, develop.

Stability

"In retrospect, the Communist hard-liners were right about one thing, though: they warned passionately that it would be impossible to grab only Western investment and keep out Western poisons like capitalism and dreams of 'bourgeois freedom.' They knew that after the Chinese could watch Eddie Murphy, wear tight pink dresses and struggle over what to order at Starbucks, the revolution was finished. No middle class is content with more choices of coffees than of candidates on a ballot." - Nicholas Kristof, New York Times op-ed.[119]

Beyond significantly upping the standard of living in many of these nations, a middle class provides political stability by making upward mobility an achievable possibility for millions of malcontented poor - the proverbial American Dream. Once people attain middle-class status, they also gain a political voice through their buying power, education, and media access. Their money literally talks, and people with stable jobs and homes are much more desirable for governments than lower-class workers with little impact on the larger economy. A stable middle class creates a more stable nation, with far less social and political unrest, and with more democratic tendencies, even in China.

Once key nations gain stability via a middle class, they help stabilize entire regions around them. Countries focused on building their economies and supporting their populace have far less reason to quibble with neighbors for access to resources and political power, though nationalistic politicians can always stir things up. Post-WWII Europe has been a good example of such stability; while not everyone was happy with the various borders, there were far more important tasks at hand than arguing about the past.

Also, India's prosperity means less reason to argue with Pakistan or threaten them with nuclear weapons, just as China's economic success hopefully leads to fewer concerns regarding Taiwan. As such, one country's burgeoning middle class has spillover effects for an entire section of the world, even if neighboring countries aren't yet experiencing the same level of economic or political success.

And, as the benefits become clear, other countries can even change their systems to join the bandwagon. This has yet to occur in the Middle-East, but it's already visible in Vietnam, Cambodia, and Indonesia.

Investing in and fostering growth in developing countries, especially in Asia, is similar to military investments made in prior decades to promote regional stability. America long ago realized that stability in the Asian region was critical to the global economy, so much so that aircraft carrier battle groups and forward bases around Asia keep relatively stable. In the same vein, newly minted industries and the middle classes they develop will be the new engines of stability for the 21st century.

Jobs, a Future, Consumption

The reality is that developing world citizenry needs good jobs. And this is precisely what off-shoring and Western companies offer them. These aren't always perfect jobs at the lower levels, but certainly a stepping stone to a more prosperous future, individually and collectively.

Jobs with western companies also may be better paying and more secure than other opportunities available to them, especially when one considers the other options for girls in most developing societies. Many sadly end up in very early marriage, prostitution, and even slavery in some places. However, as more families become middle class, many good things happen, like girls getting into school, houses getting built, and health care improving.

Perhaps most importantly, hundreds of millions of people can see a good future for themselves and their children; this is a powerful force that can never be underestimated since such optimism drives success the world over. In short, the whole world can aspire to its own version of the American dream. In fact, many would argue that the lack of such a dream in much of Africa and the Mid-East is the strongest driver of many current challenges in those important areas of the world.

And, as noted, when stability and income rise, so does consumption. While massive increases in consumption raise issues of over-use of natural resources, they are surely the ticket to a better future, both in the developing country and for the Western world who supplies the market and technology for that growth.

Off-shoring Challenges

Off-shoring provides advantages for numerous businesses, but like everything it has drawbacks. Many businesses try off-shoring and determine they aren't well-suited for the practice and often regret hiring overseas workers. Some companies find that foreign workers aren't as productive as they hoped, or that their cost savings aren't as large as promised. Others run into cultural and language barriers that create awkward interactions for their employees and customers. Like any initiative in business, off-shoring is not without challenges and may not be right for every company or at every stage of a company's development.

Unforeseen Issues

For some companies, the expected gain in savings from off-shoring ends up being illusory. They are told that they can hire workers for fractions of the price while their productivity remains the same. Often, though, the numbers don't quite work out that way. Though employees in places like India are always cheaper, they can be less productive, especially as they come up the learning curve or experience distance or culturally-related challenges.

For instance, employers often complain of Indian workers requiring more detailed instructions or more hands-on training, given that they are less familiar with the U.S. products and customers. One CEO who took his business off-shore reported that though his new employees cost only 1/3 of his old staff, they were only 1/6 as productive.[120]

Productivity is also a particularly difficult issue in areas experiencing rapid innovation, as employees more geographically removed from clients have a more difficult time catching up. Bassab Pradhan, senior VP of worldwide sales at Infosys Technologies, India's largest software services company, has spoken on this challenge. In a New York Times article, he said, "Whenever the pace of innovation is very rapid, is when the work should be done closer to the client."[121]

This reality dictates that new, creative business processes can only be developed by face-to-face interaction between developers and clients, something that is impossible to outsource or off-shore effectively (though people are trying). Experience in Silicon Valley, the fastest and most innovative place on earth, tends to confirm these challenges, though many are trying innovative ways to circumvent them, as the off-shoring benefits to cash-strapped startups is very compelling.

Companies also often forget how much built-up institutional knowledge they have in their domestic workforces, a lesson often painfully learned by manufacturing firms sending work abroad in the 1980s. "The loss of tacit knowledge is often understated, and unfortunately, not many companies realize this and even fewer have specific plans in place for capturing, or at least transferring knowledge before it walks out the front door for the last time," said Dan Trimble, Managing Director of the Convere Group, a global knowledge management consulting group.[122]

It's easy to forget how difficult it can be to send work across the state, let alone the world, especially when a firm does it on the cheap and without proper planning or preparation. This is in part why consulting firms in this area often say, "Just pick a process and send it off-shore." They know a company needs to start small, make mistakes, and figure out what they don't know; they just have to try it once or twice on a small scale before making a well-planned move with significant risks and rewards.

Another challenge is rising wages. While India is still generally inexpensive, wage pressure and increased turn over in the IT and call center sectors are raising concerns about where the industry goes from here. Some of this pressure comes from a hot Indian economy, though schools are still turning out very large numbers of graduates across the educational spectrum, providing a strong back-bench of workers for many years to come.

Even in sectors where technology and processes aren't changing day-to-day, cultural gaps among employees, bosses, and clients can create challenges that mire productivity. Language and cultural differences are most obvious, often causing challenges in the interface between domestic and foreign employees, though relationships with customer are often even more difficult.

Many people get irritated when they call their phone company and realize that they are talking to someone in Asia, especially if they already have a negative perception of Americans losing jobs. Even if foreign non-call center employees speak English, they often have heavy accents or limited fluency, which poses a problem for passing on critical information clearly. This can be especially difficult for detail-oriented phone work, currently a major source of off-shoring. If customer service or trouble-shooting representatives cannot effectively communicate with clients because of language barriers or cultural differences, the effort is probably in big trouble.

Most of the time, these problems can be countered with increased training and better recruiting. English language and U.S. culture classes are often a part of the investment in foreign workers, especially for multi-nationals and large outsourcing firms such as Infosys, WiPro, and TCS.

Sending jobs abroad is obviously not the perfect solution for every American business. Moving work overseas involves numerous complicated challenges, from technological to cultural to economic. However, this does not mean these often-minor setbacks will reverse the trend. Some critics believe off-shoring and outsourcing are being heavily hyped and that once the challenges become identified, jobs migration will slow or even reverse.

Critics think everyone will realize things are not as good as they sound, and the problem will simply go away. Unfortunately, while evidence of language and productivity problems and inflated savings predictions is wholly anecdotal, the hard statistics show companies continually increasing their off-shore investments, at attractive prices. Further, a recent Stanford survey interviewed over 1,000 outsourcing customers, and most indicated they are pleased and plan on sending more work abroad.[123]

Security Concerns

In today's post-9/11 world, everyone is more concerned about security and, to some extent, privacy. Both of these issues have come into question in the quest to push more activities abroad.

Security concerns have been raised when certain "sensitive" materials go abroad. For instance, the California utility Pacific Gas & Electric (PG&E) out-sources some of its routine engineering work to various American firms, for things like tower construction and power line design. These firms, in turn, send some of that work to their foreign offices where qualified engineers do the work. While this is not unusual, the idea of critical electrical infrastructure designs being available to foreigners has given pause to some.

In this case, the work was sent to a captive facility in Thailand owned by an American engineering firm, who claims strict physical security and background checks for its workers. As such, this is probably not an issue, but it does raise concerns about some of these efforts on a broader scale, or when more sensitive information is involved.

Privacy issues have also arisen when private or personal information goes abroad. The most prominent case involved medical transcription for a University of California San Francisco (UCSF) hospital, which routinely sends out this type of work to subcontractors in the U.S. The American company that UCSF contracted with sent some of the work to another American firm, who then sent some of it to Asia. A woman doing some of the work in Manila was apparently not paid properly and threatened to put the private data she had on the Internet.

The issue was resolved, but it does point to the larger issue of transnational data movements and especially the legal and other frameworks surrounding them. There are not easy solutions, since the U.S. and Europe fought for years on this very subject and essentially ended up agreeing to not do much. Regardless, enforceable privacy legislation is needed in the countries doing this type of work, along with more transparency to the process to insure sensitive information is protected.

Host Country Challenges

Just as off-shoring poses difficulties for America, it is also not without challenges in the very countries it helps. This is especially true given the rapid pace of globalization and change, when suddenly billion of dollars and millions of people are involved in something that did not even exist five years ago.

Cultural

Cultural changes in the host country are of particular concern, given that developing countries have a deep and rich culture that cannot always withstand continued contact with, or interference from, some of these efforts. Many would argue that getting young Indian women into the workplace and giving them real responsibility, independence, and social lives for the first time is a positive step, but it is having a variety of effects in the traditional Indian culture. This is especially true as young women go to work and meet men of other castes or begin dating outside of their family's social or religious network.

To a large extent, these challenges mirror those of America more than 150 years ago, when young women migrated to urban factories such as textile mills. Given the morals of the time, it was necessary for the factories to advertise that the women were always supervised in women's dorms, that strict rules were enforced, etc. These same types of hiring processes and assertions are seen in India today to allay parents' fears, but the overall concerns and process are challenging nevertheless.

There are sometimes also fundamental cultural mismatches that make it difficult for foreign workers to easily understand the products or services they are delivering. For instance, even though Korean animators help create the Simpsons TV show, Koreans in general don't watch the show, whose humor is too American. Further, in an example of some of the challenges of cross-border work, the animators reportedly had difficulty drawing a scene where Homer fired a gun; the Koreans had no experience with guns (they are illegal) and had to be told precisely how to construct the scene.

Labor Standards

Labor standards remain concerns, especially those regarding minimum wages and ages, worker safety, and the ability to unionize, and especially in China. Codes of conduct for manufacturers are increasingly becoming required before Western companies such as Wal-Mart will purchase, though many companies ignore those and the laws (corruption is still a challenge). Many of these issues are limited to the blue-collar factories, though they can creep into some white-collar work, probably mostly in the BPO area. They are unlikely issues in engineering, research, or medical work.

Though many labor and human rights groups want to impose American standards and benefit packages on everyone, it pays to remember such standards and benefits are the result of prosperity and wealth, not its cause. America and other Western countries added these things only after they prospered, not before; it is the same for China and others. Pushing them to adopt fully Western packages would probably raise their costs sufficiently to destroy their economies and keep them permanently underdeveloped (especially when their productivity levels cannot support such a cost base).

In the end, there is a complex mix of benefits, challenges, and risks in the rapid rise of off-shoring, but on balance, the benefits certainly outweigh the challenges. Further, as the process is accelerating it behooves everyone to focus on leveraging the opportunities while working hard to mitigate the downsides for everyone involved.

Chapter 8.

Solution Overview

"As the U.S. encounters new global realities policy makers face a choice: we can compete in the international arena or we can retreat. America can only grow jobs and improve its competitiveness by choosing to compete globally, and that will require renewed focus on innovation, education and investment."

Chairman of the Computer Systems Policy Project [124]

The world is ever-changing, and those citizens that do not evolve with it may well be left behind. For better or worse, the economy is a ruthlessly efficient ecosystem whose job is to provide the most economical products and services, not to guarantee employment for those falling behind competitively. Americans and their developed-world siblings must fundamentally accept that the world economy has shifted in character, and like their blue-collar brothers before them, white-collar professionals must continually adapt to compete.

Off-shoring is a powerful and dynamic force, one that possibly threatens the foundations of western middle-class society. As noted, portions of the potential future are already visible in European stagnation, where 10% of Germans remain unemployed (nearly 20% in the east), and though many of their challenges are self-inflicted, off-shoring jobs may only accelerate their decline. When aging workforces and restrictive work rules are combined with off-shoring of blue- and white-collar jobs, economic prospects can become truly dismal.

Fortunately, it is not too late to recapture economic momentum to create and retain valuable jobs and industries before they are drained away overseas. Despite an inevitably tumultuous transition to the new realities, there are many ways Americans can adjust and even take advantage of the opportunities afforded by these changes.

Ideally, the most effective range of solutions amplify and take advantage of America's existing strengths, including flexibility, agility, productivity, diversity, and rapid innovation cycles. Conversely, moving the world toward industries and innovations that go to America's strengths may cause serious conflict with existing business and cultural norms in Japan and continental Europe. In fact, Americans may event want to accelerate some changes to help overwhelm developed country competitors with rapid change and dot-com speed innovation. As the U.S. military would say, "get inside the enemy's decision cycle."

Regardless, America and especially individual Americans have to focus on remaining (or becoming) globally competitive. This includes focusing on long-term, multi-level solutions in numerous areas, as there is no silver bullet and neither sound bites nor short-range quick fixes help insure real economic success over the next century. In the end, competitiveness through entrepreneurship, innovation, training, exports, and global business and cultural integration are the only solutions.

Solutions

Given that competitive nations are rapidly increasing their ability to provide quality services at substantially lower prices, the only way to fix such an economic problem is to change the whole equation. Back in the 80s, Americans had to rethink how they made steel, cars, and electronics, making painful decisions and transitioning entire industries in the eternal pursuit of competitive advantage.

In the end, Americans studied hard and made a fair number of changes, to both manage and innovate their way out of the problem. These included adopting a number of Japanese manufacturing practices, focusing on innovative products in fast-moving markets, and the big transition to knowledge-driven industries.

Some industries also had to be largely abandoned, as frankly it's very difficult to compete in commodity services. After all, a commodity always sells for the lowest price, and typing insurance claims into a computer, much like sewing sneakers or making toys, simply can no longer be done efficiently in America. Companies and workers in such commodity areas must either find a differentiator or find new work; it's that simple.

Fundamental Challenge

The challenge, then, is to move to, or even create, markets where Americans can thrive or perhaps even dominate the foreign competition. These industries and markets are increasingly difficult to find, but frankly, that's why American innovators get paid the big bucks, to constantly invent economic and technology revolutions for the world. They get paid to see the future, take the risks, build the global teams, and execute their plan to change the world – think Dell, FedEx, or Wal-Mart.

Americans have to find an edge, however temporary, over their foreign counterparts. This will most likely be a mix of quality, productivity, and proximity, though the big gains are, as they have always been, in inventing whole new industries and dominating them until they become more easily globalized commodities.

Though the speed of this invent-innovate-commodity cycle is ever increasing, catching it at the right place in the curve can provide employment and success for millions. As is often said, the only constant in this process is change, and everyone involved, from governments to companies to individuals need to begin preparing for continuous change right away.

Solutions also require a complete re-thinking of how Americans look at the world. First and foremost, America is no longer the center of the planet, as very large economies can exist just fine without significant U.S. involvement (as Japan and India have for decades). And massive trade in materials, technology, and products can easily occur between Europe, Japan, and the rest of Asia without any American involvement whatsoever.

In addition, individuals must begin to consider how they will personally stack up, as they really are competing with the entire world's workforce. It is simply no longer sufficient to be a mere cog in the works, content to go on one's merry way in one's little mid-Western town, earning a paycheck every day. In the end, such a worker will have serious difficultly competing with a Chinese peasant, perhaps working twice as hard for half as much.

Thus, simultaneous changes are required along political, economic, personal, and cultural dimensions. In particular, efforts and adjustments are needed by all of the players, be they governments, corporations, or individuals.

First, Admit the Problem

This sort of shift at every level can be compared on some level to an alcoholic on the path to change and recovery. The first step is always admitting the problem before seeking to undertake the solution. It takes a lot of courage and a lot of support, and only once the problem is out in the open is there any hope of actually fixing it.

Today the entire developed world has serious challenges, and while folks are aware of the big picture challenge, they fail to understand their own culpability or how they must personally change and rise to the challenge in order to have any chance of success. Unless each one person admits it is their personal problem, and not really the government's or other nations' people, success is elusive indeed.

While a good bout of public hand wringing and discussion will very likely do some good, politicians and citizens also need to avoid the current analytical paralysis present in Europe, especially Germany. Even though major reforms are needed, the Germans are rapidly depressing themselves by thinking they have lost all of their advantages; this, in turn, could drive their economy (and the rest of Europe) into a self-fulfilling recessionary spiral. So, while pondering the challenges, it's critical to look forward and upwards to the opportunities provided by the continual evolution of technology and the global economy.

Admitting the problem is also an area where political leadership can add real value, by not sweeping the issues under the rug, by tackling the problems head-on, and by inspiring others to do the same. Leadership can also help change priorities at all levels, from governmental taxation down to individual choices about education and personal choice.

Potential Paths for the Future

There are many paths people, companies, and governments can take as they work through the challenges and/or leverage the opportunities provided by off-shoring. The first possible path is to resist the whole thing. Just grandstand, ban, tax, and build walls against the competitive onslaught. This is hardly a winning strategy, though it has long been tried by countries such as India and Brazil over the years, with predictable results of inflation, stagnation, and poverty.

Second is to subsidize or otherwise support the industries most at risk, i.e. the common European model. Politically deciding which companies or industries are important (typically for political, rather than economic, reasons) and then supporting them on their death spiral (e.g. numerous banks and state airlines such as SwissAir or Air Italia) is an all too common scenario that at best masks the problem and prolongs painful solutions.

Finally, America and its siblings can chose to compete and innovate in the face of such competition. This is the only viable solution in the long run and far superior to ineffective quick fixes that nibble around the edges of the problem.

Much good can come from off-shoring, but it is a delicate challenge that requires thoughtful handling. Many people are already incensed over the issue, creating tensions that can only rise as the job shift accelerates. These pressures unfortunately make it more difficult for politicians to take the long view and do the right thing. After all, rent control persists in some big cities despite decades of evidence that it fails on nearly every level, a clear illustration of politics over simple economics.

Changing the Entitlement Mentality

As noted, many Western workers feel entitled to their success and don't expect to have to fight for it as their forefathers did. As a result, it will not be easy for them to accept the fact that not only are they not entitled to their jobs, they have to fight every other citizen of the world just to keep them.

For example, it is one thing for a company to hire overseas during general expansion, but quite another to take away a "rightful" job and give it to a foreigner. As Geoffrey Moore, Silicon Valley-based author of the best-selling marking book Crossing the Chasm, has said repeatedly, American culture is very much "if I've had it before, I am entitled to it," but that "when entitlement becomes politically successful, it becomes economically unsuccessful."[125]

Unfortunately, at this point, feelings of entitlement are working at several levels, including within the anti-off-shoring groups that typically promote America first and that Americans deserve the best jobs. For example, in lower-level positions, unions have done a good job of making people feel that jobs are theirs, so much so that rigid work rules, lack of individual achievement, and limited labor flexibility are often entrenched in the workplace. And at higher levels, people have gone to school for years or achieved various certifications that they feel isolate them from competition.

Education and Preparedness

The reality is that most white-collar workers are probably unprepared mentally or economically for one or even many new careers in the coming years. Further, increasing career path uncertainty paints no clear picture of the proper path on which to embark. While higher-end white-collar workers have traditionally been more receptive to additional education, the lower ranks generally did poorly in school and hardly regard new training as a panacea.

This is especially true if one pictures the blue-collar worker's high-school educated wife who has spent twenty years evaluating insurance claims, or for a single mom struggling each month to just keep things together; for her, taking a risk on a two-year degree in a field with unknown prospects is truly daunting. Her current job will likely be caught up in the business process outsourcing (BPO) movement, leaving her with few options that match her previously modest salary.

Don't Trade Middle Classes for Poverty

A significant challenge will be insuring those displaced by the job shift have a home in the new economy. In particular, care must be taken not to trade India's middle-class for America's, just as Japan's manufacturing employees leapt into the middle class in the 1980s while putting Americans on the unemployment line. This is especially a concern as millions of modestly paid professionals come on-line and depress the wages of those they are replacing.

The reality is that the current job shift isn't much different than when new technology replaces old. For instance, when cars replaced buggies and direct dial telephones replaced operators, scores were put out of work. Their world had changed forever, and the new economy had to absorb the losses wrought by the change.

Things are now changing in much bigger ways as jobs are moving and the marketplace becomes truly a global one. While difficult to accept, the global march of globalization and job market realities will force workers everywhere to get on board with the program of global competition.

Compete, Compete, Compete

For the first time, every American needs to assess their competitive position in the global economy and sort out how they can leverage themselves so that they aren't left behind. This is a seriously different mindset than most people are used to - they often look around their company, village, or country to see how they measure up against others - looking beyond the borders at another country or culture is often beyond them.

Essentially, everyone must consider where he or she stands vis-à-vis every other person on the planet. For example, data entry clerks must contemplate their Ghanaian counterparts. They must identify the various competitive facets and factors evaluate how they measure up. Further, they must think about how they'll compete in five or ten years' time, along with a strategy for how to continually increase their competitive position.

This not only includes individuals, but corporations and governments at various levels -- as states have recently seen, their attractiveness as a hub for economic growth is constantly evaluated against other states and countries -- it really is American Georgia vs. Guangzhou vs. Goa vs. ex-Soviet Georgia in a never-ending quest for economic growth and prosperity for their people.

Efforts at Three Levels

These challenges require concerted efforts at all levels of society, specifically governments, corporations, and most importantly individuals. While companies simply competed against each other in prior decades, globalization in the 21st century requires serious work on everyone's part. The stakes are higher, the players bigger, and the pace of change faster than anything in the history of civilization.

The following sections summarize essential challenges for these three levels, with subsequent chapters detailing the efforts required by each.

Government

While government's overall role in the solution is probably limited, it can do great damage if misused, or be very helpful through great leadership and leading-edge public policy. Given that governments are very blunt instruments, though, they need to focus on the broad issues while generally staying out of the way as the marketplace builds winners and losers. In essence, the American government needs to lead its people, allowing things to change and prosper on their own by promoting the few key initiatives as outlined in subsequent chapters.

Government's role falls into just a few categories: leadership, accelerating America's innovation and entrepreneurship, assisting displaced workers, and mending structural economic issues.

The first of these, leadership, entails amplifying the messages in this book, namely that things have changed and America has to work harder at its core strengths to stay ahead of the world. This involves politicians really getting out in front of the issue, acknowledging the problem, and laying out serious programs and initiatives to move forward towards success.

Perhaps most importantly, government can focus on encouraging and accelerating entrepreneurship and innovation, as these twin pillars of American prosperity are both major sources of strength and quite difficult for others to duplicate. Silicon Valley is the perennial model for this, as it's an amazingly prosperous, dynamic, and successful place many others have tried to replicate without success.

Imagine if the entire country could be turned into a massive Silicon Valley -- after all, the Valley merely reflects every traditional American strength, all concentrated in the same place. The government must essentially do all it can to make it easier to invent, innovate, and build companies, including improving education, reducing taxes, funding key research, lowering health costs, and fostering free trade in absolutely everything.

At the same time, proper care is required for those displaced by such exciting new innovations, industries, and trade shifts. Assisting displaced workers entails working to both help insure the displaced land on their feet and more importantly, help equip them with the skills to prosper in the next phase of the American economy. This is somewhat like the GI Bill, which has educated and trained legions of ex-soldiers for productive work (and being consumers) in the economy.

In addition, unassisted employees not only stir things up politically, they also do not fully participate in the economy as producers or consumers, which reduces overall economic growth. As such, they also may not easily provide for their families, retain good health care, or raise good families in stable households.

Government also needs to set the stage for better integration and collision avoidance by more fully integrating America into the world. This includes efforts to improve language and cultural study, increase student and worker exchange, and generally move towards a more integrated European-style model, where other countries, cultures, and people are better understood and interconnected.

Finally, government can work on structural issues, such as rapidly rising health care costs, social security reform, and pension portability. In particular, the health care and social security challenges are sufficient to sink any economy, so they must be dealt with forthwith. After all, it's difficult to find new jobs when each new employee places a huge burden on a company's health care costs. Further, the projected need to substantially hike the social security tax to keep the system afloat will surely derail future economic growth.

Corporations

Every layer of the American economy is in on this problem, and so everyone must be in on the solution. While governments have to provide leadership and manage the big picture, companies need to focus on their future and that of their employees. This is especially true when companies are the ones actually pushing the jobs overseas in the first place and thus reaping the benefits. As such, there is some responsibility at that level to help mitigate the negative effects of their efforts while working to keep pushing the American and global economies to the next level.

Given that one of the primary issues for individuals will be retraining and preparing for new jobs in a new economy, corporate handling of workforce training is crucial for both their current and displaced workforces. Both groups of workers, and indeed all citizens, will need continuous training and empowerment to compete globally.

While it's not yet clear which training programs and methods work best, especially for white-collar workers, additional skills and preparation are clearly necessary for the 21st century. Additionally, companies advocating training and assisting with next-generation preparation can help stem the political backlash against the job losses they create.

Further, in addition to training, corporations often have to rethink how and where they do business, both to keep themselves afloat and continue to employ people at home and abroad. While coupling the proper mix of labor and capital with good product strategies has always been a corporate challenge, the new world provides an enormous range of possibilities, opportunities, and pitfalls.

While care must be taken to not over burden companies in the European manner, broad initiatives can be undertaken which don't create negative incentives to hiring or domestic expansion. In fact, market-oriented initiatives and incentives in just the right places may well entice companies to design, select, and execute the best programs all on their own.

Ultimately, companies, like governments, can only set the stage for the real work that needs to be done by the workers themselves. That sort of individual change and achievement is both an American strength and a weakness, as the most directly affected workers are not used to fending for themselves in a rough-and-tumble global marketplace. Preparing them while continuously optimizing the proper public and corporate policy will be the principle challenge in the 21st century.

Individuals

Individual preparation is where the most challenges, and the most opportunities lie. Individual success in the new economy is likely to revolve around each person finding, or better yet creating, the right job for him or her. This is especially true when life is too short to do work one hates, especially when the Chinese will do it for 1/3 the price. Further, the future of American work surely does not lie in punching the clock every day at boring, monotonous jobs. If workers view their jobs as life-sucking ordeals and go through the motions every day like a zombie, then someone else, somewhere else, will do a better job, faster and for less money.

In addition, many Americans need to take the high road and start valuing their own capabilities enough to take risks on careers that may not pay as well or be as stable, but truly speak to their interests and passions. The reality is that all jobs are tenuous at best, so why not take a risk and do something one really likes? People need to start seeing their jobs as opportunities to enrich their communities, their lives, and the world at large.

As difficult as losing a job to a foreigner half one's age and salary may be, it can sometimes be the opportunity of a lifetime. As such, it is each and every individual who will make or break the future, for them, their children, and their country. Instead of being bitter, they have to look ahead to the future and focus on what's important: innovation, education, and entrepreneurship.

In particular, individuals need to go back to school to learn how to learn, and to gain new skills that will make them attractive to employers that have the pick of the global litter. They also need to prepare their children for this brave new world, no easy task in a country where education is mediocre and interest in useful academic skills weak at best, especially among the lower economic classes.

Understanding more about business, technology, and the world are also key to success in the 21st century. Gone are the days of the one-trick-pony style worker; today more variety and breadth of knowledge are critical to maintaining an edge over others in the global workforce.

Innovation and invention must be the new watchwords, as millions of minds are brought to bear on the problems and opportunities of the day. By leveraging American innovation, can-do attitude, and following the American Dream, individuals can truly rise to the occasion and retain their position at the top of the global value chain.

Chapter 9.

Government's Proper Role

"The U.S. has a whole series of complacencies about it. It is complacent on its economic development platform. It is complacent on its infrastructure platform. It is complacent on the whole issue of promoting research and development. So you go down the list--education, infrastructure, research and development--and the U.S. is basically complacent. It is very difficult to go to Washington, D.C., and discuss those three aspects of competitiveness (education, infrastructure, and R&D) with anybody."[126]

CEO of a Multi-national Technology Company

While government's role is essentially to provide a framework in which to compete, it can do both great damage and provide great 21st century leadership (often at the same time.) Given that government initiatives affect large swaths of people and are thus very blunt instruments, its focus should be the broad issues, generally staying out of the way as the marketplace sorts itself out. At the same time, the government has a moral and social obligation to help temper the effects of the pure marketplace outcome that produces millions of unemployed.

With globalization blazing forward at a breakneck pace, what is a government to do, especially if that government runs the most powerful nation on earth? Most importantly, as physicians say, "first, do no harm"-- no easy task when a government's citizens are clamoring for protection from the foreigners.

Good answers and policies are not easy to come by, as governments respond to popular sentiment, and a multitude of polarizing forces are at work. As usual, these forces are divided rather sharply between two opposite views of the world. One side sees globalization and lowered costs for all, while the other sees greedy companies throwing hard-working Americans out of work. At the same time, looking across the pond at Europe to see government programs, that while laudable on many levels are ineffective and have bred a society of entitlement and perhaps permanent structural recession.

Realistically, quick fixes and small-range measures that avoid dealing with the deeper issues will do little to meet the serious challenges ahead. For instance, revaluing the Chinese Yuan, adding tariffs, or sheltering domestic industries will not lead to any solution. Instead, dramatic new thinking is needed about how Western economies will fit into the new global economy. In particular, nearly every industry, process, and individual must be realigned to become part of the ever-dynamic global value chain.

Leadership

"I have a real degree of difficulty with the fact that we are spending some five to eight times as much on the industry of the 19th century than we are on the industry of the 21st century," Technology CEO.[127] (Spending $40 billion a year on agriculture subsidies and just $5 billion on basic R&D in the physical sciences.)

Leadership entails amplifying the messages in this book, namely that things have changed and America must work harder to extend its core strengths and stay ahead of the world. Leadership must also introduce and explain a range of well-thought-out programs and initiatives to take advantage of the opportunities while addressing the challenges.

It is important to just begin talking about the challenge beyond the usual sound bites. One global high-tech executive said he was hard-pressed to find a comprehensive statement on what the government is doing to address the issue, noticing that "We haven't even articulated the problem."[128]

On the other hand, the Bush Administration thinks they do understand the challenges. "We certainly understand the challenges there," said Phil Bond, undersecretary of technology at the Commerce Department. He noted that the government has a policy to make sure that all children are "`technologically literate" by the eighth grade. Funding for science and math education was also recently boosted by $1 billion. [129] Unfortunately, while education is important and will bear fruit in the decades to come, it pales in comparison to the immediate challenges.

Governments everywhere set the tone for their nations and citizenry, especially providing leadership in difficult times. In particular, governments must not let recession or declining fortunes drive isolation and undue nationalism (as has happened in the past). Globalization provides convenient enemies in the form of foreign nations and outsiders who are "stealing" jobs that citizens feel entitled to, setting the stage for protectionism and even militancy against foreigners and their homelands.

Politicians, who rarely show a penchant for grasping economic fundamentals, need also to understand globalization and trade as it affects every citizen on earth, including how it makes America stronger. From that, they must lead their constituents into the new economic era and all that goes with it. Sadly, little of this leadership has been forthcoming, largely for political reasons. For example, one of the Bush Administration's economic advisors mentioned that off-shoring was okay and not to worry; this was immediately slammed by the opposition and had to be retracted (though his arguments were indeed sound), indicating that the time is not yet at hand for true discourse.

The only real leadership has come from senior business leaders such as Craig Barrett of Intel or Carly Fiorina when she was CEO of HP. They have called it the way they see it, saying the world beckons, American workers are falling behind, people must work harder, and fundamental systems such as education and health care must improve. These are the types of things governmental leaders need to begin saying, though realistically they have a poor history of telling citizens things they don't want to hear.

Nearly as bad as staying in the dark about the challenges is glossing over them as a minor speed bump on the road to prosperity; some Republican administrations and fervent free-traders simply talk about the benefits of trade and the need to improve education. They never acknowledge the challenges or talk about how to manage or even assist this economic transition.

Regardless, while the Bush administration and especially the Office of Technology Policy are pondering these issues, their statements and endorsement of off-shoring need some adjustment. In particular, more specific attention needs to be paid to the difficulties created by off-shoring service jobs, especially for those losing their jobs and their economic stability and future.

The current message touts President Bush's plan of economic growth via tax cuts, some Research and Development (R&D) credits, and the "No Child Left Behind" education programs. Realistically, little is asserted beyond a "Don't worry, off-shoring is good for us," byline. Rarely are hard data or adequate descriptions of the situation included in such standard political spouting, robbing it of credibility and thus of any leadership value.

While having a central government czar on some subjects has failed (such as drugs, where the policy is itself a failure), others such as for trade have been quite useful, especially in the effective negotiation of numerous trade agreements. As such, a larger office, perhaps even Cabinet or sub-Cabinet level, should be created to focus on trade and global competitiveness.

Perhaps even the Commerce department itself can be renamed or refocused on international and global trade (since all trade is now global, even when it takes place within the same small Kansas town). Such a name change or new department would hopefully focus people's minds on the overriding need to stay competitive, perhaps the single more important national priority after national defense (which itself depends on a strong economy, which depends on being competitive). After all, losing competitiveness can easily result in the loss of nearly every other aspect of American leadership and power - just ask the British and other old-world empires about their diminished role in today's world.

Such a cabinet-level leader could also deal with the touchy problem of communicating with the public and ensuring that the perception on trade is positive. President Clinton essentially took this job himself during the NAFTA days, as chief trade promoter, but someone today really needs to focus on this full-time. Further, a focused group could also develop specific export promotion and global innovation competitions designed to extend America's growth in these important areas.

Though leadership on the actual economic issues such as taxes, repatriated income, and training is important, it is even more critical to influence the popular perception of off-shoring as a negative phenomenon. Numerous websites and aggrieved ex-employee groups have sprung up in the last year or two, touting slogans such as "U.S.A First" and "Save our Jobs." It is important to not only dispute their data and claims, but also to counter their anti-corporate, anti-government, and anti-economic temperament.

The final leadership message should be that the American spirit, despite sounding like a cliché, is precisely what will prove most crucial in this difficult transition. Instead of an unsolvable crisis, Americans should see another instance of the creative destruction that has long been at work in American economic development.

As noted, this destructive process ruthlessly eliminates inefficient or overpriced work and frees up resources for new and ideally more productive endeavors. For better or worse, this has already transformed blue-collar work, forcing workers and companies to improve productivity and quality over the last decade.

In the end, the government can serve to help American workers overcome their fear of change and embrace an exciting future. Further, Americans will have to change jobs and indeed entire careers several times in their lifetimes, so preparing them for this challenge may be the single best route to 21st century success. In the end, politicians must lead their citizens into a century where new and more interesting jobs await, as the rest of the world races quickly to take their existing ones.

There are several broad dimensions to consider in the public policy arena, each of which is discussed in depth in the following chapters.

Public Policy Improvements

"The structure of the world has changed and policy has to change as well," said Craig R. Barrett, CEO of Intel.[130]

There are many arguments on what governments should do, if anything, to rise to the challenges posed by off-shoring. And while eventual success will be on the backs of individuals making personal improvements, contributions, and innovations, there is much the government can do to help accelerate the process, or at least not get in the way.

At the same time, some have argued that the government should do nothing except focus on taxes, education, and health care. Unfortunately, the track record on these three areas ranges from poor to terrible, and connecting the future of the economy solely to those improvements is unlikely to help anyone. Realistically, more specific and more attainable programs must be thoughtfully considered, implemented, and adjusted as needed.

Accelerating Innovation & Entrepreneurship

As noted previously, the government should focus primarily on maintaining or increasing America's economic and technological lead wherever possible. This begins with understanding what these advantages are and their underlying causes. Chief among these are America's lead in innovation and entrepreneurship, both rooted in culture and business practices going back a hundred years or more. The American

Dream is alive and well and must be carefully nurtured and fed at every turn, otherwise it will be found only in China.

In fact, fostering innovation and entrepreneurship is perhaps the most important element of public policy and the best thing the government can do in response to off-shoring's challenges. It is likely the only way for America to actually outperform its competitors, as pure knowledge and technological advantages rapidly decline.

Even though Americans are far ahead of others in this area, especially as Europe falls further behind, the developing countries are not sitting still. They are increasingly pushing entrepreneurship as the key to success, especially in fundamentally entrepreneurial places like China. In a sign of how valuable they are to the country's future, entrepreneurs have recently been allowed to join the all-important Communist Party. And while innovation is difficult to teach, many smaller countries such as Taiwan and Singapore are very focused on technological progress, designing their own chips, introducing new products at a rapid pace, and insuring their place in the future world of invention and knowledge.

Displaced Worker Training

While working to foster innovation and growth, governments arguably also have fundamental responsibilities to their citizens, including workers displaced due to this off-shoring process. Even laissez-faire economists who favor an "every man for himself" approach should appreciate the economic benefits of helping workers adjust, lest they fall into poverty or welfare and end up costing even more in both hard and soft costs (e.g. poorly educated children, uninsured health care, reduced aggregate demand and productivity).

At the same time, there are good arguments to be made for retraining those displaced by automation, probably a much larger group than those lost to off-shoring. This raises the larger issue of using public funds to continually train and retrain the populace, long after they've left high school. Given that training before, during, and after employment is critical to insuring displaced workers obtain new and well-paying employment, such ongoing training may well be the best investment a society can make in its people.

Mending Structural Challenges

Government should also focus on the broad factors influencing economic progress, such as lower taxes, better education, pension reform, regulatory reform, and lower health care costs. Numerous other books discuss these topics, so they are not covered here in detail, but that's not to say they are unimportant or have no influence on the topic at hand.

And finally, the government should work hard at globalizing America, its thinking, and its culture. While globalization for others usually means adopting American values, economics, and culture, America is very poor at overtly accepting those things from others. In the long term, vastly increased understanding of, and integration with, the world by average Americans will go a long way towards fostering real globalization.

Things Governments Should Not Do

While subsequent chapters outline in more detail the thing governments should do, there are several directions on which it should not embark, as often the things not done are at least as important as those that are. Further, while these recommendations apply to the federal government, state and even local governments can also cause problems and wreak havoc, such as with state-level anti-offshoring legislation.

Perhaps the scariest path is the demonization of others, blaming the problems on foreigners. There was a fair amount of this with the Japanese in the 1980s, though it was not as startling as the recent rapid and intense dislike of the French in the run up to the Iraq war in 2003. This also gets mixed up with nationalism, or "America-first" mentalities, as if the U.S. has some God-given right to be first in everything, to have every job it likes, etc. Like all nationalism, this can get out of hand when the government gets involved, even with such absurdities as serving "Freedom Fries" in Capitol Hill. As such, the government should neither engage in such demonization, nor tolerate it in others.

The next danger after nationalism is protectionism, whose evils have already been discussed. In the 1980s this took the form of all sorts of tariffs and voluntary restraints against the Japanese. While often difficult to avoid in the face of real or perceived unfairness by the foreign country (such as Japan's very real structural impediments), in the end the whole world is served by ever-increasing fair and free trade, not retreat into Fortress America.

Major trade issues should be pursued vigorously, such as actual dumping below cost, but trade issues far too often descend into politically-motivated quagmires, such as for steel, textiles, agricultural products, and even catfish and shrimp. Real structural reform needs to be pursued, but such political foolishness is quickly seen for what it is and calls into question American credibility on a range of issues. Again steel tariffs and sugar quotas are cases in point, where Americans look foolish and then lack the credibility needed to get other countries to make real changes that matter to everyone.

Government's goals ought to be clear: to aid workers in the transition by calming nationalistic reactions; to increase global awareness; to remove the barriers to innovating; to create new ways of doing business; and finally to provide training so that each American can see the off-shoring phenomenon as an opportunity to get a more exciting job that they truly love.

Finally, a major challenge in any reform or program is to pursue it systematically, instead of in a haphazard fashion. Governments have a poor history of well-coordinated or well-thought-out programs, but citizens will be far better served by effective leadership, an integrated viewpoint, deep understanding of the issues, and a strong program to meet the off-shoring challenges head-on.

Chapter 10.

Entrepreneurship and Innovation Velocity

The seed for the Whirl (a tiny military surveillance helicopter) was planted in March in talks that Mr. Small had with a Pentagon official about ideas for aircraft that can stay aloft for days. The official had a particular need: a platform for radar to track moving targets. "We think we can do that," Mr. Small says he told him, "We'll be back in a week."[131]

America has led the world in innovation for over 150 years, rapidly transitioning from an agrarian economy to mass production to the world's largest economy in the pre- and post-WWII period. As such, Americans have always known that innovation and its close cousin, entrepreneurship, are the true drivers of economic growth and prosperity in developed economies.

Here at the dawn of the 21st century, America still easily leads the pack in innovation and entrepreneurialism, but a number of countries are appearing in the rear-view mirror as they, too, pursue the American Dream. In particular, countries such as India, China, Brazil, and Vietnam have large populations, a strong work ethic, improving education, and varying degrees of long entrepreneurial history.

This is especially true for China and its environs, as ethnic Chinese have long dominated entrepreneurial powerhouses Taiwan, Singapore, and Hong Kong. Imagine what they will do when a billion Chinese (and Indians) are finally unleashed to focus on improving their living standards through global business.

These newcomers, coupled with the aforementioned technology and cost factors driving work overseas, could easily catch up with America on many fronts unless steps are taken to accelerate the U.S.'s own innovation velocity and entrepreneurial lead.

For instance, looking at the aircraft market, Europe's AirBus has come from nowhere to overtake Boeing in the last few years, but the action is shifting to the developing world. Brazilian jet maker Embraer is the strongest player in the multi-billion market for jets under 100 seats – there are no American or European makers left in this, the hottest new market for fabulous flying machines.

Embraer, based in Brazil, is the world's largest maker of small commercial jets for airlines (these are much larger than corporate jets such as Gulfstreams). These are the jets flown by regional airlines in the U.S. and around the world, typically seating between 50 and 100 passengers.

As any frequent flyer recalls, just a decade ago regional airlines were dominated by turboprops, those large propeller-driven craft that were cramped, loud, and generally uncomfortable. The airlines (and their passengers) would have loved a solution, but the big plane makers, i.e. Boeing and Airbus, had no interest in such small aircraft.

Fortunately, two foreign plane makers had the vision and foresight to propose and build the first small commercial airline jets. Priced at $20 million or so apiece, they solve nearly all of the turboprop's problems and have been a huge hit with airlines and passengers.

Finally, since these are foreign makers, it's easy to assume that buying such planes might be a drain on the American economy. But, as with all trade, things are not as they may at first seem; this is a big case of win-win, as very expensive items such as engines and avionics often come from America, while airframe design and assembly is in Brazil, which innovated to cost-effectively produce a great airplane.

Further, the airplane itself and the entire concept of small jets are revolutionizing commuter and short-haul air transport, allowing more small American towns to have good air service and thus access to larger markets; this, in turn, may well help sustain and grow their economies.

America's strongest economic advantages today can probably be summarized in two words: Entrepreneurship and Innovation. There are lots of other natural, cultural, and governmental forces at work, but small company entrepreneurship paired with constant invention and innovation constantly drives the economy and its workers to new heights.

Given that these twin pillars are crucial to economic success, it's no surprise that government should focus on maintaining and even enhancing these advantages. There are, however, differing viewpoints on how and if this should be done.

Free traders would argue that American entrepreneurship and innovation coupled to a dynamic economy are natural and sufficient advantages to prepare and propel the citizenry into the 21st century. Others would observe this is an eroding advantage and not sufficiently diffused through society to sustain 300 million people for the long term.

In reality, the real answer lies in between, as things are neither as rosy nor as gloomy as various parties describe. Those who see no problem and want to do nothing are not really paying attention, especially to the dynamics of the Asian economies. The defeatists who naturally advocate protectionism also misunderstand the dynamics of the American economy and its power to adjust and grow, given sufficient freedom, incentives, and individual drive.

Ultimately most workers displaced by off-shoring will ideally find new and interesting jobs by joining or starting small companies, just as blue-collar workers did in the 1980s. Making certain that the system allows for them to make this transition is crucial.

For example, anecdotes tell of the factory maintenance man who gets laid-off and decides to turn his love of motorcycles and mechanical knowledge into a real business making and selling custom bike parts. This story might include his hiring other laid-off workers to help him, but then deciding to off-shore some of the manufacturing and design work in order to lower cost.

Nonetheless, this is exactly the type of entrepreneurship the government ought to promote, where an old job is replaced with a new and dynamic one in an area in which the employee is actually interested. Nothing unleashes innovation and drive more than the opportunity to work at something one loves. That, in turn, provides employment and economic benefits in the community.

Governments must also respect this as a complex process, one that cannot be boosted by simply giving more money via the SBA, though that surely helps. In reality, assistance is needed all through the chain, from training and universities, to research and commercialization, to tax and employment issues, to trade and financial assistance.

In the end, though, the government's fundamental entrepreneurship efforts should focus on accelerating the formation of new companies and lowering costs across the board. After all, these new companies are where economic growth, employment, and innovation will arise in the future.

Enhancing Entrepreneurship

Entrepreneurship is alive and well today in America, where about 550,000 new companies are formed each year. In addition, there are roughly 10 million self-employed firms operating.[132] Small companies are also America's job creation engines; for example, between 1987 and 1992, small companies with less than 500 employees produced all of the 5.8 million new jobs created in the United States. During the same period, larger enterprises (17,000 out of a total of 5.7 million companies) lost 2.3 million jobs.[133]

Starting new companies are not for the faint of heart, as the challenges are legendary. The vast majority of new enterprises fail or get shut down, with about 550,000 closing each year. Statistically, roughly 1/3 disappear within two years and nearly 2/3rd are gone within six years.[134] While much of the world looks upon such failure as a weakness, it is actually one of America's greatest strengths, the creative destruction that tears down things that no longer work, freeing up resources to focus on bigger and better endeavors.

Such creation and failure rates also belie another core American strength, risk-taking and individual drive. Created by early history and the move westward, Americans are much different than their European friends in this regard, especially when a company failure can brand a man a loser for life on the Continent. Contrast that with Silicon Valley, where a company failure is practically a badge of honor and often a good sign someone has learned what not to do. The relative success of Silicon Valley versus the European model speaks for itself in this regard.

Further, the dynamics of the American economy should not be underestimated, at any level. In particular, as with individual class mobility, companies move up and down the ranks all the time. Back in the 1950-1960s, it took 20 years for 1/3 of the Fortune 500 to turn over. In the 1970s, it took ten years, but in the 1980s, only five years were needed to swap out a third.[135] This tremendous dynamic illustrates how rapidly new and useful ideas can be generated and rise to the top as very large enterprises are formed, such as FedEx, Dell Computer, or CNN, each of which invented whole industries or economic models from scratch, typically in the face of much derision.

In addition, there are numerous advantages to building businesses in America, including a very large and unified market, and a relatively consistent regulatory and intellectual property framework. Entrepreneurs can still start with nothing and rapidly build a successful enterprise, thanks in part to the swift and efficient nature of the American system. For example, an American can start a company in less than twenty-four hours, and though most Americans perceive the government and legal system as far too slow, in reality what takes hours in the U.S. can take weeks in China or even months in India. Asian nations are catching up, but still remain bogged down in bureaucratic labyrinths that simply make entrepreneurship more challenging.

Accelerating Formation

America already has the highest entrepreneurship rate in the world, and it's accelerating, so what should be done to enhance it? This question might best be answered by examining why companies fail - it's very easy to create a company, but not so simple to keep it running.

Financing

Anyone who has started or thought of starting his or her own business would probably opine that the main challenge is finding sufficient money. Being able to finance a startup business is an obvious challenge. Unfortunately, the most interesting new businesses rarely rely on traditional sources of non-personal money, such as banks or the public markets. Instead they rely on private capital from friends, family or even venture capitalists. Realistically, they have to scrounge up money from wherever they can, never a simple endeavor for those without independent wealth.

While the government is largely responsible for regulating (and perhaps promoting) the banking and public securities markets, it generally ignores the private equity industry beyond requiring arcane and expensive offering memoranda, accredited investors, and compliance with every state's "blue-sky" laws regarding private investment. This hands-off approach is attractive on many levels and allows individual financiers and small business owners to come to their own terms using a wide variety of instruments. But, the government should also look at reducing regulation (e.g. Blue-sky laws) and stimulating private equity to get more people funded, more often.

For instance, cuts in capital gains taxes in 1981 helped spur venture capital investments and usher in Silicon Valley as it is today. In addition, more favorable tax treatment can encourage more individuals to take the leap into the unknown and start their own business. Addition studies should be undertaken to identify other key financial factors that can accelerate an already successful industry. Regardless, it will take some effort to re-align the tax system away from taxing the rich and instead promoting risk-taking and company formation – after all, getting rich and keeping their money is what makes entrepreneurs take risks in the first place.

Even if private equity becomes more available, some small companies will still have trouble finding funding for their projects. Many cannot effectively use or compete for private equity due to their size, business, or lack of stellar growth potential. Helping this group will require the government to find ways to expand already existent programs that aid small businesses just starting out.

SBIR

The Small Business Innovation Research (SBIR) program is especially interesting, as it provides $2 billion dollars in federal funds for small companies to do research and commercialization. This program can greatly assist very small companies in moving their technology forward to a point where others will help fund it, nurturing true entrepreneurship while simultaneously spurring innovation in key economic and national security sectors.

Unfortunately, the up-front dollars are often too small to do anything useful and banks are not nearly aggressive enough in pushing and assisting with these loans. Typical SBIR Phase 1 funding is $70-100,000, which supports only a single full-time technical employee for less than a year, making it difficult to really accomplish much. Increasing this to $250-500,000 would enable a company to acquire several researchers and their equipment for 1-2 years, ushering in a tremendous innovation boom. Fortunately, Congress is looking at this very issue and there is talk of raising the first and perhaps second phase SBIR funding levels.

One issue to consider during this process is that increasing the number of funded startups also inevitably increases the number of failed start-ups. It may also increase the ratio of failed businesses to successful ones. Unfortunately, as venture capitalists well know, some (even a lot of) failure is inevitable, as one can't make an omelet without breaking a few eggs. In the end, even when lost, these funds are investments that encourage the most cutting edge innovation in companies that are taking big, important risks.

STTR

Another interesting program is the Small Business Technology Transfer (STTR) program, which is smaller, but funds cooperative research between small companies and universities or national labs. This program, which should be greatly expanded, helps cross the "valley of death" that very new technologies face when trying to escape from the university laboratory to private funding and commercialization. (More on the valley of death problem follows in the section on commercialization of university research.)

Importance of Failure

The U.S. economy has prospered precisely because the U.S. system allows for companies to try and fail as part of creative destruction. It's very important to quickly determine if a company can succeed and if not, to recycle its people, money, and equipment to other endeavors to try again. People may make fun of the dot.com bubble, but Silicon Valley, like the railroads and other bubbles before it, was able to see a good thing, deploy lots of capital and labor, sort out the winners, and then rapidly destroy everything that was not working. As a result, all of the people and equipment have been redeployed in more fruitful endeavors. What was seen as a disaster was perhaps a bit excessive; perhaps the system was at its best.

One should not think of these failed businesses as a waste of capital, but rather as a necessary consequence of the growth to the entire economy provided by creative young companies. Innovative businesspeople willing to put their necks out there will continue to keep the U.S. on the cutting edge and provide for a prosperity that renews itself with every new technological advance and cultural change.

By contrast, in the European model, troubled (usually larger) companies are given tax benefits and even funding to keep them alive, essentially propping up the walking dead. The Japanese tend to have this habit, too; in fact, they call such entities zombie companies, who tie up valuable resources and do nothing productive at all. The Europeans and Japanese tend to value stability above all else, though in the end they miss the use of instability to create growth and long-term stability.

Entrepreneurial Training

Even if a newborn business finds funding, those at its helm may be without the appropriate training to effectively build and run a business. Not every startup entrepreneur has an MBA, Silicon Valley connections, or knows all the intricate ins and outs of business success.

First-time entrepreneurs obviously need most of the training, including learning how to raise money to get business going. But, just because a company's leaders require education does not mean that their business plan is unviable; often quite the contrary. Given a little business background, many more individuals could turn creative ideas into actually successful ventures.

The need for such business background is one of the key lessons of Silicon Valley, where partnering good ideas with good business people and constantly nurturing them along is the real key to success. This is especially true given that most businesses are quite dynamic, where fundamental ideas, products, and services often have to be continually adjusted in the face of customer needs and economic realities.

Training future entrepreneurs is part of the Small Business Association's (SBA) mandate and these programs have been relatively successful, although many members of the startup community remain untrained or even uninterested. It is difficult for the SBA to reach everyone, given that it is often difficult to get potential entrepreneurs and the government together. Someone from the SBA cannot merely show up at the doorstep of a startup and say, "Hi, I'm here from the government and I want to help," and expect to be well received.

Given these difficulties, involving the private sector in the training process would probably be a benefit to all. Alternatively, programs like the SBA could be tailored to individual sectors and also include an outreach program that could partner with other agencies to integrate more seamlessly into the business community. New programs may not even be necessary, since many government organizations that directly affect small businesses, including the IRS, FDA, and OSHA, already have underutilized and poorly-understood free training programs.

Further, while there may be new solutions to the problem of training entrepreneurs, it may be most prudent to fix programs already in place, insuring they help those in need. For example, the SBA should set stretch goals of doubling their training program every five years, with some benchmarks of getting companies started and then surviving one and five years, plus various employment goals – after all, that's their true measure of success and their leaders and employees should be rewarded as such.

There are several non-profit groups such as Pacific Community Ventures (PCV) and BizTillery in San Francisco, that help train and mentor small companies, particularly those with disadvantaged or minority employees. These programs are extremely successful and should receive funding and encouragement as mechanisms to assist small companies in both challenged and traditional entrepreneurial communities.

In addition, groups like PCV are also creating whole new financial structures and programs to educate low-income and immigrant employees about finances, saving, and retirement plans. This, in turn, sets the stage for employees to not only own their homes, but perhaps some day launch their own entrepreneurial enterprise.

Finally, BizTillery is creating an incubator-like facility to actually directly support entrepreneurs with shared services, training, and sales support to jumpstart their success. While this model has long been used in the high-tech sectors, broadening its application to general small businesses could well be the key to fostering growth and success.

Accelerating Hiring

Once the small businessperson gains funding and learns how to set up his or her enterprise, they next consider perhaps the most vital question for increasing jobs in the U.S., what employees to hire. Clearly the best way to increase jobs is to accelerate the hiring process.

European countries facing similar problems have chosen to make it difficult for companies to reduce their staff in bad times, thereby hoping that they hire too many people at first and later get stuck with them. Companies are smarter than that and thus are very slow to hire. As such, building impediments to downsizing are obviously a backwards approach. Instead, the U.S. should promote hiring while still allowing for companies to be flexible about their workforce as times change.

The rise of the temporary worker in recent decades is but one manifestation of such flexibility. While not ideal for everyone or without problems, they have allowed numerous people to control their work life while giving companies flexibility to maintain optimal staffing levels.

Other models also encourage companies to hire more workers. For instance, programs already exist that subsidize salaries and/or training costs for certain workers and industries. A variety of states also offer tax and partial salary subsidies and incentives to business owners when they hire more workers, though a rigorous study of the results of such incentives needs to be undertaken to insure taxpayers are getting the most out of their investment.

Government programs in this area, as in others, may have more of a psychological effect than cause a significant increase in net job creation, but such emotional benefits are equally important. If entrepreneurs believe the government is there to help them, encouraging them to expand their companies and workers, inevitably they will be more confident in their business pursuits and make decisions that benefit the entire economy. In essence, this is a modest risk-reduction policy.

In fact, minimum wage reductions for some categories are probably in order. This is difficult to manage and politically dicey, but the financial needs of high-school kids are not the same as 50-year-old fathers; nor are all jobs or industries created the same. Sorting this out is a challenging problem, but careful consideration should be given to whether or not it's better to have one person employed at $7 per hour, or two employees at $4 per hour. Further, are there businesses that could exist with $3 per hour that cannot at $7 per hour? This off-shoring phenomenon suggests the answer is yes, as the market may well create additional jobs in this area if given the opportunity to price labor at market rates.

In the end, if the system reduces the risk to employers when they hire workers and allows them to let them go easily if they cannot afford them anymore, hiring will increase. This reduced risk combined with funding and training assistance from government programs will inevitably lead to small companies not only becoming successful but taking a lot of employees with them.

Lowering Costs

If there is one thing small companies complain about, it's government-imposed costs, for everything from health and worker's comp insurance to excessive regulation, and taxes. For example, California Governor Schwarzenegger wisely recognized these challenges in that state and campaigned on lowering costs for business by reducing the onerous overhead that was forcing companies to flee the state.

Unfortunately, governments take a very narrow view of the costs imposed on business, in the form of licenses, permits, fees, and perhaps the minimum wage. In reality, costs should be much more broadly defined, where as any cost imposed on a business acts as grit in the wheels of commerce, employment, and innovation. Cost, especially transaction costs that rise with sales, must be considered evil at every turn, something to be continuously re-assessed and minimized.

Tax Reform

When thinking about encouraging small business growth, nearly everyone immediately thinks about tax reform. But despite taxes being everyone's favorite area ripe for change, any large-scale overhaul is probably improbable in today's political climate.

Instead of thinking of broad reconstructive measures such as a flat tax and no corporate tax at all, any improvements in taxation probably must work within existing frameworks. Despite these limitations, a handful of well-placed tax adjustments can still do much to encourage entrepreneurship and job growth.

These adjustments fall into many categories. For instance, more credits for training and hiring could help both these problems elucidated above in the discussion on hiring incentives. Training expenses could be double deductible or otherwise encouraged, for instance.

Reduced or eliminated taxes on S-Corp, LLC, and small C-Corp income would be a huge boon to generating startups. Imagine if small startups, say from 5 (to avoid abuses by single person or family-only companies) to 100 people, paid only 50% of the standard tax rate on S-Corp pass-through income. There would be a huge rush to form such companies as people figured out how much better off they'd be running a company with employees rather than slaving away at a big firm. That would truly be putting taxes to work for Americans.

Existing Disincentives

Further, there are several tax disincentives to starting one's own company. The first is the Social Security and Medicare (FICA) System that all workers pay into at a rate of 7.65% up to roughly $87,000. What most people don't realize is that companies also contribute 7.65% of an employee's income to the system. That in itself isn't bad, but it has two negative effects on new company formation.

The first is that any person leaving employment to start their own company has to immediately pay an additional 7.65% tax on the same income, on top of the 7.65% that everyone already pays (called the Self-Employment Tax, of 15.3%). Making $87,000 in one's first year on their own costs them nearly $6,700 in extra taxes. Hardly an incentive to jump out on one's own.

Second, and perhaps more important, is this tax weighs heavily on small companies, as it is a 7.65% corporate tax on their highest cost, wages. Imagine a 25-person software firm with an average $60,000 wage; that's $115,000 they are paying for the privilege of employing those workers. That $115,000 would hire another two employees (i.e. adding about 7.65% to employment, if all else was equal). This is not small change for a startup company. So, while that tax is great for retirees, it loses sight of the true goal, to grow the economy and provide good jobs. As such, perhaps there are programs to gradually introduce this tax as a company grows, or provide various credits for the early period in a company's life – after all, saving 7.65% may make the difference between success and failure in many industries.

The next challenge is health insurance. Never cheap for anyone, it's taxed extra for entrepreneurs. While Congress finally made entrepreneurs' insurance deductible, it left on the FICA taxes, meaning a startup's owners still get to pay 15.3% of their health insurance in tax. For an average monthly premium of $250, that's $500 a year; again not a big incentive to run out and start a new company.

Further, the National Association of the Self-Employed says that 70% of companies with fewer than 10 employees do not offer health insurance, usually due to cost.[136] While the cost of health care hits everyone, it also acts as a further disincentive to start a company or join one in the early stages when one can really make a great contribution.

Health care costs are also hurting larger companies. For instance, General Motors reports that the price of every car includes $1,500 for health care for employees [137] . This encourages them to outsource and move their employees abroad, where there are often no such costs.

While solving that issue is beyond the scope of this (or any) book, there cannot be enough emphasis on getting this under control from a company point of view. This will likely involve much higher premiums for workers, who after all, are the ones consuming the health care services; until they feel the real pain of their health and health needs, there may be no way to enable companies to free themselves from such costs.

There are likely many other strategies and tax programs that would also encourage people to start and grow companies, but the overriding factor has to be on growth, not short-term tax revenue, or the perceived "fairness" of the tax code. After all, "fair" taxes are useless if they wreck the economy they seek to extract revenue from.

Income Averaging

Another challenge for the self-employed and small company owners is the lack of income averaging. Many years ago, entrepreneurs could average their income over a few years to determine their tax rate, but this expired and now citizens must pay according to that year's tax bracket. This is of little consequence to those with stable jobs and incomes, but can easily cause entrepreneurs to pay a higher average tax rate. It also disproportionately affects job seekers or others moving from job to job, who may have high earnings in some years, but less in others.

For a system that should be encouraging entrepreneurship, this is hardly a good idea. Instead, income averaging should be reinstated, again to lower the cost of starting and running a company, particularly in a turbulent economy.

Workers Compensation Insurance

Worker compensation reform is another tax-related issue that is currently a hot topic in both California and smaller states like Maine. Some businesses with decent loss records can pay insurance equal to or even exceeding the actual payroll of their employees; how can doubling payroll expenses in this manner be good for anyone? Clearly such a burden would cripple any business, and needs to swiftly be fixed.

The answers lie in a number of areas, but include finding ways to reduce rates, such as cracking down on fraud (both employee and physician), reducing the absurd benefits of California-style programs, and generally tuning the system for reduced costs instead of maximum benefits. Again, it's all about priorities and growing the economy --providing decent coverage is critical, as is additional training and other measures to help prevent injuries in the first place.

Regulatory Reform

All of the above recommendations focus on the central question of how the government can best support and yet regulate businesses. The regulatory environment always has two perspectives, the government as a surrogate for society's need for orderly markets and safe environments, and the business side with its perspective of too much regulation and bureaucracy.

Given the goal is increased hiring and economic success for small businesses, it seems prudent to actually listen to the complaints of business people actually trying to build successful businesses. They are typically good at complaining about the things that hinder them most.

For instance, there used to be a commission, the National Performance Review, led by then Vice President Gore, to reduce the cost of regulation. This group never even came close to reaching its goals, but should perhaps be revived in some form to really focus on serious concerns in this area, reducing costs, regulations, laws, and other unneeded government interference and friction. Throwing out whole programs, legislation, and regulation is a good place to start; perhaps one could over with minimalist activity to support the basic public good.

At the same time, it's important to recognize that regulations also help businesses in ways that are not always obvious. The system of laws regulating businesses provides for a level playing field, if they are instituted fairly. Oftentimes the solution in these areas is just making sure that all companies, even the bigger ones, play by the rules already in place; in such cases, new rules are perhaps rarely necessary. Enforcement is obviously important to the success of regulatory measures, but lack of follow-through prohibits good laws from actually making an impact.

In addition, state-level regulations also often get in the way of entrepreneurs freely doing business, though some states such as Washington help by having a single point of contact for nearly all business/state interaction. On the other hand, states such as California seem to go out of their way to make life difficult, usually to serve a varied list of "good social causes." Unfortunately, driving business out of the state has had the perverse outcome of depriving the government of the tax revenue needed to support those very causes.

While these kinds of problems cannot be solved overnight, it's important to be mindful of how these regulations stunt economic growth. Finding ways to listen to the SBA and other small business advocates is critical to actually increasing their numbers and success. Again, a benchmark should be set, such as a 25% increase in new company formation over the next five years.

Encouraging Innovation Velocity

Innovation.

This is what most people say when they think about how America will transcend the current difficulties and grow out of the problem. Americans dominate at innovation, they say, and will use their brilliance to beat everyone else.

This is hopefully true and American is the undisputed leader in innovation, but there are warning signs to consider. Long the leader in almost every technology and especially in research and development, America is fairly rapidly losing its advantage. For example, nearly 50% of American patents are awarded to foreign entities and more than half of the scientific papers in key areas such as physics are published by foreign labs. With countries such as China and India rapidly building world-class research labs in areas such as biotech, it has never been more important for America to assess and maintain its lead.

In addition to foreign competition, the general pace of innovation has increased dramatically. The U.S. Patent and Trademark Office (PTO) reports that throughout the 20th century, patent applications averaged 60,000 per year. By 1995, however, this had climbed to 120,000 and in 2000 stood at 300,000 per year; a 500% increase in just a decade or so. And of patents actually issued, only 54% went to U.S. citizens.[138]

As one might imagine, in order for entrepreneurs to create millions of new jobs, they need interesting and valuable things on which to work. In addition, the success of entrepreneurship, as mentioned, is heavily determined by implementation speed and its associated cost. This is where the government can be especially helpful, by greasing the wheels of invention and allowing entrepreneurs to move quickly through the economic and legal systems to bring technology to the market.

On one level, innovation is an elusive term, and the forces behind it tend to be poorly understood. But the stages involved in bringing new products to market tend to be conception of an idea followed by research, development, and then commercialization. Fortunately, there is some agreement among theorists as to how the government can help at each of these stages and make them work quicker, though following through on those ideas remains difficult.

For instance, research normally takes place at a university, a corporation, or some blending of the two. Currently, the U.S. does 50% of the world's research and has a long track record of success, but there are many ways to improve this process, especially when the overriding strategic goals should be more innovation, new companies, and jobs.

Along this value chain, product development is the process of turning research or an invention into a product someone will pay for. Despite the clear importance of this stage, it is a critical gap in government and corporate support for innovation, nicknamed "The Valley of Death," when inventions die on the vine because no one is willing to put up the capital to see them through to completion. This is perhaps the most serious challenge in innovation today and while several programs such as DARPA and the 1980 Bayh-Dole Act are addressing it, no overall solution is yet in sight.

On the other hand, true commercialization, or getting developed products into the marketplace, is something at which Western companies generally excel. Still, there are things to be done, especially regarding leveling the global playing field, encouraging investment and venture capital, ensuring global intellectual property protection, and expanding global trade assistance to small businesses and emerging markets.

America's strongest assets in this process remain speed and creativity. America cannot, however, rest on its laurels, as these advantages do not persist forever and other countries can certainly move faster than Japan in the innovation game. In fact, the whole world is moving faster, making staying ahead ever more challenging – things in the rear view mirror really are closer than they appear.

DARPA

If there is a single government program that deserves the most praise and emulation, it's the Defense Advanced Research Projects Agency, better known as DARPA. Started in the 1960s, DARPA funded the early Internet (called ARPA Net) and many of the technologies connecting the world today.

DARPA works by giving very early-stage grants for specific projects with specific near-term goals in mind. Whether it's a particular weapons technology or a universal language translator or an autonomous robot, they have an endpoint in mind though usually no idea how to get there. That's where private industry comes in.

The agency does not usually provide large sums of money, typically \$2-\$20 million, but private companies usually add plenty of their own. Why? Because they, and not DARPA, end up owning the technology. This is an extremely important point, for like Bayh-Dole, it realizes that companies will not invest if they cannot see a return.

DARPA says essentially, "this is what we need, here's some money, and you can sell it to us when you are done." Needless to say, this is perhaps the best model ever invented to foster innovation and get technology to market.

DARPA also has short time frames; these are not 10-20 year- military or NASA projects, but usually 2-3 year- (if not shorter) projects with specific and usually attainable goals. This lets everyone check the process and make important decisions with real information on a quarterly basis, unlike common multi-year government contracts that run for five years and are then found to be five years late and $10 billion over budget.

And, DARPA has stayed amazingly apolitical. Unlike military contracts in general, they do not choose projects or vendors in states with important Congress members; they do not favor industries with large employment bases, or otherwise make non-technical decisions. They think about what the military needs and work very hard to get industry to develop it rapidly and for tiny amounts of taxpayer money.

Lastly, there is perhaps no better example of the value of DARPA's model than the on-going "Grand Challenge" desert races. DARPA believes the military needs autonomous vehicles that can move cargo and fight without human drivers or even human guidance. Needless to say, this is quite difficult, especially on unknown terrain, with roads, bridges, forests, obstacles, friendly and enemy forces, etc. Such technology is also useful for civilian use, for everything from oil fields to natural disasters to a wide variety of applications not yet foreseen.

Rather than spend what would undoubtedly be billions of dollars developing such vehicles, DARPA decided to run a contest and actually invest essentially no money at all. The contest is simple; teams must supply a vehicle that can cross about 150 miles of Nevada desert, operating completely on its own at high speeds. The route includes roads, bridges, desert, obstacles, etc. The first vehicle to win gets a $2 million prize, but the team retains ownership of their technology so they can further develop it for both military and commercial uses.

When first run in 2004, DARPA was amazed at the number and diversity of the teams that turned out. They even had to add an extra judging round to limit the number of participants. Teams ranged from a guy in a garage to experienced entrepreneur teams to large corporations and powerhouse robotics universities such as Carnegie Mellon.

Unfortunately, very few vehicles made it out of the starting gate and the best vehicle went only 7.4 miles. Essentially, everyone failed, but no one thought of it as a failure; instead, the process worked perfectly, as DARPA originally estimated it may take years of races and significant breakthroughs to get a vehicle that can complete the course.

It turns out they were too pessimistic, since several teams successfully completed a more difficult course when the race was re-run in late 2005. The wining team, from Silicon Valley's Stanford University, proved that American ingenuity and innovation are alive and well. This is especially true considering that large companies had spent billions on the problem and the race itself was considered absurdly difficult just two years before.

In the end, there will be such a set of vehicles and technologies, serving the U.S. military, the American public, and the world at large. Plus, numerous companies, innovations, and jobs will be created along the way. All for the few million it costs taxpayers to run the contest. A very good deal, indeed.

The X-Prize and its Siblings

Beyond DARPA are a few larger private efforts, including the X-Prize and other prize-driven R&D. The X-Prize was created to award $10 million to the first team that could get a three-person spacecraft into space twice within two weeks. As with the DARPA road race, the sponsors were not investing any money other than the prize, the rules are simple, and the resulting efforts are enormous.

Dozens of teams were started all over the world, several with real spacecraft already flying around. Even a team in Romania worked on the problem and though they were unlikely to win, such efforts helped build morale and visibility for the importance of science and engineering, much like the moon landings. And who knows, some day key components of new rocket engines may come from small companies in Romania.

The leading contender, which won in 2004, was Burt Rutan's Scaled Composites. With $20 million in funds from Microsoft founder Paul Allen, they have already sent a spacecraft to orbit by designing a myriad of new technologies for a fraction of what it would cost NASA.

Rutan and Allen are doing this, not so much for the money, but because they believe these technologies and space in general are the future. Such technology will not only inspire young people, but also provide numerous long-term opportunities for employment and economic progress.

By the way, Burt Rutan, who is a national treasure, is precisely the type of entrepreneur that these efforts should support. The first to fly all the way around the world without stopping, he is an aviation pioneer in numerous vital technologies. All that is needed are ways to induce him and others like him to get out in the hangar and dream up new fabulous flying machines.

In fact, people like Rutan (and the late Seymour Cray, inventor of the super computer) are so powerful as innovators that they can invent and change entire industries. Rutan recently commented, "I would like to see affordable travel to the moon before I die, so I am starting relatively soon on developments for orbital-space tourism."[139] In other words, he wants to see people visiting the moon in a few decades and is very likely to single-handedly make that a reality. That's vision, innovation, and entrepreneurialism all rolled into one.

So, the X-Prize and others like them for other scientific endeavors, should be encouraged at every turn, and for nearly every problem facing society, including energy, safety, and medicine. Such efforts provide rapid innovation and commercialization, typically in industries where America usually holds a commanding lead. Further, by focusing America's strengths of rapid innovation and commercialization, these efforts dovetail nicely with the need to provide employment and economic growth over the long term.

As an example of the power of this method, today's X-Prize was patterned after the $25,000 Orteig Prize, famously won by Charles Lindbergh in 1927 for flying from New York to Paris. Designed to spur transatlantic aviation and tourism, it prodded nine teams to spend $400,000 in the quest for its $25,000 purse.[140] Lindbergh's winning of the prize via his trans-Atlantic trip then ushered in decades of investment and rapid innovation to make aviation one of the wonders of the modern world.

Robinson Helicopter

One example of how powerful innovation can be is Robinson Helicopter, based in Torrance, CA. Robinson is the world's largest helicopter maker by volume and dominates the industry for light helicopters. Employing 1,500 people, the company's founder, Frank Robinson, essentially invented the market by himself in the late 1970s.

At that time, other helicopters were either very expensive or very unreliable, and he undertook an endeavor to solve both problems. Using nothing other than his own efforts and vision for the market, he designed an extremely reliable and very inexpensive new helicopter that is today the world's most popular model.

He didn't invent any new technology, manufacturing practice, or really anything other than a new design and business philosophy. From that grew a company that made him rich, employs thousands of people, and perhaps most importantly provides inexpensive helicopter training to generations of new pilots.

This is truly innovation at work, as he didn't really steal business from competitors; instead he created a whole new market, expanding the role for helicopter on a global basis. And, Robinson is a big exporter, selling $500,000 machines around the world.

University Research & Commercialization

American universities are clearly at the top of the world in education, research, and until lately, publishing scientific results. And while these vaunted institutions continue to attract and educate the world's best and brightest, it's not clear whether the current system maximizes innovation and economically valuable research, nor is it sufficiently strong to maintain leadership into the 21st century.

First, it's important to understand that if a graduate student creates a wonder drug at a top school like UCSF or a new Internet search engine at Stanford, it is still very far from being a real product. For instance, one recent study indicated that 45% of licenses are for technologies that are only a "proof of concept" while only 12% are "ready for practical use."[141] Someone has to invest millions or even hundreds of millions of dollars to do real commercialization and bring the technology to market as a real product, especially as nearly half of technology licensed from universities fails (46%), with only 26% of the very early stage technologies eventually succeeding.[142]

Prior to 1980, the government funded most research and retained ownership in the inventions created therein. It also always licensed them non-exclusively, to insure everyone could use the invention. On one level this makes sense, as the taxpayers should presumably get paid for a product for whose development they funded, and why should publicly funded research benefit only a singe company?

However, the very real problem was that if government owned all of the inventions and never licensed them exclusively, private enterprise found it difficult to invest capital to fully develop a product actually owned by the government. The result was stifled innovation and limited return on public money. Trying to make inventions available to many ended up making it available to none.

The Bayh-Dole Act changed all of that in 1980, by letting the universities own the inventions. Further, it provided for licensing those inventions to companies, and very importantly, mandated some ownership or royalty rights for the professors doing the actual research.

Suddenly, universities, inventors, and companies were all strongly incented to build real products and bring them market. To a large extent, this act has functioned as designed, bringing billions of dollars of products to market, especially for biotech inventions (which arguably need the most private capital to get to market).

Columbia University is the king of all royalties, earning $130 million per year from the so-called Axel Patents on recombinant DNA technology, widely used by pharmaceutical and biotech companies. Another big winner, the University of California, earns $85 million annually, 40% of which came from UCSF, the leader in biotech and medical research.

Stanford University is also one of the top earners (at $53 million) and has a very diverse portfolio, with 7 licenses earning at least $1 million, and another 42 earning over $100,000. As the core of Silicon Valley, Stanford is probably where innovation is most rewarded and thus should be the model for all American schools. They have over 1000 active licenses, run by a technology office with 25 people, patenting about 50% of their inventions and licensing about 30%. Stanford also takes equity in new ventures and is currently holding stock in 66 firms, the biggest being Google, which may earn the school $250 million or more when they cash out.[143] Royalties are generally split in thirds, going to inventors, the department, and the school, insuring strong commercialization incentives for everyone involved.[144]

Even with these multi-hundred-million-dollar success stories, the reality is that not nearly enough inventions and innovation are flowing through this system. The entire U.S. university system earned $1.3 billion in licensing fees in 2003.[145] Extrapolating that using an average royalty rate of 2%,[146] these inventions have built industries with annual revenue of $65 billion. Further extrapolating that with average revenue per employee of $150,000 implies that over 400,000 jobs have been created by these inventions (not including older industries already beyond patent protection).

That seems like a great success, but only a half million jobs is not that high for a university system with 16 MILLION students at over 4,000 schools.[147] So, while the Bayh-Dole act essentially opened the invention floodgates halfway, now is the time to swing them wide, and to flood the world with invention and innovation. As such, the goal should be to create an additional million jobs based on university research.

Sadly, just as many universities do not properly value good teaching, many do not value research that can be turned into real products. The all-important tenure process that drives most faculty's goals and work never takes into account inventions and commercial products produced. Further, many faculty simply are more interested in the science than building companies or products; they can't be bothered with patent applications or even describing things in a timely manner short of their next all-important publication. As one university licensing officer commented, "We teach innovation but don't practice it."

Improving this situation is not easy, given the foundational nature of university research, but ways need to be found to get technology from the lab to the shelf and to induce absolutely everyone involved to insure they are doing valuable things for the economy and society as a whole. One way to help insure commercialization is to take this into consideration when funding initial proposals.

For instance, DARPA and other Department of Defense-(DOD) driven funders look to explicit problem solutions and capabilities they need when funding various activities. As 2003 testimony to the House Committee on Science mentions, "Because the DOD has clear needs, it requires that each research proposal include a section on potential applications. This forces scientists to focus on realistic and practical uses of new knowledge. The Federal Government can improve innovation by requiring most research proposals to include such sections, but should also require a cost/benefit justification. Taxpayers deserve a return on their investment in research." - Professor Thomas Eagar, Massachusetts Institute of Technology.[148] This should apply equally well to the NIH, SBIR, and other government funded research programs.

There is also growing concern that the current system of researchers working on their own, with no sharing between groups (or downright secrecy), is not serving society well. This is because it often takes many years from discovery to publication and during that time no other researchers can benefit from the new discoveries. As such, many funding sources are requiring immediate collaboration and sharing of data as part of the grant.[149]

This is completely changing how laboratories interact, as they have to share results they would normally have kept under wraps for years. This, in turn, can greatly accelerate the speed at which inventions can be brought to market, especially at a time when many new technologies require bits and pieces from others to become viable. One team's small breakthrough can also greatly assist other teams struggling in the same area, moving the whole discipline forward.

There are dangers of universities becoming too "applied" or worse, profit-seeking, but there is surely some room to move in that direction, even at top schools like Harvard that shy away from anything commercial. Stanford and UCSF are the models, though their goal should be to double revenue every five years. While some big schools may get overly focused on making money, surely there are thousands of universities that should be making a bigger effort to delivery innovation to society. Further, recent research has not indicated any trend towards inappropriate university priorities or academic research due to the profit motive.[150]

Further up the West Coast from Stanford, there is quite an interesting contrast in commercialization between the University of Washington (UW) in Seattle and the University of British Columbia (UBC) in Vancouver. It has been argued that UBC, which has only 25% of the R&D funding as UW, is far more successful at creating companies, getting patents, and growing licensing revenue. UBC also encourages business connections, with lab space and other accommodations for companies. The UW's licensing revenue exceeds $20 million a year, but some press reports describe continued challenges in building new companies, for instance in not allowing faculty to run a startup or serve on boards of directors.

The UW is also hardly supportive of commercialization; Alvin Kwiram, former UW Vice Provost of Research indicated the university has potential to spin out 10 to 15 companies a year — not two, as it did in 2002. But the UW's culture stymies cooperation with business, he said. "The attitude here is, 'Don't stick your neck out, because if you make a mistake, you'll get hammered.' It's an underlying, systemic malaise."[151]

Ed Lazowska, the Bill & Melinda Gates Chair of Computer Science and Engineering at the UW, says, "Research revenue is as high as ever, compared to peers, so it's not the research activity that's slipping. It's the licensing, the patenting, the company formation."[152] Such schools must bring their commercialization efforts up to Stanford's level if their research and invention output is to ever reach the consumer, benefit mankind, and produce jobs.

Finally, there is the general business climate of a university. Some schools, such as Harvard, are generally opposed to business, even going so far as to prohibit faculty from doing external consulting. Others, such as Stanford, take the opposite approach, with faculty routinely moving between school and business – the results are fairly clear, with Stanford driving Silicon Valley and a fair portion of the advanced technology in the world today. Shrouding great universities like a monastic sect worked well in earlier centuries, but great technical research and innovation today requires collaboration and entrepreneurial activity throughout the process.

Valley of Death

The aforementioned "Valley of Death" also needs significant assistance, since even if faculty starts miraculously pouring out inventions for licensing, there is often no one to pick them up and invest to get real products to market. Such work is beyond the mandate of universities and government agencies, but the inventions are too immature to attract venture capital funding or interest from industry. As such, many potential drugs or inventions "die on the vine" in this valley of death between invention and product.

Public/private partnerships are needed, with real funding, to help span this valley. This is no small challenge, as these are endeavors too risky for even venture capitalists, the most risk-seeking of investors. Governments and companies spending money in this area can make an enormous difference in success in many technological areas.

This is also one area where private foundations can assist, as there is increasing belief in transitioning from public to private money during the innovation cycle to bridge the valley. For instance, the Department of Energy has begun building linkages between public and private sector investors.[153]

On the government side, SBIR grants can be helpful to a company picking up these technologies, especially after Congress increases the grant value, and the STTR program is focused on this area, but is probably still too small by a factor of 10 or more. The NIH also has a new "Translational Research" center program which, though targeted at specific problems, tries to advance technologies into real therapies that can be commercialized.

In another governmental effort, the Advanced Technology Program (ATP) supports emerging technologies for improved products and industrial processes. Funded at $150-$180 million, the ATP program focuses on bridging the gap between the research lab and the market place. ATP does early stage investment to "accelerate the development of innovative technologies that promise significant commercial payoffs and widespread benefits for the nation."[154] ATP can provide up to $2 million in funding over three years, which is serious enough money for most endeavors to prove they can get somewhere and attract outside investment.

As such, ATP should probably be expanded, perhaps doubling every other year, up to $1 billion or more (some of which might be taken from NIH or other R&D programs, as ATP-like programs may well produce more real innovation). Further, today ATP only provides funding in response to its own RFPs, which locks out promising inventors in other areas. Thus, consideration should be given to funding peer-reviewed proposals, more in line with how the NIH funds activities, as this could greatly expand the scope of funding into new areas not previously identified. A casual look at the ATP proposal and subsequent grand and payment process looks overly bureaucratic, especially for very small firms.

One challenge is that these types of directed efforts at commercialization run afoul of critics who think government funding should be strictly limited to basic science. While there is some merit to moderating a government's mercantilist approach to picking industry or products winners, broad support for private efforts seem prudent, especially when competing with countries heavily investing in all of these areas.

For example, the Technology Ventures Corporation, a non-profit funded by Lockheed Martin, helps companies commercialize the technology currently buried within the national laboratories. While it does not fund companies (perhaps it should), it takes the first step-- it helps inventors and startups write business plans and obtain private funding. Their end goal, appropriately enough, is to get the technologies to market to create jobs. Just as in the university sector, many of the technologies are available for free or at reasonable cost, but it takes real effort and capital to get them to market. TVC reports that they helped 55 new companies receive $410 million in funding, creating over 5,000 new jobs.[155]

A number of universities have also started helping with direct investment and venture capital funds. For instance, Boston University has its Community Technology Fund focused on commercializing that school's inventions. Cornell University and others have similar efforts.

R&D Tax Credits

Some programs, such as temporary R&D tax credits, are helpful to business large and small, but serious study should be undertaken to better understand how these programs can be better tuned to the needs of small and medium-sized businesses. It's not clear today that they are well matched to true innovation, especially when many large companies use the credits for run-of-the-mill R&D, such as drug development.

Looking at this problem, the think tank Progressive Policy Institute (PPI) recommends the credits be made permanent and the rate increased from 30% from the current 20%. Further, in a move to accelerate the aforementioned innovation-oriented research, they would like to see a flat, non-incremental, 30% credit for company expenditures devoted to collaborative research at universities, federal laboratories, or research consortia. And finally, they would like it to be easier for smaller and start-up companies to take the credit, further encouraging their work to create the next generation of American technologies.[156]

In addition, there may be other tax incentives that can be employed here to help induce companies to invest in such risky ventures. This is clearly the area of big risk, big payoff, and any risk mitigation or upside-enhancing tactics can help spur things along.

Expanding Promising Economic Sectors

Innovation and entrepreneurship are clearly two important ways to feed the overall goal of economic growth. But growing the economy has clearly been a goal for a hundred years or more, so the question becomes, how can government prepare and nurture the economy for the new challenges in the coming century?

In which sectors of the economy should entrepreneurship be encouraged? After all, it may be possible to provide incentives to grow the call-center or even the buggy-whip industry, but what would be the point?

Instead, the focus should be on encouraging economic growth in promising areas that will fare particularly well given the global competition. Unfortunately, these are broad goals for which specifics are difficult to pin down. There are also serious disagreements about which specific policies are actually useful, especially after they wind their way through Congress and the Washington special-interest gauntlet.

Thinking about promoting specific economic sectors reminds people of the mercantilist policies of Japan and the Asian Tigers in the 1970s and '80s, who believed it was critical to identify the areas in which economies excel and then ensure that these sectors were also top growth areas. Despite promotion in the U.S. at the time, the managed economic concept never really caught on, which some would say is for the best.

Instead of a broadly mercantilist policy focused on many sectors, the government might look at incentives in areas of strength and relative advantage, especially by aiding innovation and entrepreneurship in those areas. The first step in terms of policy is to determine what areas have the highest potential success and long-term vitality. Examples of such fields now are biotech, fuel cells, aerospace, and nanotech, though there will always be new and interesting technologies to add to the list.

After identifying key sectors, the government should minimize regulation, enhance R&D efforts, and work to accelerate research and commercialization in every area. The Internet is a prime example of minimal regulation stimulating growth, where only protective measures were made, like a moratorium on sales taxes. If new, exciting economic sectors can be given the same room to grow, the U.S. will be far better equipped to innovate its way out of the coming economic crisis.

In addition, the recent legislation covering private space launches was well done, in terms of creating a very loose legal framework in which the nascent industry can prosper without undue regulatory and liability burdens (those can come later). As in the early days of aviation, this hands-off approach will allow numerous companies and technologies to move in numerous directions, creating enormous value for everyone as they sort out how best to get to space.

Specific Industries

Looking at specific industries, some of the nanotech initiatives currently funded are interesting, although ways should be found to both funnel more money to private work, and to insure that there are commercialization paths.

Further, there is a plethora of work in the private sector in this area (really a cluster of areas, from materials to biotech to electronics), such that avoiding overlap and duplication in a fast-moving space is an ongoing concern, especially as billions of taxpayer dollars are deployed. Nanotech is not exactly biotech, as the former has few (if any) of the latter's regulatory hurdles or timeframes; thus, companies can commercialize the technologies at a very rapid pace.

Other interesting industries continue to include anything aerospace, especially lighter and more efficient engines and airplanes. This is a high-employment industry with only a few major players that could use some shakeup to keep the growth rooted in developed countries.

Biotech continues to be a major interest, as the U.S. performs the bulk of the work here, though other countries, especially China, are rapidly improving their facilities, education, and funding in key areas such as stem cells and genetically engineered crops.

In the end, though, it's difficult to really pick where the next telephone, television, automobile, or Internet will come from. As such, while promoting key industries, it's important to remember to set the stage for success in all industries.

Silicon Valley Model

Finally, the entire governmental effort for entrepreneurship and innovation might be summed up in something called the Silicon Valley Model. The Valley is a prime example of cutting-edge innovation and entrepreneurship, with a high-risk environment where innovation and growth rule the day. Money, talent, technology, and drive – all these things have converged in the Valley and transformed it into a hotbed of rapid development. The Valley's break-neck pace causes businesses to be in constant upheaval, always fighting for new ideas that will allow them to prosper in the near future. Further, though Silicon Valley is slowly globalizing by looking at Chinese and Indian investments, it's still a mix of interpersonal networks and an interconnected-ness that defies replication.

A recent study sums it up best: "It is not simply the concentration of skilled labor, suppliers and information that distinguish the region. A variety of regional institutions -- including Stanford University, several trade associations and local business organizations, and a myriad of specialized consulting, market research, public relations and venture capital firms -- provide technical, financial, and networking services which the region's enterprises often cannot afford individually.

These networks defy sectoral barriers: individuals move easily from semiconductor to disk drive firms or from computer to network makers. They move from established firms to start-ups (or vice versa) and even to market research or consulting firms, and from consulting firms back into start-ups. And they continue to meet at trade shows, industry conferences, and the scores of seminars, talks and social activities organized by local business organizations and trade associations. In these forums, relationships are easily formed and maintained, technical and market information is exchanged, business contacts are established, and new enterprises are conceived. This decentralized and fluid environment also promotes the diffusion of intangible technological capabilities and understandings."18

Granted, this structure does not always lend itself to mom-and-pop grocery stores and other traditional small-scale endeavors, nor to the more conservative business cultures outside of New York, Miami, San Francisco, L.A., or Seattle. But it does tend to generate the enterprises and opportunities that best leverage sectors most vital to overcoming the challenges of off-shoring.

As such, finding ways to emulate some of Silicon Valley's key characteristics around the nation will likely be key to insuring future success. In particular, it's important to realize that the Valley's success is largely driven by the convergence and co-location of important factors, since individual elements such as money, talent, or technology cannot succeed on their own.

Much has been written about Silicon Valley in recent years, though it's often derided for the dot-com bubble and subsequent burst followed by recession. As mentioned previously, while not ideal, the bubble merely follows in a long line of historical bubbles that resulted in crashes followed by sustained recoveries leveraging the bubble's technologies, such as planes, trains, and automobiles.

In the end, it's critical that the American government and society in general be able to rapidly create innovations, quickly deploy capital and people, and swiftly commercialize ahead of everyone else. And, when it's moved off-shore or become a commodity, tear it down, re-educate, and re-deploy everything for the next wave. Any incentive or program that supports and indeed accelerates this process will serve America well for many decades.

Chapter 11.

Economics and Trade

Introduction

Given that America has the world's largest economy and participates in a fair portion of world trade, it is only natural that governmental focus on properly managing both its economy and global free trade. In the long term, there is nothing more important for a government than growing its economy. Even nominally more important tasks such as national security and social safety nets are highly dependent upon a strong economy, as economic might really does determine military, political, and cultural strength.

Unfortunately, this reality has been lost on many countries, at least in terms of the need to promote growth over nearly everything else. They have tended to focus instead on social safety nets while ignoring the need for strong economies and misunderstanding how to build them. And while many developing countries are now starting to realize how economic growth should be their first priority, they have historically very basic services such as water, housing, and health care, without really working on sustained broad economic growth along with the required education, empowerment, and innovative freedom.

Some would argue it's going to be difficult to build a strong economy if all the jobs are drained away to Asia, and to some extent, that's correct. But America's job market has also been extremely dynamic over the last century and a half, as slaves, immigrants, factories, agricultural machinery, imports, and service jobs have come and gone in great waves. Through it all, government's role was and is to foster economic growth, which in the 21st century unsurprisingly includes sourcing low cost services and components from Asia.

Economics

A strong economy is the foundation on which everything else is built and while in truth there is probably little a government can do in this area in the short term, the long-term effects of public policy can be quite profound. One only need look at the differences between the current American, Chinese, and Japanese economies to see what a difference a government action (or inaction) can make.

Tax Policy

Perhaps a government's most direct influence on an economy, aside from monetary policy, occurs via the tax structure. While volumes have been written on this subject, perhaps two key arguments can be made here-- that complexity is very costly and that taxes must be primarily geared for economic growth.

Much has been written about the need to simplify the existing tax labyrinth, though the true cost of just complying with current regulations is probably vastly underestimated. One only need add up the fees and salaries for all of the accountants and lawyers involved to get a handle on the drain on the economic productivity of a nation. One source puts this at roughly $265 billion per year while others report over 6 billion hours lost just to filling out tax forms.[157]

Beyond that, taxes that attempt to meet social goals tend to be anti-growth, forcing individual and corporations to forever make uneconomic decisions based on avoiding taxes rather than on growing their business. Just witness the entirely unproductive contortions necessary in estate planning, when businesses are carved up or even sold to avoid taxes.

Further, the tax structure tends to disfavor desirable activities such as investing in plants and machinery, innovation, and new companies. Some relief on capital gains has helped over the years, but Democrats often cannot bring themselves to focus on growth by leaving the money in the hands of a few rich folks in an effort to make everyone rich. Again, giving everyone the chance to be rich is key, as it's nearly impossible to become well off without helping many other people along the way. Holding them back or taking away their rewards hardly seems a productive way to grow the upper-middle class. As Nobel Prize Laureate Milton Friedman has said, "We have a system that increasingly taxes work and subsidizes non-work."[158] That is surely no way to run a 21st century economy, or else 22nd century Americans will be making plastic toys for the Chinese and Indians.

Taxes can even be horribly destructive, providing instructive lessons in the power of government to wreck a good thing. For example, the luxury taxes imposed on boats in 1990 to soak the rich ended up raising only ½ of the projected revenue, but cost 7,600 well-paying jobs in the boat building industries. The net effect, after unemployment and employment taxes were figured in, was the loss of $7.6 million in the first year – hardly a winning tax strategy.[159] The damage was so great that Congress wisely rescinded the tax after a few years, though they left it on automobiles, since they didn't care about the largely foreign producers of such luxury cars.

All of this complexity naturally stimulates discussion of the flat tax. Vastly simplifying the current structure, but not politically popular due to much misunderstanding, such a simple system is being increasingly adopted by various countries around the world. Stunning simplicity not only takes cost and friction out of the system, but also it frees up enormous resources at the high end to be more productively employed in entrepreneurial investments, housing, technology, and even international travel (raising incomes of foreigners who buy American goods, like computers and airplanes, as mentioned elsewhere).

Regardless of the various views on social implications of taxes (either soaking or sparing the rich), the focus needs to be on growing the economy. As California recently learned the hard way, a growing economy pays for all sorts of things, but economic stagnation is fatal to nearly everything. Further, they found that becoming overly dependent on the incomes of the rich only causes a spending spree that rapidly comes to an end when times are not so good. The resulting tax swing for California was tens of billions of dollars, creating additional state debts to support the binge spending on recently created programs now curiously seen as necessary entitlements.

As noted in the entrepreneurship section, the tax structure must especially favor startups, small companies, and their financing above all else. The 1981 capital gains cuts during the Regan administration were especially helpful in boosting the Venture Capital community, as they liberate tied-up capital to be invested in new, growth-oriented enterprises. That community is certainly comprised of the rich, but their money and management is precisely focused on what will continue to sustain American leadership well into this century. At least 11 other developed countries have seen the light on the importance of using capital for growth and have eliminated their capital gains taxes. [160] Perhaps America should do the same, and soon.

Trade

Given that globalization is an unstoppable and ever mounting force that can power whole economies, it is natural that governments consider economics and trade as essentially one and the same. Therefore, they should be considered an integrated whole, with the major goal to increase trade in all directions, under the premise that any trade can only help every economy.

Countries as States

Immediately following the American Revolutionary War of 1776, the United States were a loose confederation of largely sovereign states, each with its own economy, currency, taxes, and most importantly tariffs. While this arrangement managed to function for a time, leaders quickly learned of its challenges and downfalls, especially in the folly of allowing individual states to have their own economies and trade regulations. Especially noxious were interstate trade regulations and tariffs, which together imposed enormous costs and complexities on the fledgling American economy.

As such, when the American Constitution was written in the summer of 1787, one of the key points was the prohibition of states from managing economics or trade. Support for this was so strong that states were (and remain) unable to manage the flow of goods across their borders, which naturally led to the single, unified market that has helped make America so strong. It's also notable that many of the challenges put forth by today's anti-traders were also true back then, including wide economic disparities between states and weak governments coupled to corruption.

Today, as was true over 200 years ago, there exist numerous "states" that have considerable trade among them, though with all the same regulations and tariffs that proved so toxic so long ago. The difference today is those "states" are called countries.

Realizing this, think tanks such as Progressive Policy Institute (PPI) and others are urging leaders to think of the whole world as a larger "United States," with each country as a state. The natural progression of this line of thinking, embodied in the WTO and free-trade agreements, is that trade among the "states" should be free and fair.

The Framers very rapidly understood the serious costs imposed by any other structure and wisely embarked on a widely successful free-trade experiment 200 years ago, with the successful results for everyone to see. The task now is to scale up that model for the whole world.

Trade Promotion

America is the world's largest international trader, moving over $2.5 trillion dollars worth of products and services in

2003. Amazingly, though, Germany exports more goods than the U.S., despite having less than 1/3the population. This surely indicates there is much work to do in growing American exports and in increasing trade in general, as reaching even 1/2 of Germany's exports per capita would instantly erase America's trade deficit.[161]

Therefore it is crucial that global trade and American exports in particular be promoted at every turn. The U.S. Trade Representative has been doing a reasonably good job of this in the World Trade Organization (WTO) and throughout global trade rounds, but a redoubling of efforts is needed in order to foster continued success. Key areas of new innovation such as aviation, telecommunications, pharmaceuticals/biotech, and general technology need to be assured complete and unfettered access to global markets.

Such work includes lower tariffs and subsidies, restrictive local content and other structural rules, and harmonizing a wide variety of technical issues globally. This also will naturally lead to significant reductions or elimination of agricultural subsidies in the developed world, which could dramatically transform the very poorest countries, lifting their people from poverty and providing new markets for American goods and services. Plus, the tens or hundreds of billions of dollars squandered annually on such subsidies can be better applied to educating workforces, developing technology, and making the world a better place.

The U.S. government also has various programs that assist companies in selling their wares overseas. Some of these even focus on small and mid-sized enterprises, though it's not clear how successful this effort is. Even if today's programs have only limited efficacy, it's important to really step this up by listening to what companies in various sectors say they need and then giving it to them.

Such efforts are especially useful when more and more American work is virtual intellectual property in nature, such that a company no longer has to ship big machines overseas to make money. Given that today a $1,000,000 product might be shipped by email, everyone can be an exporter.

It used to be that visibility was a problem, though the Internet has largely eliminated that problem, although embassy-run trade shows are still useful for getting people together (especially important in Asia). Subsidizing trade-related travel, giving tax incentives to export, and providing assistance for the legal, linguistic, tax, and cultural challenges would seem appropriate, perhaps with a one-stop-shop exporting office in major trading states.

Benchmarks should be used for such programs, with measurements such as total exports for companies with less than 100 and 1,000 employees. Beyond that, really listening to what the various sectors need and keeping the goal of maximum exports in mind will ultimately lead to substantial success for company, employees, customer, and taxpayer.

Intellectual Property Protection

Innovation is generated by ideas, particularly revolutionary new concepts coupled with improved methods for existing processes. America's founding fathers foresaw this dynamic engine of growth and enshrined its protection in the Constitution in the form of patents.

Known today as intellectual properly (IP), patents and related legal protection for inventions and innovation are critical to the future of information, knowledge, and innovative societies. Given that America leads in innovation and new ideas, few things are more important to protecting and promoting the development of intellectual property on a global scale. Towards this end, the government should continue to expend significant effort on expanding and standardizing protection for these future ideas, technologies, and innovations.

This especially includes improvements covering the patent process both at home and abroad. The international patent situation is certainly improving and America has been working hard on these issues, especially with the recent semi-convergence of U.S., Japanese, and European patent law. But significant issues remain unresolved in many foreign nations.

For instance, the "first-to-invent" versus "first-to-file" issue remains unresolved; the former is critical to American innovation, while the latter favors larger companies and will probably stifle innovation. It's not clear how to resolve this issue, but innovation in both developed and developing countries needs "first-to-invent" protection to insure the American Dream is available to small innovators everywhere.

In addition, lowering the cost of global patent filing via a more coordinated system would be a big help to small companies. Such filings can cost $50-$250,000 per patent and are often prohibitive for the most innovative companies. Finding ways to harmonize and lower this by an order of magnitude are critical to small companies being able to build the products of the future. This is especially true as the world globalizes, as a U.S. patent becomes less and less protective if a Chinese company can freely use American technology and sell it to India, Indonesia, and Ireland. There really is no excuse any longer for not having a global patent office and clearing house, which would rapidly expand global innovation and IP generation, protection, and licensing.

The real global IP challenges lie in developing nations, particularly in China, India, Brazil, and Vietnam. These countries are both new engines of development in both products and services, and important markets for Western invention. They must bring their IP structures in line with global norms, partially for themselves and the benefit of developed economies, as everyone wins when new ideas flourish.

In addition, current government IP policies are far too entertainment-focused, trying to rein in music sharing and movie piracy. These efforts have gone nowhere and are a waste of time, as these challenges will resolve themselves over time, both as viable legal downloading improves and as developing economies mature and fall further under the rule of law.

Instead, efforts should focus on where the real innovation and economic growth potential are, on better patent processes and protections, since these are the real engines of growth and employment. It's nice to protect Hollywood movies from DVD copies sold in Shanghai, but this pales in comparison to the value of patents for the next generation of microprocessors, nanotech materials, aerospace, or miracle drugs.

Further, the issues dragging on regarding copyright extensions and public rights erosion should be terminated in favor of the public. As Stanford's Lawrence Lessig has argued for years, the Founders, especially Jefferson, intended copyright to last for a modest amount of time so works would pass into the public domain. This has, unfortunately, not really happened, as Disney and others have successfully lobbied Congress to extend copyright virtually forever.

This unfortunately undermines the Founders' brilliance, as with patents; they wanted those works to be available without license or cost for derivative works, free publishing, and dissemination to a wide audience. This is even more relevant in today's global Internet-connected world, where global artistic and economic creativity could use America's copyrighted materials to create so many new things. And they would likely use American computers, software, and technology, all far more valuable than additional royalties to Disney.

On the positive side, on the piracy issues, efforts are being made to get local populations, especially artists and inventors, to understand the value of IP protection. For instance, Chinese and Indian companies are starting to generate their own patents, especially on biotech products. And local musicians and film makers are starting to see their own works sold on the street for pennies, making them realize how useful copyright laws really are. In turn, this pressures the governments involved to improve IP legislation and especially enforcement, protecting everyone everywhere, allowing them to invent everything.

Upgrading the U.S. Patent & Trademark Office

Barriers to innovation in the form of IP issues still exist on the home front as well, at the Patent and Trademark Office (PTO). These generally fall into two areas: speed and accuracy, with speed being more critical, given that any delay in obtaining patents directly impacts innovation. This disproportionately affects smaller companies, since their ability to attract funding often hinges on patent issuance; for them, the typical 12-24 month patent cycle is literally a lifetime.

Congress has become aware of some of this, with New York Congresswoman Nydia Velazquez observing: "The current U.S. patent process is also impacting our ability to quickly develop new innovations that could spur economic growth. Many U.S. firms are being hindered by the slow process of receiving patents. Their competitiveness is threatened as they fail to see rewards for their innovations due to significant lags in processing time."[162]

In addition, the entire world patent system is "under siege" according to the PTO's 21st century strategic plan. There are approximately 7,000,000 applications in the global pipeline, growing at 20-30% per year. Frankly, it's a miracle the Patent and Trademark Office (PTO) manages to keep operation under this rapidly increasing onslaught. Given that, the IP and PTO issues are so crucial to the future of innovation and the American economies that it is clearly the most important of all government agencies and functions. In fact, after the Pentagon and State Department, Trade and Patents are probably the most important components of the government, as they fuel the economic engines that pay for everything else.

The PTO is making strides in improving patent review speed, but their goals and resources are far too modest. The current average patent issuance period is 18 months, with a strategic goal of 27 months total pendency (the time from filing to final disposition.) Note that not all of this time is spent inside the PTO, as pendency is partially dependent on the PTO receiving quick responses from applicants.

Regardless, the goal should be revamped to 3 months for first action, if not allowance -- there is really no reason this cannot be achieved (1-2 months would be even better). While the PTO is complex, if run like a traditional service or claims bureau with adequate resources and incentives, work would begin on an application in the same week it is received, not in the same year, as happens now.

Such a change would take substantial change in PTO operations, but would also have an enormous effect on industries dependent on patents, i.e. most of the important new ones. New companies and inventions could gain protection faster, significantly increase their ability to raise capital, and thus accelerate their rate of innovation and commercialization.

The whole world of global technology and its financing really could be revolutionized by a three-month patent process. Further, with that sort of time frame, there would probably be a huge surge in applications as independent inventors could see the fruits of their efforts in reasonable time frames.

While going faster is vital, accuracy is also critical. The PTO must retain experts in every one of the world's vast and rapidly expanding technology. Given that they must also work quickly, the process often results in questionable patents. This tends to generate litigation, which helps employment in the legal sector, but is hardly useful for anyone else. Faster patents help growth, but not if they are given to the wrong companies or individuals. The PTO has embarked on additional training and quality programs, but these programs need to be expanded in order to ensure both speed and accuracy.

Doubling the PTO budget would be a good place to start, followed by growing it with volume, especially since the PTO is self-funded. Unfortunately, it actually earns money for the U.S. government, which shamefully takes some of the patent fees for the general fund. Diversions are particularly offensive to patent applicants and technologists, as they are not getting the services they are paying for, and the whole world suffers from reduced innovation.

The Bush administration has proposed cutting this diversion by 50% in FY 2004 and providing a $1.4 billion budget, but the diversion should be terminated, once and for all. Finally, letting the PTO retain its own fees is a start, but still not sufficient to add the additional several thousand examiners needed to handle this decade's global innovation. FY 2005 should spend an even $2 billion on the PTO, growing at the application growth rate plus 10% until average pendency is under 6 months.

Don't Neglect Traditional Sectors

It's easy in this world of the Internet and high-tech gadgets to forget more traditional sources of employment, particularly in heavy industry. Many states or regions, such as the San Francisco Bay Area, have given up on heavy industry as they see their future in the transition to service or "clean" industries.

Unfortunately, this path is considerably riskier than has been generally appreciated as those clean jobs move overseas or to lower costs states such as Nevada or Arizona. In addition, heavy industry or other more traditional jobs tend to pay higher wages to lower-skilled workers, creating considerable benefits in the form of secondary jobs among suppliers and related services. And while many manufacturing jobs are moving overseas, there are numerous industries where America either has advantages in technology, productivity, or proximity, such as pulp and paper, automobiles, specialty chemicals, foods, and even steel.

As an implicit measure of importance, the U.S. economic census notes that the manufacturing payroll is 14 % larger than the next two largest sectors, even though it employs 15 % fewer people.[163] That 30% wage gap certainly argues for substantial work in maintaining or even expanding manufacturing work, especially in higher value sectors such as aerospace, electronics, and advanced machinery.

While software and call center jobs are easily moved abroad, traditional industries such as manufacturing are also quite difficult to move abroad, as these companies have invested tens or hundreds of millions of dollars in plants that are meant to last for decades. These factories provide permanent jobs, but the government should focus on incentives to get more plants built or upgraded to remain competitive with foreign producers. Doing so will not only create long-term jobs for Americans but will also spend money locally on construction and domestically on advanced equipment.

Along these lines, a commission ought to be formed to work on ways to improve competitiveness in these important traditional industries. Unfortunately many of these politically well-connected sectors have long favored protectionism. Instead of paranoid protectionist measures, these industries need to focus on increasing investment in plant and equipment, employment, and productivity. This will include reforming union thinking on work rules and flexibility, improving training, and increasing worker involvement to maximize productivity.

Beyond improving traditional businesses, more energy should be spent understanding why various industries move overseas. Often industries with minimal or modest labor input relocate anyway, despite America's seeming sufficient advantages. Taxes, health care costs, environmental regulations, and other issues all come into play, but a better understanding might assist governments at various levels to retain more enterprises and their related jobs. In some cases, companies are simply serving their global customers by building facilities closer to them; those new and productive factories, in turn, can send their wares back to the U.S. and no amount of incentive can alleviate that.

Immigration

The free flow of peoples across borders has always driven and defined positive economic activity in the developed world, nowhere more so than in the United States. As an immigrant nation, America has always relied on foreign talent on both ends of its economic spectrum, with poor immigrants at the bottom and the well-educated at the top.

Some anti-immigrant or anti-free-traders wish to further limit immigration, especially at the most economically useful high-end. They wish to cap H1B visas and don't care that fewer foreign students are coming to study in the United States, that there may be a talent shortage, or that such actions will only accelerate off-shoring and foreign innovation.

The reality is that these students and foreign workers are needed more than ever, especially when their home countries are trying hard to keep their brains at home – in fact future global competition may be for the world's best brains; this is a competition the U.S. has nearly always won, until now.

As Tim Draper, one of Silicon Valley's most talented Venture Capitalists recently noted, "National boundaries are going to probably dissolve or change. Governments, I think, are going to have to realize that they are competing for people, rather than people sort of sucking up to government." [164] This issue of individual competition is so important that Richard Florida has written an important new book about it, "The Rise of the Creative Class."

Today's reality is the world's smartest people no longer need go to America to excel, especially when family and cultural ties tend to keep them at home; further, living in developing countries such as India or China is no longer as challenging as it once was; it's very easy to live in Shanghai in a new seaside condo, eating sushi, drinking Starbucks coffee, and creating the world's most advanced technologies.

Stanford's Rafiq Dossani's survey of immigrant populations confirms this view: "The survey confirms several of the popular views about the contributions of the mainland Chinese, Taiwanese and Indian-born immigrants into Silicon Valley. Across the board, they are highly educated, entrepreneurial, and derive important benefits from their formal and informal network . . . Despite these factors, all groups look to their countries of birth as places to return to, subject to the right conditions, such as professional opportunities.[165]

In another case, cited by an HP alumnus, "One Chinese got a Ph.D., went to HP for five years, then another Valley company, but is now living in Taiwan for TSMC. He's moving to Shanghai to build a new plant, near where he's from, saying that's where the 'exciting opportunities are, not Silicon Valley.'" Further, there used to be a one-way flow, with mainland Chinese going to Taiwan and the U.S., but it's now the other way as chip processing moves to China.[166]

As Bruce Mehlman, former Assistant Secretary of Commerce for Technology Policy has observed, "… the opportunity to do high-wage, high-value work without immigrating to the U.S. clearly reduces the 'brain gain' that has been so critical to America's historical success."[167]

Such attitudes among important immigrants can hardly be in America's long-term interests. This is especially evident in Silicon Valley, where immigrants have always been a major force, starting new companies, inventing new technologies, and creating whole industries right alongside "regular" Americans.

Further, it's even worse when students do come to America to be educated, but cannot get work visas and then take all that knowledge and talent back with them, creating an instant competitor. This is especially evident amongst Japanese, Chinese, and Indian technologists, often schooled at Stanford or Berkeley, but unable to get a visa. They increasingly return home with the American spirit and dream firmly embedded, resulting in a new company in direct competition with American workers.

One of the fundamental problems is that America expects immigrants to go home after coming for school or a job, in a wrongheaded policy of trying to send the best and brightest back home. In reality, it should be the reverse, not dissimilar to what's written on the Statue of Liberty, starting with "Give me your poor . . ." In the 21st century, perhaps this should be restated, "Give me your educated, your entrepreneurial, your innovative . . ." Not only should further immigration be encouraged, it should be increasingly tied to economic success and education, similar to the Canadian policies that encourage professional and skilled immigration.

Fundamentally, immigration needs to be rethought along the lines of corporate recruiting, i.e. how to attract the best and brightest the world has to offer, as it's better to have them working for rather than against American enterprises. Further, just as taxes should be focused on economic growth, so should immigration, admitting or even inviting additional talented or educated future citizens, lest they add their talents to some other economy.

At the moment, any foreign student completing a four-year college degree gets one year of "practical training" to stay in the country before being sent home. In reality, this year is spent frantically searching for a real job, one that will sponsor an H1B visa. Foreign students by and large like America, and rather than expecting them to leave, Americans should expect them to stay and contribute. It's important to keep in mind that many of the students coming to America are the best and brightest their countries have to offer; further, they are by definition risk takers who are leaving their homeland for a great unknown future in the U.S. They don't merely want to get by, but want to excel and succeed. With luck, they will carry lots of Americans with them.

As such, everyone who graduates from a four-year school should get an automatic five- year green card. At the end of five (or even 10) years, they would keep their residency if they were making more than say $75,000, or had started their own company that grossed more than $250,000 per year or had at least three employees. These would be very strong incentives for immigrants to contribute strongly to the economy, hiring others, and building future enterprises.

Further, any foreigner with a Masters or Ph.D. in the sciences, engineering, or management should be eligible for a five-year H1B or green card as soon as they arrive. It will be argued that these people will take away American jobs and that may well be true to some degree, but that is irrelevant as they create new innovation, companies, and employment.

Recalling that the goal is to grow the economy , foreign-born technical talent is critical to doing that (as it always has been.) The important question to ask is if immigrants can create more jobs than they "take away." Certainly in Silicon Valley, where immigrants run scores of successful companies with tens of thousands of employees, the answer is clearly yes.

Another way to think of the H1B issue is that visa limits probably contribute to off-shoring and actually reduce jobs in America. In a free market with no limits, companies would use the proper mix of local, immigrant, and off-shored talent. But, with a cap, they are forced to choose between domestic employees and off-shoring. This means that visa limits force companies to import the services of immigrants, rather than the immigrants themselves, which is a very poor economic tradeoff (at least in the short term). This is because all things being equal, it's probably more desirable to have the Indian programmer on U.S. soil, paying U.S. taxes and eating/sleeping locally, but working less expensively, as this is a direct productivity increase for the U.S. economy.

As an example of how much influence such immigrants have, one need look no further than California in general and

Silicon Valley in particular, where 34% of residents are foreign born.[168] Like New York City, Silicon Valley is a diverse place with large groups of varied nationalities, races, and types of people.

For another even more telling example, Silicon Valley author Po Bronson tells a story of how he used to go sit in San Francisco Airport's international terminal, watching the flights arriving from China or other Asian countries. He looked for the lone bewildered-looking young men, who looked like they were arriving for the first time. He would interview them about what they were doing; many simply wanted to be in America, the land of the free, to live the American dream. Many had Ph.D.s or similar educations in technology and wanted to help build greatness in the Valley. He followed about a dozen of these men over a one-year period and found at the end that several had started their own companies ; one had already sold his and was rich; every other one was hard at work creating Silicon Valley's next wave of technology.[169]

These are the types of immigrants America needs. With proper incentives, they will continue to get to live the American dream and pull everyone else along with them.

In the end, infusing foreign talent into the domestic labor pool is identical to buying a microwave oven or automobile made overseas. Both have the same effect on the economy, the same benefits, and the same challenges. If importing goods is okay, than importing services must really be the same, though even more so, as imported talent continues to contribute for decades to come. Limiting immigration in this manner is simply affirmative action for Americans, with all the downsides that go with such programs.

This is especially true when the imported goods are superior, in the case of Japanese automobiles or top talent from various countries. Just as no one wants to be forced to buy an inferior and higher-priced domestic car, why should they be forced to hire such an employee?

Chapter 12.

Displaced Worker Assistance

Introduction

Globalization and off-shoring are clearly affecting the composition and distribution of white-collar jobs in America, a trend that will only accelerate over time. As such, workers are potentially facing substantial job losses at every turn, and at every level of white-collar employment. With the prospect of millions of displaced workers in the coming years, clearly one of the most significant practical and political challenges is assisting them in finding productive new jobs.

To illustrate the challenges of finding good new jobs, the Bureau of Labor Statistics reports that from the 1980s to the '90s, 31% of those losing jobs to international trade were not fully re-employed. Further, while 36% of these displaced workers found work at the same or higher salary, over half made 85% or less of their prior wages. And, a quarter of the employees took at least a 30% pay cut.[170]

Free traders argue that things will take care of themselves and government participation can only make things worse. They believe innate American flexibility and entrepreneurial spirit will eventually win the day, and there is some truth to this line of thought. After all, the above-cited heavy losses in manufacturing employment didn't destroy American spirits or the economy; to the contrary, in many cases it freed up poorly utilized talent and capital to focus on the future.

While the American tradition of prosperity and its built-in advantages will undoubtedly be helpful, the government also has a role in improving the prospects of displaced workers. That, in turn, will help boost the economy as a whole as it keeps people productive, encouraged, and engaged.

As noted, the 1980s blue-collar shift was a migration from manufacturing to services, from blue- to white-collar work, and theoretically from hands-on to knowledge-based employment, moving up the value chain to higher-order functions not easily sent off-shore at the time. A similar shift is now underway, though with some challenging differences.

There is no "next" portion of the economy to move to, as there was in the shift from manufacturing to services. Services were always considered the "next" step from manufacturing, but from here the next step is murky, as developing countries and especially China begin to compete at all levels of the economy. Hands-on service jobs might be the next frontier, but those have always existed and in many cases are a step down in expertise and compensation.

For the first time, many white-collar professionals need to look at new occupations. By definition, a professional is an expert in their profession, so forcing them to change vocation necessarily creates challenges. For instance, they have "suffered" through many years of education, often at a great expense, and have usually been working in their field for at least a decade.

Now these long-entrenched professionals are being uprooted, and they aren't even necessarily moving to secure new places. Once people find new professions, it isn't even clear that the position will last long, as they may easily be forced into yet another occupation in a few years.

This is especially problematic if the change in careers occurs faster than the training cycle time in that profession – one can imagine the hypothetical challenge if physicians needed to switch specialties every three years in a world where it takes five to ten years to become proficient in a specialty.

Regardless of the these challenges, the white-collar workforce has to begin looking at how it will transition to new professions, and this naturally brings up the issue of education and fundamentally how to train people to be trainable.

Training Programs

How can we grow, educate, attract and retain the best and brightest scientists and engineering students? How do we avoid a disconnect between the jobs we want to keep in the U.S. and our workforce's ability to do them – Bruce Mehlman, Undersecretary of Commerce for Technology Policy, in testimony at House Committee on Science, January 24, 2004[171]

Congress and some states have long recognized the need to help train or otherwise assist displaced workers, creating a number of programs over the years. These programs are almost universally focused on blue-collar displacements. In fact, the Bush Administration and Congress have recently failed or even refused to extend these benefits to white-collar workers, though in one sense this provides a good opportunity to create new and effective programs from scratch.

Unfortunately, no one has ever attempted to retrain scores of professional white-collar workers across a wide-spectrum of sectors or job levels. One probably does not just hand an ex-accountant or attorney a pair of pliers and send them off to install phone lines, or hand them a scalpel for surgery. Further, while clerical employees can probably transition to other related occupations, it's not even clear how to retrain a professional with multiple years of education and experience.

While there are numerous similarities with the historical retraining of the blue-collar workforces of the 1980s onward, there are significant differences that make this transition both easier and more difficult.

Who Needs Help

In the old days when moderately skilled labor made up the bulk of the displaced workers, they could usually seek new, yet similar work across town, across the state, or across the country. However, blue-collar workers found in the 1980s and beyond that they needed to retool themselves as their skills were either obsolete or simply not in demand. Thus, pipe fitters, welders, weavers, and even roughnecks became appliance repairmen, skilled construction tradesmen, or fiber optic splicers.

So, sorting out who needs training assistance and distinguishing between the various types of requirements, opportunities, and needed programs is a key challenge. Unfortunately, this is not as simple as it may seem, for displaced workers vary considerably in age, education, experience, and flexibility. As such, no one-size-fits-all approach is likely to be successful.

As with a retirement or investment program, it's critical to properly analyze the market's needs before embarking on numerous government programs at considerable cost. Today's blue-collar oriented programs are almost certainly ill suited for the task; considerable thinking and experimentation will likely be needed on the federal and state levels before effective programs are developed. Programs born of public-private partnerships that offer for-profit delivery of training and incentives to students are likely to be the most effective in the coming years, as the market will sort out what's needed where by whom.

As mentioned, incoming trainees differ in many ways beyond just the jobs they previously held. Many different age groups, cultural backgrounds, and educational levels will be affected by the job shift. For instance, a 25-year-old unemployed engineer's needs will differ from those of a 50-year-old computer programmer, though both are high-end professionals.

The engineer, given his youth and probable lack of financial responsibilities, is likely to be far more flexible than the more mature programmer. A 50-year-old with a mortgage, a husband, and kids is presumably more risk-adverse and less likely to uproot and try something entirely new. Programs that are sensitive to these differences will be much more successful, as they will not try to push either worker into a field or decision that isn't right for them.

It's also very important to draw distinctions between retraining a welder to fix appliances and moving a lawyer into a new career in public relations or financial management. Many of these new skills are soft and often ill-suited to people coming from other professions.

Fortunately, white-collar workers tend to be better educated and therefore theoretically better able to absorb new training, especially at the high-end; however, the unanswered question is whether it's really possible to train higher-end professionals in new lines of work on a large scale, especially at the same salary. This has never been attempted before and will certainly be more difficult and costly than retraining displaced coal miners. It may well take a decade or more to sort out how best to manage these transitions, so the time to start is now.

There are numerous training distinctions to be made, as MBAs, CPAs, and corporate attorneys all have a fairly good grasp of business and operations, probably sufficient to work in nearly any industry. On the other hand, some of these folks have become so specialized, such as in foreign exchange hedge accounting or stem cell intellectual property law, that they may well lack the broader skills necessary for generalized work such as managing an international product team at Proctor & Gamble.

Worker Categories

Among the many possible categorization schemes, assessing prior job level may be a good method to evaluate training needs. The previously-described white-collar divisions of low, medium, and high are probably useful here. As a reminder, low-end jobs include clerical positions, transcription, or claims processing. The mid-level covers engineering, IT and programming, accounting, and call centers, while high-level roles include professionals such as lawyers, scientists, and physicians.

Given such diversity, a one-size-fits-all approach is clearly doomed to failure. In fact, in such a diverse environment, it's almost certainly best to empower individuals to guide their own transitions, with assistance from a mix of public and private resources.

Low End

At the low end, in clerical and similar jobs, the employees have spent considerable time in their type of position, or moved over from blue-collar factory work, such as when women exit the textile industry. Their jobs are the most easily moved abroad and they are perhaps the most difficult to train to move up the economic ladder, given their lack of formal schooling and often more advanced age. There are also probably more single parents in this category, making it more difficult to attend evening school or other time-intensive training activities, especially without adequate and affordable child care.

Realistically, their future probably lies in other service jobs that are more immune to export, such as in health care. Ideally they will be able to function at a higher level, say as a nurse or nurse's aid, which may be educationally accessible to them and for which there is a global shortage of workers (so much so that America imports nurses from developing countries, especially in Africa, destabilizing their health systems).

Regardless of their eventual destination, low-end white-collar training is probably best handled in the existing context of community colleges and specialized training schools. These institutions are well versed in the challenges of older and less-educated workforces, and merely need to tailor their programs for the future professions of those at risk in this new economy and world order.

Mid-Level

The mid-level white-collar professionals are perhaps the most difficult to retrain, as they have often spent years in a relatively narrowly defined, yet often well-paying profession. The nature of these jobs drives them off-shore, given that they are computer-driven specialties that only require a good education and some experience, both of which are readily available in countries like India and China. It is not at all clear how to retrain or re-purpose a 40-year-old engineer or computer programmer accustomed to making $100,000 a year, since most of their available occupations, even after retraining, are also ripe for off-shoring.

In the end, each individual will need to examine his or her circumstances, where they can fit, and possibly also look at the plethora of opportunities in other sectors, including non-profits and specialized niches. In addition, even though this mid-level group is very much at risk, there are many opportunities for those that can expand their skills, especially by combining business and technology or mixing in various international perspectives (international and cross-cultural management, languages, global operations). Workers with this cross-functional or cross-cultural experience will always be in demand, especially as business and the world at large increases in complexity.

Further, as noted above, training for this group may best be focused on preparing for many jobs, rather than a particular position. As such, the mini-MBA courses, an introduction to international trade/culture, and specific training in an area of interest might be best. Such a broad set of knowledge will ideally position the trainees to hold different positions in a wide variety of industries over the following decades.

High-End

High-end white-collar professionals will likely require a whole new approach to retraining, as they have years of specialized training, professional certifications, and perhaps decades of service in their industries. While some, such as attorneys, can more easily transition into other businesses, doctors, researchers, and many other professionals will find this much more difficult, especially on a grand scale.

Since very little is known about what sorts of programs (if any) will be most effective for this group, careful study of the factors involved will be critical to designing new initiatives. Fortunately, individuals are leaving these professionals all the time, so an analysis of where they are going and the skills necessary might be instructive. And, unlike their mid-level siblings, many high-end professionals have the financial resources to weather some professional storms and to spend the time to work on a new profession.

Training Goals

It is important to examine and properly set the actual goals of the various training programs that might come into play. While it may seem obvious that programs should help employees get new jobs, it's actually more complex than that, especially in a dynamic environment where it's not at all clear which jobs will exist in a decade.

For instance, should programs focus on short programs that provide specific skills that are in demand, to help insure a rapid transition to a new job? Or should they focus on longer-term programs that provide a stronger foundation for job categories likely to be available in the future? For many groups, the latter is more likely to prepare them for a strong future in a wider variety of industries and positions.

Such programs might resemble mini-MBAs, focusing on accounting, marketing, and operations in combination with more focused training in technology, health care, or other promising areas of interest and commerce. That sort of training provides bridging skills that are not yet present in developing countries Perhaps more importantly, it sets the stage for entrepreneurship for many displaced workers. In addition, having multiple skills that cross functional boundaries may be where Americans of all stripes may add the most value in the coming years.

For different ex-employees, programs might cover basic math and science skills needed in an array of possible positions, from fiber optics to project management to non-profit finances. The key is to prepare every citizen for life-long learning and flexibility, rapidly providing as many skills as they can handle at any given stage, at a level commensurate with their needs, background, and perhaps most importantly, interests.

In addition, it's crucial to involve the actual "consumers" of these workers, namely the companies doing the hiring. While they tend to focus myopically on their most immediate needs, their input at least insures a better overlap between what the courses teach and what companies need. Various sectors are also likely to have different training needs, so programs must be tailored to the various specifics. Community colleges in particular have been fairly good at this and are probably a good lead group to direct some of these efforts.

Enhancing Current Methods and Programs

Despite continual concerns about program structure and training methods and efforts forward, much good work is already being done in the retraining area. Though the current job crisis in white-collar work poses a special challenge to the system, workers have been going through "dislocation" and displacement for as long as economies have existed. Many existing programs work well and ought to be evaluated for enhanced support and expansion.

If the government is to have a role, then the next consideration is the most effective nature of that role. As with welfare and other governmental direct-action programs, it's far from clear that the bureaucracy is actually capable or even best suited to undertake the training itself. Therefore, careful consideration needs to be given to the proper public/private mix of funding, management, and delivery of these services.

Existing programs

Existing training programs fall into several categories. As noted, a major challenge is that existing programs are almost exclusively focused on blue-collar positions, like training the ex-welder or assembly line worker to repair cars or computers. Considerable work remains to determine how to best re-position a mid-career professional and many programs are likely to fail along the way as part of the training optimization process.

Company-paid Programs

Many companies run, or at least pay for, outplacement programs for their workers. Typically run by an outside placement firm, these are often short-lived and, especially for white-collar workers, tend to be more focused on resume and job-search skills in the same profession. These programs can be helpful, but they are probably quite inadequate for the coming job shift, as they are merely window dressing to help find a new job just like the old one.

Realizing this, companies such as IBM have created the Human Capital Alliance, a $25 million effort to train workers in new skills. This program is targeted at employees being replaced by foreign workers, focusing on technology training in things such as Linux and the intersection of various technologies and business. Unfortunately, it is still very ill-defined; hopefully IBM will accelerate its activity in this area, as much may be learned from their well-funded efforts in a key industry.

Government Programs

There are a wide variety of state and federally-funded programs serving displaced workers. While worker training has been around for decades as part of the Job Training Partnership Act (JTPA) of 1982, more recent adjustments have focused on workers being displaced by global competition. The Economic

Dislocation and Worker Adjustment Assistance Act (EDWAA), Worker Adjustment and Retraining Notification (WARN-1988) Act, and the Trade Adjustment Assistance (TAA) are among the most prominent.

These programs provide a variety of diverse benefits for works, including training vouchers, support after unemployment payments run out, training services, coaching, and many other options. Some programs include classroom, occupational skills, and/or on-the-job training in addition to basic and remedial education, entrepreneurial training, and instruction in literacy or English as a second language (ESL).

A major challenge of these acts, however, is that they generally only support manufacturing and thus mostly target blue-collar workers. Certainly that group needs assistance, but legislation needs to catch up with today's realities. Fortunately, there are recent efforts in Congress to update these programs to at least include white-collar employees in existing programs, though the Bush Administration has resisted this expanded coverage.[172] The real challenge may not be the funding, but the proper designing of programs that serve the unique needs of these newly displaced persons.

Other more experimental programs are also in the works. For example, the Department of Labor ran a $10 million pilot project providing skill vouchers to workers in a few diverse states. These vouchers are called "career management accounts" and are designed as the consumer-choice model for worker training.

From the excellent final report on this project, this overall objective was precisely in line with the needs outlined here: "Built on the premise of consumer choice, this new approach to doing business will be a significant change from established practice. Rather than being dependent upon case managers to prescribe a training regimen, individuals will be allowed and, indeed, expected to take an active role in managing their employment futures through the use of Individual Training Accounts.

This pilot project involved 13 different state training sites, which used considerably different methods to explore the best solutions. The report also points out numerous lessons learned and various innovative programs and operational tactics that appeared particularly effective. Key findings included how well trainees felt about control over the process, the flexibility of training choices, and feeling personally accountable for the money spent and results obtained. Many states provided between $3-$8,000 over one to two years, and some saw dramatic increases in the number of private programs offered to their trainees, along with lowered prices and more individual customization.[173]

Such programs are probably the future of white-collar training, allowing the worker to individually choose from a variety of plans that suit his or her age, profession, education, and interests.

There will be the numerous bureaucratic challenges posed by greatly expanding such programs, especially to serve a dynamic workforce with diverse needs. In some ways, this challenge is similar to welfare, with its diverse constituency and needs; it's not unreasonable to expect that citizens probably would prefer the retraining program run more smoothly, and with better results, than Welfare.

States also are providing postsecondary tuition assistance to help dislocated workers pursue alternative career paths. For example, Washington funds tuition waivers for dislocated timber workers and commercial fisherman. State legislation requires community colleges, technical schools, and some four-year universities to reserve 750 student spaces for dislocated workers. Tuition waivers also can be used for state-sponsored distance learning programs.

About one third of the states report that one-stop career centers created by the Workforce Investment Act (1998) have improved services to dislocated workers by providing a more efficient delivery system and streamlined access to comprehensive programs and services. Services include resource rooms with career information, computer terminals with data on services, and registration for programs.[174]

The Workforce Investment Act also provides $4 billion for training of existing employees that are likely to be laid off; this is essentially a preemptive program that presumably shortens the time between jobs. There is some concern that this training focuses on relatively entry-level work, so its horizons should presumably be expanded to a wider variety of skills and professions with their associated higher demand and compensation.

Other players in this training process include organizations such as the Eastern Kentucky Concentrated Employment Program, which has supported displaced worker training since 1968. The EKCEP has both adult and youth programs, and focuses on getting workers the proper training they need at other facilities. It provides tuition, required books, commuting assistance and even meals or child care for workers getting retrained.

This program, though it does not directly train workers itself, provides all the means to get workers trained as well as advice to help them decide what training is best for their new career path. These sorts of programs need to be all over the country and available to every worker in need, perhaps as training ombudsmen to help (or actually) manage and monitor each individual's training money, choices, and programs.

In addition, Congress is working to consolidate some of the array of overlapping programs. Numerous bills are in progress that also help move decision-making closer to the end-users at the state and local level, since Silicon Valley's needs are not the same as those of Michigan or South Carolina.

Things could always be more efficient. The congressional General Accounting Office reports that there are 44 separate federal training programs, run by nine different agencies, spending $12 billion per year.[175] Expanding or doubling this to cover the plethora of white-collar needs may not the be wisest use of taxpayer funds, so consolidation into either a master program or providing funds to states to run their own best practice programs may be the best route.

In addition, there are other interesting efforts that seem to help this training process along. For instance, prodding unemployed workers to really look for jobs by giving $500-$1000 bonuses seems quite effective, as trials in several states suggest that unemployed workers who are given cash incentives to find work get jobs faster.[176] Clearly there needs to be experimentation and a variety of approaches, along with appropriate follow up and tracking to ascertain what works best.

Community College Programs

In addition to any government-funded programs, there are a very wide variety of community college-based vocational programs. These usually focus on teaching a trade, though they do stray into many advanced areas such as computer programming, laboratory work, and even molecular biology. Such schools include the University of Phoenix and other hands-on, direct-to-consumer programs. Even though the student usually pays tuition at these schools, the states and local communities typically also subsidize the school in an effort to simply improve the education in their area.

Private Programs

Finally, there are private training programs for specific industries or professions, such as computer work, commercial diving and welding, flying, etc. There is a wide variety of options, from very focused single-course schools to very large operations that overlap with community colleges, such as the University of Phoenix.

Program Choices

Combinations of the aforementioned delivery and funding methods provide a considerable array of current and future options. As noted in the Department of Labor pilot program, the best choice is probably a cluster of user-directed programs where money flows directly or indirectly to the ex-employee, who decides among the available programs best suited to their needs. Considerable guidance is presumably needed, almost like a high-school guidance counselor for mid- or post-career professionals.

This is also another area where diversity among the displaced workers becomes a challenge. Some individuals may have a good handle on their future direction and training needs, but this is much less likely for some, e.g. a single mom laid off from an insurance processing center. She will need considerable guidance and education just to understand the opportunities open to her, both in terms of training and potential careers (many of which she may never heard of). One size definitely does not fit all in any of these circumstances, so both creativity and deftness will be needed to properly match trainees with programs in a cost-effective manner.

Paying for Training

As with any program, there is the funding question. There have probably not been sufficient funds available for blue-collar displacement, but white-collar needs are likely to be much larger, as the new-career training programs will presumably be longer and more complex. After all, training a microbiologist is a bit more difficult than showing someone how to splice fiber optics.

As such, today's reality is that students have no shortage of educational opportunities, and funding can come from a variety of sources, but it's not clear that this is either effective for existing displaced white-collar workers or for the coming growth in this sector. In particular, it's not clear there is anywhere near sufficient money to run millions of people through multi-month, if not multi-year training programs.

After all, quick math for a million people annually doing a one-year $25,000 program is $25 billion just for tuition, in addition to their housing and eating needs. Those same people could easily cost $50-100 billion to support and retain in such a scenario; these are levels of funding far beyond anything being currently contemplated, in public, private, or mixed-funding models.

Company Funded

The first and most obvious possible funding source for training is direct company funding, where the company laying off workers pays for their training. Unfortunately, there are two drawbacks to this approach, the first being that smaller companies simply do not have the resources for this, especially if their layoffs are driven by downsizing or going out of business, essentially leaving the employees in the lurch.

Second, and perhaps more important, is that mandatory employment-related fees such as lay-off-driven training can act as a hiring disincentive, much like minimum wages or European-style layoff penalties. There are, however, a number of tools to mitigate this challenge, especially limiting the fees to larger companies or finding other ways to carefully tailor the costs without creating hiring disincentives. Overall, there is a balance to strike, though it needs to err on the side of promoting employment.

Tax Funded

The next possible funding source is essentially indirectly company-funded, through taxes, fees, or other mandates similar to Medicare or Federal Unemployment (FUTA). For instance, the latter has a cap of $434 per employee per year, which could be doubled to raise $50 billion. That would probably hit small businesses pretty hard, but raising the cap by only $66 (to $500) would still raise $8 billion, surely enough to kick start any training program focused on insuring workforce education and employability in the long run. Even if a million jobs were lost each year, that's $8,000 each to assist with their training needs.

Regardless, while these taxes are broader-based than direct funding and therefore less of a hiring disincentive, these are still real costs for companies and a direct drag on the economy. It's also not clear how to apportion these "taxes," as companies or industries that never outsource will surely scream they are being taxed unfairly. In the end, however, these types of fees may be the best broad-based method to fund training that presumably benefits everyone.

Closely related to the direct tax, another source is simply from the government via general taxes, which fall disproportionately on the employed via income taxes, rather than companies themselves. As always, taxes are evil and raising them to pay for this process is hardly desirable, especially when one needs to explain to the employed citizens why they need to support their unemployed brethren when large companies are paying nothing (since they often pay little in income tax). This is generally how current programs are funded today, but raising the financial commitment several fold does not seem likely.

Also on the tax front, it's important to factor in community colleges, which are usually partially funded by local and state taxes. They are also presumably efficient at service delivery, given their modest tuition costs; as such, heavily utilizing their programs, facilities, and resources can only be beneficial to these retraining efforts, though their costs in taxes will surely rise with enrollment.

As an alternative, given the toxicity of taxes, community college subsidies may be best used as a DARPA-like catalyst, leveraging private and other money to efficiently retrain large numbers of people at modest cost to the taxpayer. Tax money can also help seed a diverse array of local and state programs in an effort to sort out which are effective and which should be discontinued before they inefficiently consume vast sums of money.

Individually Self-Funded

Finally, retraining can be self-funded by the ex-employee getting displaced. This has obvious challenges, especially for professionals. While they tend to have more savings due to their higher previous salaries, their training period is often much longer and more expensive than a blue-collar educational process. In addition, any worker and his or her family used to a high income is likely to find it quite difficult to substantially dial down their expenses in the short-term.

Regardless, making displaced employees pay for their education might seem unfair politically, given that they are the ones thrown out of work. However, employee self-funding at some level may well result in the most efficient tuning of training needs, not to mention insuring very efficient selection and utilization of public and private education resources. If they are footing a portion of the bill, workers will be sure to get their money's worth and pay for only those programs that are actually helpful.

Careful planning will be needed, however, as individuals may also find themselves trapped in a chicken and the egg situation without money to pay for training to get a job that can pay for training. Regardless, some type of meaningful self-contribution is important, lest the country end up with a health care-like system of spiraling cost and questionable efficacy.

In addition to funding various training courses, a low-cost loan program is obviously highly desirable and should probably be instituted immediately, similar to existing Perkins or Stafford Loans. Outright grants should also be used based on need, using a structure similar to existing Pell Grants for undergraduates. Getting those least able or interested into training should be a major goal and measurement for such programs.

Even for a single layoff of 500 employees from a call center, who will pay the $2.5-$5 million cost of retraining them? How does society pay this kind of money for every individual that needs retraining, and how much responsibility falls on the individual vs. their ex-employer vs. society at large?

In the end, some combination of these efforts seems most likely, though each of these funding sources must be used judiciously. None of these groups ought to be solely responsible for funding training programs, as this sub-optimizes the results. High taxes, reduced hiring, and displaced workers going broke are all quite undesirable and thus to be avoided as the plans progress into previously uncharted territory.

Regardless, letting funds come from all three sources (company, government, individual) in different ways may be the most interesting way to go. One can imagine a training program partially subsidized by the government, held at a company's facility, and aided by reasonably modest fees to its students. Whatever way these problems are worked out, it is clear that questions of funding are delicate and that the burden cannot be placed on one group alone.

Society's Commitment to Adult Education

A major challenge for students of even the best training programs is how to survive financially during the training period and what to do when the resulting new salary is substantially less than the old job's compensation. There currently really are few options, as American society expects adults to take care of themselves and their educational needs, especially at the white-collar or professional level.

It can be argued that there should be a considerable government role, based in large part on the societal benefits of retraining and maximum utilization of human resources. For instance, all developed countries provide universal free primary and secondary education. They also usually provide a relatively inexpensive (U.S.) or free (Europe) college education for the same reasons, namely that an educated populace is critical to progress, economic growth, and a better society.

Unfortunately, once someone graduates from high school or college, they are on their own. Part of the premise here is that once a citizen reaches adulthood, they are on their own and responsible for their own future, especially in America. This generally makes sense. However, a structural economic shift of the magnitude described herein may require a revisiting of this tenet and commitment to a program to boost the education and training of the general population.

For instance, society is almost certainly best served by getting displaced workers retrained and productive as quickly as possible (perhaps at nearly any cost). This is especially true when there are considerable dangers of the white-collar classes coming unglued or leading to destructive protectionism, not to mention more direct and immediate challenges such as the lack of health care insurance.

Under this theory, society, and therefore governments, should expend considerable resources to retrain workers for the brave new world. To some extent this is similar to the need to spend more money on public and preventative health to avoid spending much more later in health care (though America is quite bad at this).

There are obvious dangers to throwing around too much money, but modest controls and state-level experimentation (as used in welfare reform) will ultimately develop optimal solutions and help keep things on an even keel. Regardless, while difficult financially, it may well be good policy to expend billions of dollars on these efforts, especially for significant improvements to one of the best components of American education, the community college system.

Wage Insurance

There has been recent discussion in various states about helping displaced workers via wage insurance, which tries to compensate for the lower wages earned when a worker transitions to a new industry, usually as a novice. This is especially an issue for older workers with poor educational backgrounds and considerable financial responsibilities.

Wage insurance essentially acts as a supplement to their new salary, so that their income would not substantially decline in the new job. A fair amount of work has been done on this idea by Lori Kletzer at the University of California, Santa Cruz and Robert Litan at the Brookings Institute. One or more states are also contemplating a trial. Still, the cost is projected at $4 billion per year, hardly small change (and bound to increase once the bureaucracy gets involved).[177]

Congress has expressed some interest in this type of program and included a tiny (and overly-restrictive) pilot program in a 2002 trade bill, but the Department of Labor does not know if it has yet been utilized by anyone.[178]

One of the primary advantages to a program like wage insurance is that it will increase hiring, as it both helps workers stay afloat and reduces new hiring risk and cost to companies. If the government is willing to cover the difference between what a company is willing to pay an employee and what the employee expects to make, the company is much more likely to take the employee on.

Given that wage insurance can probably be deployed fairly rapidly, it may be a good way to begin helping workers while developing more comprehensive training programs and tuning them to truly fit workers' needs.

Other Worker Support

There are also numerous other areas in which the government could help individuals weather this off-shoring storm. Each poses varying degrees of challenge to those who are laid off and trying to put their life in order.

For instance, affordable child care is a major challenge, whether one is employed or not. This problem is especially acute for single parents, or when both parents are forced to work due to the loss of a single high income. While this hardly seems an issue for off-shoring, it is a major challenge for working mothers, especially when they need to work part-time and improve their educations at the same time. Providing free training and other assistance may not be that helpful if there are still two children to take care of during the day.

Welfare programs have looked at this problem, as they have similar issues, though cost-effective solutions are still elusive. Even so, this must be addressed so ways can be found to allow these women to move on and be productive in the new century.

Health Costs / Portability

Another challenge to job mobility is health care costs and plan portability. For the former, obtaining health care coverage after being laid off imposes an often very high cost on a family, upwards of $1,000/month. COBRA has certainly helped by at least making coverage available, although ex-employees often find it difficult to afford the expensive corporate plans when they'd prefer a more economical plan.

Further, portability is always a challenge, as being "in network" in a new plan can force families to change doctors, sometimes multiple times over several years, in what must surely be a disruptive process, especially for children.

The solutions here are not clear, other than extending COBRA and perhaps providing some lower-cost post-employment options for individuals, entrepreneurs, and families. The need to support a family's health care is one reason heads of households often stay in jobs much longer than they should, for the benefits. This can have the perverse effect of delaying their entry into a new and more promising industry or profession at the right time, so that when they finally get laid off abruptly, there is no where to go.

Pension Portability

Pension portability can also be a major challenge for employees moving between companies in some industries, though this is being eased by the widespread participation in defined-contribution plans such as 401(k) plans (though only 52% of them allowed inbound roll-overs in 1997).[179] For many older pension plans, there is significant risk of company failure (e.g. the airlines), and moving between companies often leads to a loss of seniority and other factors that eventually determine the paid-out benefit.

Such challenges potentially create a barrier to changing careers or industries until the last minute, hindering an employee's ability to learn, grow, and re-position for the coming new economy and its job shifts. The Economic Growth and Tax Relief Reconciliation Act of 2001 eliminated some of the barriers in this area, but more work may be required for single employer-defined benefit plans, the most difficult type to transfer.

There also remain significant difficulties in transferring pensions between countries, which is becoming a hot topic in Europe, given that professionals are more often moving within the EU. The U.S. has signed some agreements on Social Security portability, but should probably go much further as the economy and population globalizes. After all, if one chief way to combat off-shoring is to specialize in global management and to work in many countries to get experience, it makes no sense to lose one's pension benefits in the process.

Bringing workers' skills into the 21st century must be regarded as a component of any response to off-shoring. Companies, countries, and societies that learn to instill learning in their workforces will be best prepared to handle the increasingly dynamic nature of modern economies and globalization.

Chapter 13.

Bridging the Cultural and Language Divide

A major poll finds that 77% of respondents say that high school programs in the U.S. do not adequately prepare young people to understand current international affairs.[180]

"We must increase our exchanges with the rest of the world. We must work closer than ever with educational institutions, the private sector and nongovernmental organizations and we must encourage our citizens to engage the world to learn foreign languages, to understand different cultures and to welcome others into their homes."

Secretary of State Condoleezza Rice[181]

Globalization of Population

The world is moving unstoppably towards globalization and the U.S. must ensure its populace globalizes as well. In addition to being prepared to compete economically with China and India, citizens of every country should have an informed perspective and understanding about other cultures. While it's always been important to understand and appreciate other cultures, today's globalization requires and rewards global citizens able to move among, and work with, the world's peoples.

Even though America is perhaps the world's most diverse nation, its citizens continue to display an astounding ignorance about, or lack of interest in, the rest of the world and its people, language, and culture. As the old joke goes: "What do you call someone who speaks three languages? Tri-lingual. What do you call someone who speaks two languages? Bi-lingual. What do you call someone who speaks one language? American."

Sadly, this isn't far from the truth. One of the most important long-term roles of any 21st century government is to globalize its population, setting the stage for global understanding and economic participation while avoiding the natural nationalistic and protectionist reactions. Non-American countries are fully aware of this imperative and thus are trying to insure all of their citizens learn to speak English.

It's difficult for a government to help globalize its citizenry when government officials themselves are clueless. For example, House Majority Leader Richard Army (R-Texas), once publicly said that he had no intention to travel to Europe, because he had already been there once.[182] Further, Foreign Affairs magazine noted that about two-thirds of Republicans elected to Congress in 1994 did not have passports.[183]

This ignorance of the world is astounding and destructive on many levels, including an inability to really participate in the new high-tech economies that are increasingly driving the world. Americans, in particular, are unbelievably fortunate that English is the lingua franca of travel and business. However, it understandably encourages laziness among Americans and masks the difficulties they encounter when interacting with people from various cultures. The fact that Japanese or Chinese businessmen speak passable English does not change the fact that they will inevitably encounter significant cultural confusion with their American counterparts.

As seasoned travelers know, there is far more to cross-cultural interaction than knowing the same words. One need look no further than some of the cultural challenges with off-shoring to India to see some of the barriers, even for countries that ostensibly speak the same language, have similar governments, and share a history with the British Empire.

People have been crossing cultures since the dawn of time, but no developed country does it as little or as poorly as America. This is a key area where government leadership, and perhaps a little funding, can go a long way towards changing this self-limiting mindset, especially in a world where America has only 5% of the population and speaks only one of the 5,000 or so languages in daily use.

Given the incessant march of globalization, language training and cultural programs are vital to surviving the coming job crisis for two reasons. First, to insure that the U.S. is not overrun with xenophobia and possibly violence, and second, to give workers every advantage in the economic rat race. Programs such as student exchange, language training, travel, and general cultural awareness, can do much to create more globally literate Americans.

Beyond language, Americans are chronically underexposed to anything non-American, often regarding such things as "un-American." And, much to their surprise, Chinese food and Japanese cartoons hardly count as Asian culture.

The U.S. also unfortunately harbors a fair number of xenophobic and prejudiced people, whose attitudes are not confined to fringe right-wing militia groups. Given the current political tragedies caused by terrorist groups, this sort of anti-foreign (and anti-immigrant) fervor is only likely to rise. These are the folks that say that immigrants should all speak English and that there are too many foreign cultural influences in America today (forgetting the exact same things were said of, and by, their ancestors).

This can be especially dangerous when driven by xenophobic radio hosts and in both left-wing anti-globalist and right-wing isolationist campaigns. These types of groups and their media were directly responsible for Yugoslavia coming apart in the 1990s, when the "us vs. them" fires were fanned by politicians seeking to increase their own power. Some would agree that talk radio and Fox News could be the forerunners of such movements today.

After all, jobs have been shifting from places like Chicago to South Carolina for decades, yet no one complains that it's unfair or destroying the economy. But, when jobs move to Mumbai or Manila, it's going to an alien place, to "those" people. Xenophobia is born of ignorance and the only cure is education and exposure.

Beyond the extremes, there are tens of millions of Americans who are simply ignorant of other cultures. The coming decades will render these attitudes not only socially undesirable, but economically unfeasible; the most prosperous individuals in the new economy will be globally-focused and able to coordinate business, technology, and people in new and innovative ways. These will be people unafraid of other ways of life and knowledgeable about varied cultural norms.

For instance, the businesswoman who can gracefully move between meetings in China, France, Jordan, and Mexico will be the most valuable element of the new economy. These skills have always been valuable in Europe, but few Americans prize them; fewer still possess them, let alone the language skills to work with foreigners in their native tongues.

Fortunately, some portions of the U.S. such as the San Francisco Bay Area and New York, are already well down this path. In fact, a recent study of the Bay Area indicated that one of its core strengths was the ability to manage far-flung global businesses operating in a variety of cultures. San Francisco acquires this highly compensated ability through its greatly diverse citizenry and outward-looking focus, which goes back to the Gold Rush over 150 years ago.

Underneath the language issues lies a more challenging issue, that of distrust of anything not American that naturally leads to an "us vs. them" mentality that was all too evident in the Iraq War. This was also obvious in the 1980s when the Japanese were treated like the enemy. That sort of anger as Asians took jobs in the 1980s is visible again in depictions of the Chinese as aliens taking today's jobs. It's fortunate that many, if not most, of the proponents of protectionism go out of their way to say they are not racist or anti-immigrant, though this could change over time and turn increasingly unhelpful.

Things need to be handled differently this time around, both to affect a different outcome and because the nature of the competition and the world has shifted. For instance, there is no longer a single "other" competitor like Japan; this time, it's the whole world.

As in the 1980s, it is particularly easy to blame foreigners for what is essentially an American competitiveness problem. People are understandably angry after being laid-off and watching their jobs move overseas, but they are often misdirecting their anger. Foreigners who benefit by getting jobs and higher standards of living are not the enemy. Instead, those hurt by economic loss ought to look at themselves first, look at their firm's management second, and finally push the U.S. government to offer reforms and programs that boost U.S. technology, innovation, incentives, and thus employment.

In addition, America is not on only one side of this competition, as many European countries are moving work to the U.S. to escape numerous economic problems. As such, America also plays the role of host nation, reaping benefits as companies flee even more difficult (or repressive) economic environments.

Language Training

The first task in the long road to cultural awareness is substantial expansion of foreign language training, clearly the best method to learn a foreign culture. Government funding and/or promotion of such programs would send a valuable message to both American citizens and foreign nations about the importance of cultural awareness.

Looking back in time in the U.S. (or now in Europe), one was not considered educated if they didn't speak foreign languages such as French, German, or even Latin, yet this has been lost in modern America due to the global dominance of English.

In the 21st century, every American should be conversant in a second language and have spent time in countries where the language is native. And, while Spanish is important and the most obvious language to pick up, people should also think more creatively on an individual basis about which language(s) are most interesting, challenging, and advantageous for them.

Unfortunately, while millions of people enroll in language courses each year, either through private Berlitz-like firms, universities, or in public secondary schools, the languages chosen and vigor of pursuit are not impressive.

For instance, most people choose French for historical reasons, Spanish for proximity and Latino cultural reasons. Unfortunately, neither are much help on the global economic stage, though Spanish is clearly the preferable of the two. Frankly, it's not clear why French is offered at all in nearly every American high school, as few people appear to use it, and virtually never in business. Realistically, the Chinese and Indians are not wasting their time learning French; they are focused on English, Japanese, and Spanish.

Regardless, language training is a strategic process, and as such, fluency is not necessarily the goal. Even minimal effort to learn a language is a useful cultural experience and greatly appreciated by foreigners, if only as a message to children about how important it is to connect with the rest of the world.

For even if your Chinese business partner can speak English and communicate basic ideas, you knowing about his homeland's customs and attitudes will greatly increase the actual communication taking place. Again, this lesson was painfully learned in dealing with Japan in the 1980's, when yes often meant no and communication suffered at all levels, which led to numerous conflicts and economic disappointment.

Even foreign governments are realizing how important it is for Americans to speak their languages. For instance, both the Chinese and Italian governments recently funded advanced placement test development, making it easier for high schools and colleges to teach and test in those languages. They understand that getting Americans plugged into their culture and languages is a key element to their own continual economic success.

Children's Language Instruction

Children should be a focal point for language training, both to be educated directly for their future and because in reality vast numbers of adults will never take advantage of language training, even if it's free. The way to these folks is through their children, who can hopefully expand their parent's world views through international friends and travel.

As such, expansion of school language training it important, though if there is one lesson to learn from the world's efforts at teaching English, it's that education must start early, ideally in the first grade or at least elementary school. This is especially true for poor and disadvantaged citizens, whose children unfortunately tend to have checked out educationally by junior-high school.

Fortunately, there is some movement in this area in the public school system. Nearly a third of all elementary schools offer foreign language instruction, while 87% of secondary schools teach foreign languages. [184] Unfortunately, as mentioned above, the languages being taught are of questionable global economic importance. French and Spanish currently dominate children's language instruction, though the far more useful Spanish is gradually superseding French.

In terms of programs, a process similar to the one used in the Netherlands or Scandinavia should be used for selected languages, where students start very early. The Swedes require on average 1.5 hours of English a week for all nine years of their primary schooling (ages 7-16), with mandatory tests at the end of school, and as a result students speak nearly perfect English. Knowledge of English is also required for entry into Swedish universities.[185] Foreign languages used to be almost required for entry into a good American college, a practice that should be re-instituted.

Further, another 1980s trend, immersion schooling, should be expanded. Conducted largely in Japanese back then and in some Chinese today, these schools teach several subjects only in a specific foreign language. Mechanisms should be found to expand and re-emphasize this type of extremely effective education, again with processes to encourage minority and blue-collar participation, especially since such parents are unlikely to place a high priority on sending their kids to a Chinese or Arabic school.

Unfortunately, beyond the two "core" languages of French and Spanish, only Japanese and Russian have recently (1997) been increasing in availability, with all other languages declining, hardly on par with the needs for globalization. Chinese, in particular, is glaringly absent, as is Arabic and perhaps Vietnamese, Turkish, Farsi, and other useful languages for the coming decades. Recall that a third of the populations of Iran and Vietnam are under 25 and will be both great producers and consumers in the coming decades. Smart Americans will get the jump on that future and study those languages and cultures now.

Regardless of language, funding is a perennial challenge for primary and secondary school language training. For instance, elementary schools (where languages should be intensively taught) continue to report funding shortages. State and federal governments should consider how best to jumpstart this process, perhaps by issuing block grants for emerging languages in non-urban schools. As with other cultural efforts, care should be taken to focus on the rural areas least connected to the rest of the world; fortunately, rural programs are probably also the least expensive compared to more urban environments. Vouchers for presumably less expensive private instruction may also be valuable tools in various settings.

Adult Language Programs

While intensive language programs for children set the stage for future global interaction, what about the working generation? They also need assistance in getting plugged into the larger world around them, both to enhance their economic value and to better understand and appreciate important foreign cultures. As such, greatly enhanced language programs for adults should also be a high priority. Though not everyone will partake, it's hard to overestimate the impact of global language ability on even a small portion of the population. After all, fluent Arabic and Chinese speakers are pretty useful these days.

While private language schools are popular, they are relatively expensive and typically available only to a small slice of the population, often in urban areas. Further, without leadership illuminating the need, it's hard to motivate the population into seeking (and paying for) such training.

As such, the government should both provide leadership on the need for more language training and help pay for it. Language and cultural training is so important that it should be free, or at least subsidized for anyone interested in learning.

This sort of free training may sound like a frivolous waste of money, but it should be considered a key educational investment, nearly as useful as reading, writing, and arithmetic. Nearly every other country makes a similar investment in English, so America should be investing in their languages and cultures, period. America's insistence on a one-way culture is a very 20th century notion, one that will not fly with the looming trade and economic giants of the 21st century.

A variety of mechanisms are available for this ambitious language program, and not all of them involve money. Again, leadership efforts to promote universal bi-lingualism can have a strong effect on how high schools and other programs prioritize their offerings, without additional funding. The military might also start pressuring recruits to study languages in high school or in the service, if only to sensitize their soldiers, sailors, and airmen to the foreign cultures they'll be killing. And, such training will not only help globalize these young people, it will enhance their skills and marketability once they return to civilian life.

Unfortunately, those most likely to start attending language school are already globally focused citizens in diverse urban locations. After all, teaching Chinese is common in parts of California, but hardly so in the Carolinas. So, a new language training program should focus on areas not traditionally so globally oriented, which means de-emphasizing New York, Washington, D.C., San Francisco, etc. and focusing on the Midwest, South, and poor or minority communities.

Further, along the same lines, there may need to be incentives to encourage blue-collar and other less education-oriented adults to take place, as they are most likely the source of xenophobia and the lack of ability to transition into the new economy. Getting a former wrench turner or insurance claims clerk to learn Chinese will be no easy task, especially when there is no obvious immediate benefit. Regardless, it's important to keep the strategic goals in mind, which is to at least expose populace to the world. As such, they are not necessarily going to be fluent, but at least more sensitive to global culture and comfortable in cross-country interactions.

Programs should also be created at the state level to promote experimentation and to provide vouchers, credits, and financial aid in the languages (sort of like in the arts). At the adult level, this means paying to attend Berlitz or any number of schools that are likely to rapidly multiply under this program. Quality control and certification will be important, as many educational assistance programs have run into trouble with newly-minted schools whose educational value is questionable.

Further, while it may appear useful to prioritize language offerings and financial support based on what's in vogue, it's important to offer a broad array of languages and options. While Chinese or Arabic may be the sexy language of the day, someone of Hungarian descent may want to learn the language of her ancestors. This, in turn, may lead to interesting employment or trade opportunities with Hungarian companies, NATO, the UN, or other interesting entities.

Since adult classes are offered in private settings (and not one-size-fits all public schools), they are free to offer all sorts of languages in a wide variety of formats. In addition, since adults will likely need to pay for at least part of their language education, they will choose languages that truly interest them or they perceive as useful in their future.

Companies can also require or provide employee language training, given the economic advantage of having a multi-lingual staff; perhaps a small tax incentive would catalyze such a program fairly quickly. This is already common in larger global companies and those based in non-English speaking countries, especially as business marches ever forward towards globalization. For example, many large European companies such as Siemens use English as their main working language, even for meetings where everyone is German.

Subsidized Travel

Learning a language is but the first step towards understanding a culture, closely followed by actually going there and spending time among the people. As such, Americans must find ways to go abroad more frequently, literally broadening their horizons.

Travel and actual overseas experiences are absolutely vital to understanding the new global world, especially given how parochial most Americans are. These sorts of experiences transform the "other place" into something familiar and make the unknown known. As Mark Twain once said, "Travel is fatal to ignorance, small-mindedness, and backwardness." This was true 150 years ago and is more so today.

There are several ways to increase physical travel and interaction. One way is to actually send people abroad; perhaps supplement free language programs by sending anyone who passes a language test abroad to try out their skills, make new friends, and create new cross-cultural connections.

Again, this might be viewed as frivolous, but there are many ways to structure an economical program that gets hundreds of thousands of Americans out there "in the wild."

Such programs also need to focus more on real interaction and less on tourism. Americans will of course want to see the sights, but inter-personal interaction is critical, perhaps including round table discussions of various viewpoints and spending time in the schools. Just sitting with French or Chinese people like themselves and (calmly) discussing their lives, children, and concerns can go a long way towards global understanding and appreciation. Perhaps the embassy cultural offices could facilitate real cultural interaction on a grand scale, with parties, visiting American discussion groups, home stays, partnered tours, etc. Embassies abroad should be given goals, say to double American tourism in their countries within five years; countless innovative programs to lure Americans abroad would assuredly be the result.

In addition, while the volume of passport applications has doubled in the last ten years to nearly 9 million per year, less than 20% of Americans have passports.[186] As such, there should be a program to increase passport ownership among those who have never traveled. Perhaps first passports should be free, which, coupled with a promotion program, might really get an extra few million Americans overseas.

Many will argue that promoting travel to foreign destinations just sends money overseas and reduces tourism-related jobs at home. This is true, but strategically one has to look at the larger picture and the value afforded by massive international travel by Americans. Not only do such travelers learn a great deal about foreign cultures, they also spend badly needed money in developing economies.

Ideally they will also entice foreigners to visit the U.S., as already evident with China, whose citizens are rapidly ramping up their international travel. Such inbound tourism will ideally more than make up for domestic tourism dollars lost when Americans go abroad. After all, the ideal tourism situation is 50 million Americans going to the four corners of the Earth, while 50 million foreigners visit the U.S.; this is far more preferable than everyone staying at home.

Along the same vein, the current bans on travel to Iran, Cuba, and North Korea are the exact opposite of what should be happening, as no closed country can withstand the onslaught of an army of a million American tourists. It's far better to invade with American tourists than the American military any day.

Expand Exchange Programs

Nothing prepares for the future like grooming children to be proper global citizens. One very effective method to expand foreign cultural exposure is via student exchanges, where

Americans go abroad for a year while foreign students come to the U.S. to study, typically in high school.

Further, nothing better educates an entire family about another culture than having a foreign child live in their home or their own child living abroad. And, having a single foreign child in a school can change attitudes for dozens or hundreds of students. Having a dozen in every school can change the world.

While foreign exchange student programs have existed for a long time and are relatively popular, they largely remain the province of the affluent or already forward-looking families. However, as noted, the real need is with precisely the opposite community, those who have no desire to go abroad, who live in rural areas, and who have little education or money. The reality is that relatively few families have the motivation or means to take in a foreign student, and even fewer to send their child overseas.

Substantially increasing foreign exchange programs will greatly increase the percentage of American youths that are exposed to other cultures. Further, for every child that is sent abroad, another student comes to live in the U.S. These foreign students integrate themselves into American schools and show the students that foreigners are not scary or strange, but normal kids like themselves. And American kids returning from abroad will share their experiences with families and friends, bringing back stories that raise interest in their host countries abroad. Ideally, their families and others will be convinced to go visit the foreign land.

In addition, friendships that are formed out of exchange experiences last a lifetime and continue to inform people's attitudes towards other countries throughout their careers. These sorts of experiences form international families and relationships that are rare but increasingly important. Students coming back from exchanges in other countries often still refer to members of their home-stay families as their "sisters" or "brothers." Nothing causes more impact on a person's attitude than personally interacting with, and knowing someone from another country, let alone living in that country.

Historical and cultural exchanges like this are key to insuring that the new globalized economy does not become balkanized, where people become polarized or nationalistic. When Americans better understand other cultures, peoples, and history, ideally they will be less judgmental and more understanding. The more friendships there are between peoples, the more smoothly these changes will go, and the more economic profit everyone will gain. In the end, the world of today and tomorrow will be drawn together in the way only long-term personal interaction can bring.

Finally, close personal connections between future business and governmental leaders sets the stage for continued close ties over the following decades; imagine if FDR, Mao, and Stalin had known each other since childhood; it certainly would have created a different world after WWII.

Regardless of format and who participates, student exchange programs are a greatly underutilized interaction and learning resource that should be greatly expanded, perhaps five or even ten-fold, in an effort to send every willing child abroad for a truly multi-cultural experience. Sending 2% of American high school students, or 320,000 kids, overseas in any given year is a good goal.[187] That 2% would create an impact felt in every town and city in America.

So, a typical 1,000-student school would have 20 students overseas and host 20 foreigners each year, which puts one in nearly every classroom, every day. At that rate, in 10 years even a small school district in Oklahoma would exchange hundreds of students, permanently altering everyone's global perspective.

In addition to traditional year-long, school-based exchange programs, other plans should also be explored, such as intensive summer programs and other exchanges. There are already some of these programs run by private groups for many different purposes; perhaps funding and other assistance can double such programs every five years.

In addition, college exchange programs should be expanded. Roughly 160,000 students were exchanged last year, double the figure a decade ago. Unfortunately, current college-level courses seem to be evolving towards party and tourism trips, something to be avoided if at all possible, as it fosters an attitude of the "ugly American." Students used to learn languages and really understand a foreign culture, but today it can be a party trip, especially to English-speaking countries or when too many American students go together.[188] This has to be curbed by better participant screening, itinerary, and country selection.

Media's Role in Educating

Beyond language education, subsidized travel, and exchange programs, there are also ways to use popular media to better inform the populace. For instance, popular media outlets such as the History Channel are filled with extremely interesting programs, though relatively few focus on the emerging world. For every segment on the history of China or Saudi Arabia, there seem to be ten or a hundred on Hitler or WWII in the Pacific.

While this is understandable in a historical context, the focus really should be on the future and understanding where things are going, in addition to where they have been. In addition, even though the Internet brings every country into the living room, governments should promote additional rich cultural exchanges such as bringing foreign performing arts groups to rural areas and encouraging the development of television materials regarding foreign history and culture.

Working with the media is an area where governmental leadership and little-to-no money can go a long way. In addition, other governments or bodies may provide funding to produce high-quality programming that will grip kids and parents alike, again especially those generally adverse to such topics. The goal has to be kept in mind here, which is to educate and inform those who don't care for or are afraid of the "enemy." In particular, grasping even a bit of the history of various cultures goes a long way towards understanding how people come to be the way they are, in good, bad, and humorous ways.

Fortunately, some media such as the San Francisco Chronicle are focusing on this very issue, trying to educate the population about important countries, even encouraging travel to these distant lands. The Chronicle says it best: “To appreciate and better understand these connections, we begin today an occasional series focusing on the homelands of the Bay Area's major immigrant groups, with the hope that you'll visit some of the places your neighbors hail from. -- John Flinn, Executive Travel Editor[189]

Finally, cultural awareness is the capstone of globalizing the population. Understanding the Chinese or Indians will not be easy in a country where most whites still don’t understand the black or Latino cultures in which they immersed. Still, efforts should be made to increase education at all levels, including school-level classes in Asian and Middle Eastern history and culture. The world will only be better connected and a little smaller as a result.

Chapter 14.

Corporate Role

Companies should play a significant role in preparing the country and its citizens for the 21st century, especially when they are actually responsible for sending jobs overseas. They reap the direct economic benefits of lower costs and increased competitiveness, and as such have some responsibility for funding and managing the process.

As mentioned, companies cannot and should not be prohibited from moving jobs abroad, but they should do it responsibly and with some eye towards society's need for a stable middle class. If only for selfish reasons, companies still need a stable domestic customer base on which to grow; i.e. a 21st century version of Henry Ford's model of insuring his workers could afford the very cars they were building.

Companies can also marshal significant resources in order to execute the programs discussed in prior chapters, especially for training. While all companies have some responsibility for employee training and preparation, those laying off employees due to globalization have special responsibilities to help prepare their soon-to-be-ex-employees for the future. Corporate action is vital in order to bring the potential benefits of the off-shoring process to fruition, as their activities and perspective can often mean the difference between a worker making a successful transition and a less positive outcome.

At the same time, any program that forces companies to create costly programs acts as a tax on the economy and must be judiciously applied with the lightest of touches, lest it strangle the very economy it strives to save.

Leadership

As with governments, corporations might do best with simple leadership. Simply being honest about future plans and talking about the importance of training while planning for the future may be the best route to getting everyone on the same competitive page.

Employees are generally aware of the economic forces at work in the world; while some may accuse senior management of just lining their pockets at workers' expense, most understand these processes, even if they don't like them. Unfortunately, the current political climate makes this difficult, but companies have to work meaningfully with all stakeholders to insure everything works out.

Unfortunately, most (61%) white-collar employees fear they or someone they know will be outsourced, so companies are on thin ice even discussing the issue.[190] Some, like IBM, are even admitting that some jobs will go, so it certainly behooves employees to work on their skills right now, and forever.

The key is treating everyone with respect, especially working to preserve as many jobs as possible and training employees whose roles can't be saved. Avoiding the ire of the anti-off-shoring crowd is difficult, but sufficient warning time and help for the soon to be ex-employees are the most important issues, along with being open and honest from the beginning. Companies essentially need to start leveling with their staff, telling it like it is, and then working hard to move their employees up the value chain so everyone wins.

Regardless, companies should look to the benefits that accrue from a more skilled workforce and add training across the board; this is one area where American firms can learn from their European counterparts, where continuous training is much more common. Not only does this reduce the anxiety about the lack of individual skills, it also helps lower the anger level when the actual layoffs occur.

Training

Existing workforce

As mentioned, most U.S. corporations should probably be doing more training as a matter of course. Smart companies continually upgrade their employees' skills, just to keep pace with the competition, both local and global. For instance, many advanced manufacturers routinely train their factory employees in literacy, statistics, and specific technical skills.

Indeed many such training programs can be provided at little or no cost to the employer. Often all it takes is a little coordination and a room where employees can meet with an instructor once a week after work. This works even if the workers have to pay a modest fee for such instruction, as the effort involved entails simply getting the classes up and running. Employees have no excuse for not furthering their education.

Further, companies should think about how to prepare their employees for the day when they no longer work the company, as the second most important success factor after layoff warning time is the availability of training programs. This is especially crucial in smaller cities or rural areas, with limited supplies of replacement jobs for displaced employees without retraining.[191]

While general training in useful skills is an obvious goal, such preparation might also include lessons in entrepreneurship or running a company, along with general life skills. Even if these employees never leave or found their own business, they gain a much better understanding of the complexities of running an operation; this can only make them better employees for current or future employers.

In fact, the best employees are often those that leave to start their own firm, get overwhelmed and shut it down, only to return to employment with their original company. In fact, it might behoove companies to encourage this sort of activity. While some firms consider a quitting employee to be written off or as a traitor, the common Silicon Valley practice of letting them go and then welcoming them back can really pay off. Returning employees often appreciate a stable job and the challenges in running an operation of any size, and they can make much stronger employees in the long run.

Getting companies to train and "set free" the next generation of entrepreneurs may thus be the best strategy. It creates new companies and employment, plus it educates existing personnel to become better contributors to their existing company.

General Electric has long had this strategy, training hordes of managers via its highly acclaimed Management Development Program. Many of these managers subsequently leave at some point to lead other firms, and while GE is loosing some good people, those they retain excel at leading the business to new heights. The challenge now is for all companies to train their employees in such a manner, allowing those that stay to excel and equipping those that leave with valuable skills for their future careers and the good of society.

Companies should also take a bigger hand in driving the development of training programs for their future workforces. Many trade-oriented companies have done this successfully with unions and community colleges or trade schools, but it's not clear this is going on at the higher levels. Guidance, and possibly money, should be provided to these schools as investments in the future.

Further, companies should take in more interns who provide inexpensive labor, while giving students valuable experience in new industries. Corporations might also provide more mentors or other liaison activities between existing and future employees or students.

Training the Outgoing Workforce

Given that many jobs are going to be lost, a key corporate role is to help train the outgoing workforce, especially before and right after it announces that jobs are vanishing. This is the point at which they still have an income, are still bound together as a group, and are keenly focused on their next step in life.

As mentioned in the chapter on displaced worker training, there are a number of considerations, programs, and funding possibilities for corporations to get involved with, but regardless, it's important that the company do something.

A chief corporate consideration is to examine retraining programs that might better fit together with governmental efforts and provide workers with better preparation for new economic roles.

Globalizing Employees

Americans are likely to lead the world in cross-border and especially global management, from the CEO down to junior project managers. As such, companies can play a key role in globalizing their employees. This directly benefits both the company and society at large. Such employees need not move abroad or accept Indian wages, but can instead help run or at least participate in international enterprises where everyone has to be globally aware, all the time.

Such globalization efforts might take the form of providing language training, foreign travel, or even video conferences for employees at all levels. Such programs can be expensive, but the increased ability to communicateand manage global resources seems well worth the investment, especially in fast-moving industries where cross-cultural misunderstanding and delays are expensive.

Beyond that, there are many inexpensive efforts that can make a difference: global newsletters for larger firms; distributing foreign newspapers; inviting foreign employees to talk about their countries to employees' children; or simply stating that employees need to be familiar with the world and helping facilitate that by using suggestions from employees themselves.

Handling the Off-shoring Process

Companies can do many things before they send jobs abroad, but at some point, many corporations find it necessary to actually displace existing workers. When that time comes, handling the transition properly is probably one of the most strategic things a firm can do. Poorly handled situations have led to numerous challenges in the press, with politicians, and most importantly with the employees that stay.

There are many paths to reach the point of transferring jobs abroad, but it usually begins under cost pressure on various projects or products. Off-shoring is often considered next, especially if the company is in an industry with existing off-shoring arrangements, such as IT, call centers, or BPO. Larger companies also sometimes have the option to transfer work within the company, via a captive off-shoring arrangement (see below).

One of the biggest success factors is timing, especially how much time is available before the actual lay-off date. More notice obviously allows employees and communities more time to adjust, retrain, and otherwise prepare for the transition. In fact, the most important factor in determining the reemployment prospects of workers is the amount of notice they have.[192] With ample notice employees can prepare psychologically, save money, and work on skills they will need for the transition, especially given the longer retraining time needed for white-collar workers. And, for many, it provides time for spouses and children to prepare for their parts (e.g. by taking a part-time job or switching from private to public school).

Unfortunately, as this process has become increasingly politically charged, companies feel forced to conceal their intentions until the last possible moment, lest they show up on "Benedict Arnold" lists of those who would shame them. The stigma attached to the off-shoring process may well have the opposite effect of reducing employees' subsequent re-employment success.

An improvement to this process might include involving key employees (and perhaps unions) in the decision regarding pushing work abroad. Employees are fully aware of global competition and presumably want to help the company survive; involving them in the numbers and walking through the decisions in detail can only help to build trust and understanding for the difficult periods to come. Further, their participation can also help smooth out relations and anger among the rank and file by reducing miscommunication and misunderstandings, not to mention combating the notion that management doesn't care, or is only lining their pockets.

On another note, employees are unfortunately often required to train their foreign replacements, something that tends to create a fair amount of anger or resentment. Such training is often required by their severance agreements; essentially employees don't get a buy-out package without the somewhat humiliating process of training others to replace them. As challenging as this is ethically, it's often the only way the company can execute a smooth transfer, just as if a plant was being moved from Chicago to South Carolina or Puerto Rico. There may be no good way to fully mitigate the anger this generates, other than providing adequate warning, worker participation, and excellent transitional support.

Few companies completely off-shore their entire workforce at one time. Thus there are often scores of remaining workers who are left worrying about their own jobs; they are understandably rarely energized or motivated after seeing their friends' jobs sent to India. It's crucial at this stage to level with them and be seen as an honest player -- the attitude of "they have to work here, there's nowhere else to go" will hardly produce maximum performance from remaining staff.

Instead, it pays to be as humane as possible, going over the top to warn, retrain, and generally support those being terminated. After all, the justification for off-shoring is usually cost savings, so it's important to use some of those savings up front to insure the remaining business remains successful.

This is especially true in situations where the off-shored component of the business significantly enhances domestic operations, such as moving major production work across the ocean to save design, sales, marketing, and support jobs at home. Those higher-value employees who remain must feel they are actually valued and understand the rationale behind the moves; they must also be constantly trained so they don't feel like they are the next to go, and even if they are, that they have a good chance of finding a new job with relative ease; otherwise, they continually worry about their future rather than the work at hand.

Insuring Corporate Prosperity

In addition to carrying out a number of programs and initiatives for future, existing, and ex-employees, there are also a number of off-shoring factors that directly affect the prosperity of companies involved. These range from the types of off-shoring done to the myriad of opportunities offered by the entire off-shoring process, including inshoring from other countries and newly available customers from across the globe.

Look Before Leaping

Not every off-shoring experience is a pleasurable one, as costs, cultural differences, and communications challenges can sometimes be insurmountable. In particular, the savings are rarely as projected, especially as currencies fluctuate over time; for instance, the Yuan may rise 20-40% or more over the next few years, so any project with only 20-40% savings will likely be in trouble over time. And this doesn't take into account wage pressures or lower productivity in many industries.

Perhaps more importantly, sending jobs off-shore is a rather permanent structural change to a company's business. Once numerous experienced employees are laid off, it's quite difficult to change direction and get them back. In addition, the first off-shoring phase will undoubtedly cause anxiety and morale issues within a company, which can generate negative returns in many ways, including the best employees leaving what they perceived to be insecure jobs.

Thus, any off-shoring plan needs to take the long view and insure there are sufficient savings and other strategic advantages before taking the leap into the great unknown. Then, dipping a toe in the water to get things up and running is often a good route, as only then can real plans be developed for the actual business and partners involved.

Leverage Employees

One of off-shoring's main advantages is that it leverages the domestic workforce by inexpensively amplifying their efforts. Manufacturers have long imported various components and low-end products to keep their higher-end offerings in play and their workforces applied. This can mean sacrificing some employees to save others, but that's quite attractive when compared to the alternatives, such as losing them all. And of course there are all those foreign customers to think about.

The key is to think out of the box on how foreign services can boost a company's competitiveness, perhaps even before low-cost competition arises. Maybe there are ways to handle business expansion by importing services to lower the cost base, or to introduce new services by leveraging foreign expertise in a particular area.

In particular, companies might think about how extremely cheap labor might change their business, just as Delta Airlines and Wall Street banks utilize 100% ticket or stock analysis to boost their bottom line. These efforts don't take jobs from Americans because they could never be done domestically in any case. Such opportunities might involve quality control review, documentation preparation, customer service enhancement processes, statistical operations review, or inexpensive R&D.

Along the same lines, businesses should think about how inexpensive, but highly talented services might be of assistance. For instance, teams of Ph.D. statisticians or engineers might be useful to help enhance a product or solve a problem, but are so expensive in the U.S. that such an effort can't be justified. These types of efforts are essentially high-end consulting on the cheap and might include financial models, engineering improvements, or customer problem solving.

One radical way to think about such leverage is to consider what a company might do if various useful services were free. For example, if there was an unlimited supply of free Ph.D.s or educated clerical help, what sort of new possibilities would that create for the core business? Asking these questions and then seeking out the low cost resources to execute such programs may well be the best 21st century business model. This also ties in well with the above-mentioned creative global leveraging of the best resources, wherever they may be.

After all, low-cost foreign production has lowered the cost of many consumer electronics products such as DVD players and cell phones, creating entire new industries and billions of dollars in value for associated industries and services. Companies that are ahead of the curve in merging essentially free hardware, software, telecommunications, and labor are likely to lead the way to success.

Insuring National and Global Prosperity

In addition to looking after their own prosperity, companies can also do numerous things in support of everyone's success. Many of these mirror public policy initiatives that governments should carry out, but on a smaller level. This enables companies to directly affect their industries in ways not easily accomplished by national governments. The private sector can also often move more quickly and effectively than public policy.

Stimulating Innovation

The future lies in invention and innovation, as that's the only way developed countries will stay ahead of their developing country partners. As such, companies must support innovation at every turn, even if it does not directly benefit them. Companies such as 3M have long prospered by fostering this innovative spirit among all employees. In the 1980s, 3M was occasionally emulated as a way to build new products, but today it's probably mandatory to just stay in business.

Fostering innovation at the corporate level can be done in many ways, from suggestion boxes to bonuses for inventions to more formal programs that generate new ideas. The solution is to actually gather, evaluate, and act on the enormous creative energy present in every workforce. That energy is a major American differentiator and must be nurtured at every turn if companies are to stay ahead of their lower-cost competitors.

Spinout Technology

American companies are awash in new and interesting technologies and products, though often ones that aren't fully aligned with their businesses. These products often get buried or hidden away, but they should instead be licensed or spun out to form new companies ready to compete on their own.

The best spinouts often take some employees with them that are motivated to work on the new products, adding far more value (and licensing revenue) then they ever could have added as regular employees.

Such technologies or innovations can also potentially start whole new industries, especially when they come out of corporate R&D laboratories. Companies like Xerox are famous for being unable to capitalize on their inventions, but more careful management of the process could yield numerous startups, revenue, and prosperity for all.

DARPA-Like Challenges

Finally, companies should rethink their procurement and partnership strategies. In some cases, a DARPA-like challenge or contest might be a good way to not only get R&D work done for free, but also to instantly create a whole new industry for further innovation. This is especially true in manufacturing and product companies.

For example, every company has ongoing challenges with their processes, products, or technology that could be solved by others. Dangling a few million dollars in front of hungry innovators ready to compete may solve everything from better fuel cells to video compression algorithms to very specific chemistry problems.

The best part of this is that a company only pays for a real solution, and even if a problem is never solved, considerable brain power will be put to very useful work, something that can only benefit the entire world.

In fact, this might be viewed as the reverse of the university model, where one researcher gets a grant to try to find an answer. In this case, hordes or researchers and inventors work hard to produce a real solution, only getting paid if they actually succeed.

Global Coordination, Leverage Every Country

America leads the way in coordinating global teams to build the world's best products. As such, companies should look to leverage this unique skill-set to actively build networks of high quality, low-cost organizations to deliver the best products at the lowest price. Nike took this route decades ago, running far-flung factories before anyone else knew how; now nearly everyone has to follow that model to stay ahead.

This means actively looking for suppliers, partners, technology, and customers in a multitude of places, identifying how such complex arrangements can really benefit the bottom line. While no one should build complexity for complexity's sake, the world is increasingly sophisticated, and those who can run complicated businesses should be richly rewarded.

Productivity Growth at Home

America leads the world in productivity growth, through both technology and old-fashioned process improvements.

Some would argue such productivity growth is responsible for the current economic boom and the ability of many American workers to still outperform their off-shore counterparts.

The foreigners are moving up the curve, though, so Americans must accelerate their efforts to increase productivity, to smartly apply technology, and to simply work smarter and harder to maintain their competitive edge.

In particular, continued investment in technology not only supports domestic software and tool markers, but also it pays off over the long term. This is especially true when business processes are cleaned up to best utilize the new technology; often the result is shorter lead times, better management, lower inventory and costs, and happier customers.

Modularizing the Business

As the manufacturing industries have long realized, there are many points along the value chain and a company has to decide where it adds the most value. Fortunately, manufacturing business and process are often easily split into various components, with many physical raw materials, sub-assemblies, and related services. As such, companies such as automakers design products and do final assembly, increasingly leaving the rest to others.

Service companies have historically seen themselves more as monolithic enterprises, providing complete service from end-to-end. In fact, these companies look very much like the old-line integrated manufacturers of yesteryear, which culminated in Ford's famous River Rouge plant near Detroit, making every part of every piece of every car, including the rubber for the tires and steel for the doors.

And while many law and accounting firms specialize, the larger players are often full-service, trying to be everything to all players, with the large overhead and cost base that goes along with that.

In the 21st century, service companies must consider where and how they'll fit into the value chain, i.e. what their raw materials and sub-assemblies are, and how their industry best fits together. If they do not, fast-moving competitors are likely to do it for them. The airline industry is an example of big companies milking their monolithic structures as long as possible. They only end up in bankruptcy while their agile competitors, new technologies such as regional jets, and new distribution systems such as the Internet destroy their business models.

In the end, splitting services between foreign and domestic in industries as diverse as IT, accounting, law, and research will lead to lower costs, higher productivity, and probably better service all the way around. Each of these industries is using talented, yet inexpensive, staff in developing countries to carry out designs and other work under supervision of senior domestic employees who bear ultimate responsibility for the work, in exactly the same manner as Ford is responsible for assembling the final automobile.

Small, Global Companies

While off-shoring today is largely the domain of larger companies, smaller companies are beginning to get in the game. This is particularly easy in already-modularized industries such as contract architecture and engineering, where the work is simply done in India instead of Indiana.

Beyond that, many small software companies, especially in Silicon Valley, are sending work to India and elsewhere. And while their businesses are sometimes too dynamic and disorganized for this to work effectively, it can work well for more traditional small companies.

Small companies' challenges include lack of standards, documentation, and true modularity of their businesses. Further, most probably lack the processes and documentation to send work across town, let alone across the globe. Many, if not most, are run by a few strong and talented individuals, with many interdependent parts. As such, they will likely need to adjust their internal operations to prepare for off-shoring.

Regardless, these are also the companies that should really start slowly and build up the processes and knowledge on how to send work abroad before diving in to a major project that, if it goes badly, could kill the company.

Direct small company benefits are probably likely to come via their suppliers or service providers, such as accountants or attorneys, who themselves directly use off-shore resources. As noted, off-shoring provides whole new business models for some industries, where low wages enable activities such as billing reviews that were previously too expensive.

It's also very important to not lose sight of the opposite of off-shoring, where foreign firms buy services from American companies. The globalization game works both ways -- by focusing on being the best player in a particular field, small American businesses can now service customers from all over the world.

This is very much like the German Middlestand companies, but for services. Small and medium-size German companies sell products such as equipment and machine tools all over the world, though these remain costly and complex businesses. These companies built up expertise and a reputation for high quality over decades of servicing the world; in fact, it's not uncommon to see German companies of only 50 employees with customers in a dozen countries.

The challenge for similar American firms is to really take advantage of the new customer opportunities in Asia and elsewhere. Fortunately, the challenges of shipping, customs, and equipment standards faced by material goods exporters are far less important for service exporters. For instance, designing a computer network or an aircraft wing is essentially the same the world over. Therefore the key for many small businesses is to innovate and leverage their intellectual property to expand their markets globally and focus on important innovative industries.

In particular, companies might think about the issues created by the off-shoring process itself, such as the need to keep Indians up to date on Kansas agricultural regulations or Nevada real estate law, administrating American securities broker exams, or building multi-lingual services to train global users of common enterprise software packages.

Regardless of how they participate in 21st century off-shoring, the corporate world has many roles, from globalization's driving force to preparing workers for their futures, to leading the world in global sourcing, operations, and innovation.

In the end, corporate America benefits greatly from globalization but has significant responsibilities to insure it goes smoothly for all involved. Companies need to rationally balance their cost structures by sending jobs abroad, but also focus on continuous training and skills upgrades for existing and soon-to-be ex-employees. This not only improves the workforce and continues productivity growth, it also improves morale while insuring domestic tranquility, prosperity, and economic growth.

Chapter 15.

Individual's Role

"Men are anxious to improve their circumstances, but are unwilling to improve themselves, thus they remain bound."

As a Man Thinketh

The 21st century world is indeed becoming flatter by the day. Almost any job can be performed by almost anyone, almost anywhere. Everyone competes with everyone else, all the time. Such a world has essentially no barriers, with nearly 3 billion people joining the global workforce and creating a constant stream of lower-cost competitors for every job on the planet. How shall people compete?

Ultimately, each individual will be responsible for his or her success or failure in the new economy, as governments and corporations ultimately have a limited impact. There are a wide variety of ways individuals can compete, depending on when, where, and how they begin the race, but they must compete the final leg largely on their own. In particular, people must ultimately accept that the economy has fundamentally changed and that they now must be globally competitive, each and every day.

Being more competitive means many things, including: focusing on long-term learning and flexibility; learning other languages and cultures; gaining as many useful and differentiating skills as possible; and generally working hard to move up the value chain. Further, it means finding what one loves and focusing on making that make money. Finally, it means looking at the myriad of opportunities presented by a globalized world, taking advantage of a global market, instant communications, and revolutionary technology.

As the Governor of the Bank of England recently said, "The new organization of society implied by the triumph of individual autonomy and the true equalization of opportunity based upon merit will lead to very great rewards for merit and great individual autonomy. This will leave individuals far more responsible for themselves than they have been accustomed to being during the industrial period. It will also reduce the unearned advantage in living standards that has been enjoyed by residents of advanced industrial societies throughout the twentieth century."[193]

In other words, individuals must learn, perhaps for the first time, to think critically about competitiveness, preparedness, and what they really want and need to do to remain employed. While a person's country of birth used to determine their standard of living, in the 21st century it will be individual effort that ultimately determines one's place in the world.

Someone born in America will earn the minimum wage and perhaps some social benefits, but every step above that will be the individual responsibility of the 300 million Americans involved. Some, maybe even many, will end up with living standards below those of their better-prepared foreign competitors, as one would expect from a perfect market that allocates jobs based on a market-based cost/benefit curve.

Governments will ideally work to provide the proper environment in which to compete, namely the three legs of the competitiveness stool: a proper education, coupled to an environment of entrepreneurship, supporting a dynamic culture of innovation and success. However, these are merely enabling factors, as governments themselves never create actual value – they can merely prevent, allow, or best of all, encourage it.

At the end of the day, if someone's highest skill and most loved job involves something that can easily be done elsewhere for less, they are in serious trouble. On the other hand, those that excel in one or more specialties and are at home in global markets will be richly rewarded as 21st century samurai.

No One Deserves a Job

If it's not already clear, individuals must realize that no one deserves a job, let alone a high salary. The notion that Americans deserve the best jobs and income reflects a myopic view of the world that is dangerous, both to them and the world at large when such views stray into the realm of political action. Such attitudes also hide the underlying malaise, thereby preventing any substantial discussion or progress towards a solution.

In the end, American workers are competing head-to-head with a global workforce that is less expensive, better educated, and perhaps simply better at some things. The only way to compete is to change one or more of these variables; though unfortunately, many of the individuals losing their jobs lack the tools to change said variables. In this case, the market will change the final variable, demand, by reducing jobs and thus lowering their salaries.

The blue-collar workforce learned this the hard way, as jobs, hard-fought wages, and benefits drained away to foreign lands. Their wages have not depressed significantly (yet), due in part to union support, but mostly because of the ease of movement into services, reducing labor supply and propping up price, i.e. wages. For today's service market, however, there is nowhere to go to reduce labor supply, as labor demand (jobs) can move quickly away, allowing Adam Smith's invisible hand to reduce real wages over time.

Effects on Different Groups

The changes necessary for various affected groups will differ based on many factors and individual circumstances, including age and position in the white-collar hierarchy.

Everyone will be affected to varying degrees, though there are interesting characteristics for each group – for instance, lower-end staff have fewer opportunities but are easier to train, while high-end staff require years of education for every different career.

Low end

For those at the low end of the income/skill continuum, the most serious challenge is a mixture of lack of skills and a more serious lack of ability to easily gain new skills. Realistically, the typical insurance claims processor or call center representative has limited transferable skills and probably finds further education unpalatable, at least for now. Often their prior educational journey (i.e. high school) was difficult, so new training may be the first time in their lives they really have to study and learn something; this can be a scary proposition to a middle-aged single mother living paycheck-to-paycheck.

This is especially true for those who hate "book work," or working with their minds instead of their hands. Unfortunately, there are plenty of hands in the world and not nearly enough good minds. Put simply, they must begin to condition themselves to accept continuous education and learning, or else they will literally be asking the proverbial "Would you like fries with that?"

For this group, choosing the proper training path is the most important challenge. There is no easy or safe career choice other than hands-on service such as health care, massage, Asian medicine, real estate, retail, or counseling(to name but a few). Beyond those obvious choices, the best route is probably general education in business and any technology, if only to improve their ability to learn and possibly ignite their entrepreneurial spirit.

Numerous people will continue to be absorbed into basic services, from computer servicing to telecommunications installation, though these jobs are somewhat ephemeral; constant learning will be needed for the inevitable transition when they end or as new entrants force veterans to continually move up market.

While not a growing segment, good factory jobs in numerous industries will continue to be available to those with the training in various technologies, especially computer-controlled machinery, statistics, and any sort of management or leadership. Laboratory training also appears to be helpful, as many new factories will involve various sciences, nanotech processes, or even carefully controlled clean-room aerospace assembly work.[194]

In addition, global cultural affinity is important even at the lower levels, as language and cultural familiarity provides an advantage over other job candidates for jobs involving technology and manufacturing partnerships with foreign firms. As such, someone familiar with China is more likely to get a job at a company with operations in China, if only to assist in the interaction within the far flung empire. For example, American firms often send employees abroad to both give and receive training, so interest in such cultures can only be helpful.

Those below the age of 50 or 60 also really have to think about the multiple transitions they will need to make before they retire around age 70. For many people, changing entire industries, or at least specialties every five years may become the norm. Those who master such career dynamics will end up at the head of the list for new and interesting opportunities, being able to take advantage of innovations before they commoditize and move abroad.

Along these same lines, entrepreneurship may well be one of the main routes out of the cycle of low-wage jobs for the low-end white-collar worker. Training them in business basics and providing some assistance in starting companies that provide basic services such as auto or computer repair, home service, and other related small businesses may be critical to their success, especially if they can hire their laid-off friends. In some cases, as with outsourcing's effect on companies, entrepreneurs can leverage low-cost immigrant or off-shore labor to enable interesting new business models or industries.

For instance, those that have always loved woodworking may be able to build a specialty furniture or cabinetry business, coupling low-cost labor with their artistic eye and artisan sensibilities. The same goes for ex-mechanics making after-market parts, cooks importing interesting foodstuffs, or others providing specialty services to auto garages or small construction firms. While it's difficult to imagine the myriad of possibilities in advance, general training, encouragement, and support allow members of this (and every) group to create their own future.

Mid-tier

Mid-tier employees may have the easiest time learning new skills, as they have much stronger educational backgrounds and tend to have experience in multiple industries. For instance, many computer programmers routinely move among such diverse areas such finance, health care, and manufacturing. Unfortunately, this is the area most at risk to the hordes of newly-minted foreign university graduates; any new profession typically requires extensive study or training, e.g. going from programmer to nurse takes more than a weekend course in needle sticking.

Further, many in this segment may have limited educational backgrounds and find the prospect of studying years for a new career quite daunting. Choosing the proper path and destination is more crucial than for the lower-level workers, as it does no good to study for two years to be a video animator or advanced lab technician, only to find that the job has disappeared in the meantime.

Fortunately, this group is more likely to be able to learn both the business and technology side of things and/or understand numerous portions of various businesses. For instance, a marketing coordinator might learn more finance and spend time in various operating roles to really understand strategy, tactics, and the key operational issues present in any enterprise.

Regardless of this flexibility, one critical factor for this group to remain well-employed will be continuous learning, both on the job and on their own time. Realistically, they can never know enough about too many things. This is especially true when the economy becomes more dynamic, forcing more industry and career changes.

Teaching may also be a major element of this group's future. While much is made of the need for "certified" teachers in the nation's classrooms, in reality many ex-professionals will be excellent teachers and should be accelerated into the classroom. Some states have already moved in this direction, requiring only a few months of training before allowing a whole new breed of teachers to emerge. Other states, such as California, have far too onerous hurdles to cross; once those barriers fall and if existing schools become more performance-oriented, there should be ample opportunities for mid-tier professionals to move into one of the most important professions of all, teaching the youth of tomorrow.

This mid-tier group will bear the brunt of foreign competition from educated workers, so they have to continuously think about how they will stay ahead. Entrepreneurship and driving innovation are likely the key, as this is the group starting new technology-based businesses to service the globe. They are also the ones to expand Silicon Valley nationwide, ideally employing everyone else in an innovation-driven economic boom.

This group is in many ways best positioned to compete for two reasons: they have better educations and more portable skill sets than the low-end workers; yet they are not so pigeon-holed as the high-end. They are smart and work hard, while having a business sense and a vision of how to make something better for themselves, their fellow citizens, and the world at large.

High end

The high end, while encompassing the fewest individuals, has the highest salaries and a more complex relationship with off-shoring. Realistically, many in this group are reasonably protected by various barriers to entry. Others will excel in this new competitive state, providing new and innovative services to an ever-expanding global customer base.

However, for those making a transition, either by choice or out of competitive necessity, there are some unique challenges, chiefly due to the length of time to it takes to learn and progress in high-end professions. After all, switching from patent law to heart surgery is hardly an overnight process.

Instead of switching to a new profession, realistically most specialized high-end practitioners will presumably migrate towards more generalized business roles, or even run a business itself, leaping off into the netherworlds of innovation and entrepreneurship. For instance, lawyers are always leaving the law to become CEOs or operational managers, to become bankers or finance folks, or to switch careers entirely and focus on non-profit or political work. Doctors often switch to teaching, scientific research, or developing new products and services for the health care industry. More and more professionals may be well served by taking this leap into the unknown, expanding their horizons, and leading the way towards 21st century prosperity.

Expectation Adjustments

Given the significant changes already in progress in the domestic and world economies, nearly every employee may have to reexamine his or her general expectations and perhaps recalibrate them to reality, especially those in vulnerable positions and industries. The American Dream is alive and well for Americans and foreigners alike; but as has always been true, such a dream is only attainable for those who step up and work very hard to take advantage of it.

The era of the ability to collect an unearned wage advantage is drawing to a close. In fact, with union membership at an all-time low and globalization forces on the march, the era of unearned wage advantages probably ended with the 20th century. From here on, every global citizen needs to earn his or her wage in competition with everyone else on the planet.

For those who don't figure out how to compete, who didn't do so well in school, or are occupying "me, too" sorts of jobs without any special skills or effort, the dream of a nice house in the suburbs, two cars, a boat, a big screen TV, lots of toys, and nice vacations may no longer be within realistic reach. Fundamentally, on a global basis, they may not be able to make sufficient money to afford the things enjoyed by the generation before. This may be true even if the cost of everything falls, since some people's wages may fall faster than relevant costs (especially of housing, fuel, and health care).

It used to be that their fellow citizens had to compensate them regardless of their relative worth, but globalization and strong competition allows every buyer to get the best value for nearly every good and service, for instance via Wal-Mart.

After all, it's no coincidence that the uncompetitive industries of health care and K-12 education provide mediocre products at the worst prices. Competition can only be good for everyone involved, even if it doesn't feel that way at the time. American industry is far stronger today because of the Japanese; similarly, future generations of businesses will be toughened by continual global competition.

In the end, individuals have to consciously choose their destination and what they are willing to do to get there. They have perhaps three paths: sink down towards the bottom; elevate their game to just stay roughly where they are; or become a star who loves what they do. Putting off this choice, as Americans are wont to do, leaves them automatically headed for the lower ranks, because these days conscious choice and effort are needed to just tread water to stay where they are. More than ever, superior effort will be needed to move forward and upward at all.

Global Work & Education Ethic

Intel sponsors an international science competition every year. It attracted some 50,000 American high school kids in 2004. But this pales when compared to the laser-like focus on math and science that occurs in developing countries. "I was in China ten days ago," Intel's CEO said, "and I asked them how many kids in China participated in the local science fairs that feed into the national fair (and ultimately the Intel finals). They told me six million kids."[195] That's 6,000,000 vs. 50,000, a ratio that does not bode well for the future of American science.

Some would also observe that Americans have tended to become lazy over time, both at the government and individual levels, content with and protective of their lifestyle and living standards. And while immigrants have historically tended to compensate for this effect by working harder, and at jobs citizens don't want, at least they had to come to the U.S. to get those jobs.

But hardworking, 21st century immigrants no longer need move to America at all in order to take good American jobs. As a result, distance and oceans no longer shield Americans from the global work ethic. As blue-collar workers discovered, developing country workers tend to labor harder, if not always smartly. In the case of the 1980s Japanese or Taiwanese, they worked harder, smartly.

While it's no picnic trying to compete with a poor Chinese or Indian family trying to move up the economic ladder, it is the reality. This is especially true when one competes with cultures where hard work is a cultural norm. It's also true where many employees are young and in their first real Western-style jobs. Tasting real money for the first time, along with the freedom and merit-based advances provided by good jobs, millions of highly motivated foreigners are poised to drain jobs from the West.

And while Americans probably cannot fully emulate a Chinese worker's (perhaps mythical) 18-hour-day, 7 days a week, they must find ways to do better work, in less time, for not too much more money. This is where innovation, enhanced productivity, and entrepreneurship come in, especially when leveraged by globally sourced labor and expertise.

Education & Training

CEO Barrett insisted that Intel was "still making massive investments in the U.S.," but he noted that jobs at these new facilities require two years of college "just to walk in the door. The infrastructure and education requirement of those jobs is forever increasing."[196]

Self-improvement and higher education have long been staples of American life, though they have rarely been applied evenly to everyone. Today's jobs require ever-increasing education and credentials. Today's situation clearly calls for greatly enhanced education and training, though, unfortunately, the U.S. is greatly hampered by a second- or even third-rate primary/secondary education system. Equally unfortunately, there is no evidence that this will be corrected in the coming decades. So, as has been true over the last few decades, companies, colleges, and other post-high school institutions have to pick up the slack.

Further, many, if not all of these foreign cultures value education much more highly than Americans do. After all, geeks and scholastic kids in American K-12 schools are often frowned upon and made fun of by other students. By contrast, really knowing physics or computers is admired in many eastern cultures, as are high occupational goals such as becoming a doctor or attorney. As a result, the education gap is only likely to widen, especially as older Americans compete with younger Asians or Indians.

In the old days, career and class transitions occurred between generations. A grandfather often ran a farm, his son worked in the factories, and his grandson went to college to be a computer programmer or doctor. Careers and their underlying skills lasted for decades, and individuals rarely moved between various career types.

Today, these types of changes might happen to a single individual, perhaps in the span of a few years, as they move up, down, and along life's curve. Everything is moving faster, but as noted, it's not clear that individuals or surrounding educational and training systems are geared for the pace or degree of change necessary.

Therefore, individuals absolutely must begin working on their own self-improvement and training as soon as possible. Not only will this help improve their lives, it will set a good example for their children, who will face an even more challenging competitive picture when they grow up. Constant studying and continuous learning must become a staple of every American's life or else they will simply be left behind.

Unfortunately, as noted above, adults in the lower white-collar jobs are likely to be quite difficult to retrain. After all they share much in common with their blue-collar brethren, namely that they didn't like school a decade or two (or three) ago, are not used to learning new things, and aren't terribly good at career or long-range planning.

As a result, they are left with trying to fix all of this after the fact, with retraining programs geared to the adult workforce, who arrive with varying ages, backgrounds, and motivation. Regardless, the importance of individuals taking control of their education cannot be overemphasized; as skill sets simply must improve and evolve or they will die in the face of relentless low-cost competition.

Training and education require an advance plan, as one does not lightly embark on what could be a multi-year course of action. Individuals should seek out a career counselor and think about what they would like to do--focus on not the particular job, but on what they really like about it, whether it's talking to people, problem solving, dealing with customers, complicated or exception-based processing, etc.

From there, they can identify a likely course of study or career cluster and pursue it with the assistance of various employer and governmental programs. The key is to immediately start to do so something in this direction, as any self-improvement effort is likely to result in positive effects in numerous areas. Plus, since each individual will go through numerous additional transitions later in life, just learning how to learn may be the most important initial result.

At the middle level, things are a bit challenging, as the retraining is often years in the making and the entry-level jobs needed to get experience may well be non-existent. There are no easy answers and every path is different, but there are many more technological opportunities available at this middle level. After all, these are the folks contributing to innovation in large numbers, since in the white-collar profession they are the ones actually building products and services.

At the high end, there are often diversification options within a profession. This allows existing lawyers, doctors, engineers, and scientists to branch out into new fields, such as biotech or the space business. In terms of education, it's time to get up to speed on these technologies, in Silicon Valley or elsewhere. For instance, attorneys in software firms are starting to familiarize themselves with the business and science of nanotech, better enabling them to make contacts and the jump to that promising field in the coming years.

Finally, one often-overlooked training method is interning or volunteering. Often, there is a catch-22 that it's difficult to get experience without working at the job, but difficult to get a job without the experience. Volunteering is a way out of this conundrum, as every company needs help with something, especially for free. For instance, young (or old) professionals without large fiscal responsibilities may intern in new industries or work for no pay in interesting startups to get experience that cannot be outsourced.

Everyone should volunteer in a field they might find interesting or to build experience. This looks great on a resume and may even directly lead to a paid position. In particular, small companies can always use help in a wide variety of areas, from accounting to computing to a variety of logistics and operational roles. Those that show the initiative to get this sort of experience will really impress future employers and pick up valuable skills along the way.

People should also be creative about picking up and practicing skills. For example, everyone knows soup kitchens need people to volunteer to serve food, but it's easy to forget they also have back offices where they need volunteer accountants to do their books and keep them solvent, planners to help staff and forecast needs, and managers to keep it all running smoothly. Interesting and educational opportunities exist everywhere in the economy, if one only looks and thinks about investing some time to really move themselves forward in the continual competition for extra skills.

Further, volunteering often builds a social and business network as well. By volunteering at a church or non-profit, one becomes part of a social network, which often eventually leads to a job or entrepreneurial opportunity. Volunteering is a hugely beneficial win-win and an almost entirely overlooked solution to real social problems, to improving one's self-worth, and to gaining valuable experience and connections. It's important to remember that they'll always take people who don't ask for any money in return; the personal profits are less tangible, but no less real.

Love One's Work as Talent

In the end, the key to finding the best combination of skill, opportunity, and happiness will be for each person to discover the optimal intersection of their skills, their interests, and the world's needs. In financial terms, this is called the "best and highest use," or the best possible use of each and every person in the marketplace of products, services, and ideas.

People ought to always question what the best and highest use of their time is. It may be obvious that people should like their jobs, but it's amazing how few actually do. If someone dislikes their job, they are unlikely to be very good at it. It will never be the best and highest value they provide to the economy and in today's markets someone will surely take it away from them.

Freeing a person from that monotony may be painful economically, but it can often free them up to really add value in a job they love. Often it provides the opportunity to take a risk and really do what they've always wanted, from starting a company to running a charity to writing their novel.

Funny things often happen on the way to doing what someone loves; one finds a way to make money at it. While they may not get rich or even reach the levels seen at prior jobs (especially if they were unionized), people can earn enough to live a more modest, yet balanced life, doing what they love.

Though every worker finding his or her ideal dream job may sound idealistic and perhaps impossible, globalization can enable this sort of process in many ways. It's easy to forget that America still has significant global advantages and that globalization cuts both ways –small, yet talented entrepreneurs can export their wares to a vast ocean of several billion potential customers. Leveraging the large home market, good public policy, a can-do attitude, and global focus can result in substantial success for a new generation of entrepreneurs.

Talent

Central to taking the middle or high road on the path to success will be to understand the distinctions between being a talent and just a commodity. As noted in the chapter on which jobs will remain, the key is transitioning from commodity to talent.

Most people are unfortunately trapped in jobs that are commodities, and like all such products, they are subject to harsh global price competition, with nothing to differentiate them. Talent, on the other hand, is hard to come by and can command 10, 100, or even 1,000 times the compensation. Further, this pay discrepancy may even accelerate, to the point where only talent can make more than minimum wage. This effect can already be seen in the wage split between the low- and high-end job categories.

It's possible that domestic commodity jobs will be rapidly rationalized away to lower cost sources (or countries). As with oil, aluminum, and coffee, as the price (or wage) falls, many locations (or people) become uneconomical, sometimes permanently. So, just as new technology can make an old ore mine or oil well competitive again, so can more education and motivation among people.

So, workers must sort out how they will take the high road, even if that means only a small amount of differentiation in an otherwise commodity industry or role. The important thing is for each person to identify and cultivate their own differentiator. In theory, this is not difficult, as one needs merely to love what done does. The reality is that it's difficult to find the proper intersection of where one's talents lie and what the market's willing to buy.

It's also important to remember that globalization works both ways. As jobs are drained away to faraway lands, customers are also being created. Just as it's easier to be a niche specialist in a big city rather than a small town, it's even easier to find customers when the whole world is buying.

Entrepreneurship & Innovation

Talent itself is useful at every level of every organization, but it truly comes into its own when coupled with entrepreneurship. After all, the ultimate value add is doing what one loves, providing valuable services to customers near and far. For instance, there are numerous stories in the manufacturing industries where a factory worker is laid off, only to start his or her own company in a specialized field, producing something as simple as motorcycle parts or custom hot rod components.

As an example, one man laid off from his IBM teaching job expanded his hobby to become a paintball gun expert, volunteering at various competitions. He eventually formed LAPCO, a manufacturer of custom high-end parts for the paintball aficionado, and his products are highly regarded and much sought after all over the world.[197]

Even if starting a big company is not in the cards, there are still opportunities to do thing one likes, e.g. an ex-Boeing man was laid off and subsequently started training to be a motorcycle mechanic; his observation was, "You have to do something, here's an opportunity to go learn something that maybe you want to learn."[198] He may not make it rich, but doing what one enjoys goes a long way towards making life interesting and potentially prosperous.

"Cars, or hot rods, were always a hobby," said Lauria, 62. "I got laid off from my job and went into business with three other partners." Today he's president and sole owner of Total Performance Inc., a manufacturer of $50-100K hot rods, many of which are exported to places such as Japan.[199] This sort of tiny, but global, entrepreneur is the future of American business.

Finally, the U.S. Census Bureau estimated that over 17 million Americans ran their own companies by themselves in 2002. While these are not large enterprises, they are 15% of total employment and adding value in every way imaginable.[200]

Globalization

Living in the 21st century requires each individual to understand the whole world, no easy task given that most Americans can't find China or India on a map. People must get a better handle on the rest of the planet – as long gone are the days when what America does is all that matters; now it's not only important to understand the U.S., Europe, and the Middle-East, but also Latin America, China, and Southeast Asia. There are whole billion-person societies and cultures out there, and what they think and do really does matter in the middle of Montana.

Pieces, parts, and people are now coming from, and going to, every point on the planet, and while English is spoken increasingly widely, these folks are not from Kansas in any way, shape, or form. Everyone can and will sell and buy everything everywhere, all the time, as the world becomes increasingly smaller.

So, while the government has some role in globalizing the people, in the end it comes down to the individual. This, in turn, starts with language, travel, and culture. And that starts with reading, taking classes, and making new friends in diverse and interesting communities, no matter how difficult that may be. This does not mean that everyone must learn to love the Chinese, but that they should learn about someone, somewhere that's not from their home town, country, or culture. This can be someone from the "old country" such as France or Italy, though one’s future may be better served by connecting with the newly important economies of the world. Germany, Spain, and Ireland may be ancestrally interesting, but frankly, India, China, and pan-Arabia are the future.

People should also think not only about themselves, but also about their children and how best to prepare them for the new world and all of the opportunities it presents. Given that children absorb new cultures and languages easily, parents should try to connect them with foreign language speakers right from birth, especially languages with different sounds and grammar, such as Arabic or Chinese. If speakers are unavailable, they should use tapes, movies, radio, or any other medium to provide foreign immersion from the outset.

Children will forever appreciate their parents for exposing them to new languages, and likewise forever lament their parents for not teaching them languages. For instance, such feelings are all too common among second-generation Japanese whose parents avoided teaching them the language for fear of an accent or discrimination. Japanese parents should have known better, but they were living in difficult times with difficult experiences; there is no such excuse today, especially when 21st century citizens in Europe, China, or India are not literate unless they speak two or three languages.

Children should also be pushed to have a variety of diverse friends, while parents should consider a foreign-born babysitter or nanny. Further, everyone should be encouraged to participate in foreign exchange and travel opportunities whenever possible. Children truly are the future and their breadth of experience and world view will prepare them well for the challenges and opportunities ahead.

Keys to Successful Transition

Each individual must discover or create his or her own path in this process, and sort out the proper mix of location, career, training, and economic alignment that works for them. Unfortunately, as mentioned, this is likely to prove quite difficult, especially for the lower white-collar classes who are not prepared for additional education and may lack advantages over foreign workers.

There are perhaps three paths on which each individual might embark. The first, and certainly least desirable, is to do nothing, make no changes, and thus sink down as the global workforce rises. Such a path will undoubtedly lead to working less, a lower income, and having to slave away at a job that is likely quite undesirable. Making French fries and giving correct change will probably be the most important skills on this path. Realistically, more and more workers are already choosing this path, ending up at Wal-Mart, depressing the wages for everyone in the lower classes. Getting by on a minimum wage may become a reality, which is not easy in an economy where said wage barely covers a family's monthly health care premium.

The middle path is one of continual success for individuals who sufficiently improve their game to compete against similar workers the world over. This will involve the aforementioned training, self-improvement, and working harder, though perhaps for a lower wage. Numerous industry and careers shifts will be necessary, as will a renewed focus on continual learning, technology, and attention to personal competitiveness. This group will probably change careers or industries every five years, and night school will be common. If they are lucky, members of this group will work for those in the next group.

Finally, for the adventurous, the high road will be to help drive the American and global economy into the 21st century, by leading the world in innovation and entrepreneurship. These people will be comfortable in multiple cultures as they continuously learn new industries and leverage global resources to create all of the new jobs; they will take advantage of low cost products, services, and labor to usher in successive rounds of technological advances for the global population.

Their enterprises will employ members of the lower classes who are themselves prepared to work in 21st century industries such as biotech, aerospace, nanotech, and advanced manufacturing. By stepping up to face the competition, as

Americans have always done, this group will ideally preserve the dreams of millions for yet another century.

America is also the land of class mobility, so the challenge is to mobilize those in each class to move up a notch or two. There is no reason individuals in the lower classes, perhaps laid off from a back office or factory job, cannot seize the day and start their dream company in an area they are uniquely qualified in. Employing their friends along the way, they are the new key to class mobility, living the true American Dream.

Those in the middle must follow the same track, though perhaps on a higher plane. They must leverage their talents and broader knowledge of business, technology, and the world at large to create opportunities for themselves and enterprises for others to capture real innovative value in the 21st century.

And those at the top simply have to work harder, become more global, and lead the way for everyone else. This includes continuously assisting others to get to the into the highest ranks, developing partnerships and connections the world over, and constantly striving to stay ahead of the ever faster group of competitors nipping at their heels.

Chapter 16.

Competing for the Future

"I wish to have no connection with any ship that does not sail fast, for I intend to go in harm's way."

John Paul Jones

It's easy to be gloomy about America's economic prospects in the 21st century, with endless job competition on wages, limited educational progress, reduced expectations, and a shrinking middle class. Unfortunately, most governments have no concrete plans, policies, or programs that address even one of the challenges involved. And most people are completely unprepared for these changes, with no idea what they should be doing or how to prepare to compete for the future.

Failure to embrace 21st century dynamics could force America into a Japanese or European-style decline, with disastrous effects on the whole world. Such a failure could create significant political turmoil, boiling over into hyper-protectionism and rapid decline into nationalistic trading blocs. Such decline is one thing when Yugoslavia is concerned, but hyper-nationalistic attitudes by the world's great economic and military powers are dangerous for everyone.

In John Paul Jones' time, wars were won with strong economies, deployment of large forces, good weapons, flexible execution of superior strategy, and more than a bit of luck. Little has changed, for while today's grand battles are economic, they still rely on every one of these critical elements.

Combatants still require a strong economy; without it, everything else is difficult to afford and sustain. Strong economies are themselves driven by a motivated and productive workforce coupled with a public policy stance strongly geared towards economic growth. This growth-oriented policy includes modest regulation, enlightened tax management, appropriate entrepreneurial incentives, and constant removal of barriers to growth. In particular, it's crucial to realize that modestly-regulated economic growth should be the top social priority, as an ever-expanding economy covers a wide variety of policy sins, supports those less fortunate, and provides investment for the future.

Large forces of warriors are needed, though today these are innovative companies, entrepreneurs, and employees. These warriors need strong and creative support from every level, as they are constantly in economic combat with foreign workers, companies, and countries. Given that the West's historical advantages are diminishing so rapidly, every combatant must fight harder, move faster, and stay a few steps ahead at every turn.

Neither strong economies nor armies of workers are useful without proper weapons with which to fight. Today's 21st century economic warriors need a good education, constantly-evolving skills, entrepreneurial spirit, innovation, a global perspective, a free society, and a dynamic economy that rewards success. Without these, no economic army or underlying economy will thrive, or possibly even survive.

Of these weapons, a good education is well-covered in numerous books, so the only mention here will be to agree with Bill Gates and others who feel the U.S. should throw out its educational system and start over, lest it remain a 19th century format for 21st century life.[201] An army must constantly re-evaluate and upgrade its strategies; it makes no sense to push tomorrow's economic warriors through schools best suited for the age of agriculture.

Unfortunately, no real progress on primary / secondary education is on the horizon, so the real focus needs to be on state-of-the-art workforce skills, including (and especially) the skill of learning new skills coupled to clear thinking and overall flexibility. This sort of training is under the control of the very groups that depend most on its success – individuals, corporations, and to some extent, the government.

Entrepreneurial spirit is perhaps the most important weapon the U.S. has, as America has always been a nation of individuals building and doing great things. As a result, it is critical to keep this spirit alive and nurture it by continually making entrepreneurialism easier. In fact, proper policy and incentives could unleash a new wave of startups, accelerating to 1 million new company formations per year by 2010, up from roughly 500,000 today. Asia is rapidly learning how America's economy worked in the 20th century, so it's time to move the competition to a new level.

Innovation, and its close cousin productivity growth, remains the battle order of the day, as the only way to stay ahead of the cost curve is through innovation – new products, new ideas, new industries. The American research and development machine must be enhanced and harnessed to rapidly transform groundbreaking inventions into industries and companies willing to shoot for the moon, perhaps literally.

A global perspective is a very important weapon as companies and employees look to the future, if only because everyone else already thinks, sells, and innovates globally. Long gone are the days when most companies or even their employees can look only at America as the only market or competition. As difficult as a global view is for many Americans used to a homogeneous country, economy, and culture, it will be a key differentiator and driving force in this new era. Perhaps the biggest benefit of such an outlook will be leveraging and exploiting new markets in previously unknown territory-- selling insurance in Mongolia, software in Algeria, and medical services to the Cambodians.

A free society is somewhat obvious, though the most important element of such societies is the flexibility to do as one pleases. Individual entrepreneurs will always make better decisions than those in a restricted society, as is clear by just looking at how China is doing once it unleashed the entrepreneurial spirit of its people. A free people will work hard for rewards based on their own success, creating wealth and employing many others all along the way.

The last weapon, a dynamic economy that rewards success, is intertwined with the other weapons, but also carefully allocates resources critical to the success of any enterprise—namely capital and labor. The Internet boom represents the best of these dynamics, allocating massive resources to explore new technologies, then quickly moving on to biotechnology, nanotech, and energy industries. In the end, a dynamic free market will allocate and reward all of the key elements needed to win 21st century battles.

Finally, all of these things are tied together by strategy, in the form of good public policy, corporate direction, and individual initiative. Politicians, executives, and especially citizens must understand and consistently focus on their key objectives in relation to global, corporate, and individual economic success.

In the end, America must use all of these tactics, weapons, and initiatives towards continued success in the face of new 21st century challenges, principally by innovating and moving up the value chain. The country, its companies, and citizens must work hard in new and interesting ways, literally inventing the future, for themselves and for the world. Everyone has to look at really changing themselves, their country, and the world, as their personal initiative and leadership will decide who prospers in this brave new world.

Fortunately, for all this talk of effective weapons, armies of combatants, and economic battles, there is a stark difference in today's warfare – everyone can win! While there are individual winners and losers, well-orchestrated globalization and the continuation of centuries-old shifts in capital, skills, and labor can bring continued prosperity to every developed country while propelling the whole world into modern life, liberty, and happiness for all.

Opportunity abounds everywhere, as the world's largest economies benefit from global economic growth. Further, everyone benefits from the additional geopolitical stability brought about by such growth and economic interdependency;

after all, wars and related poverty, disease, and stagnation take unimaginable tolls on the weaker members of every society. Alternatively, with global economic success, every person on the planet becomes a customer for every possible product or service.

More specifically, as the global innovation and technology leader, America has key elements of what every country needs and wants as it works its way up the development curve. After all, there is little to sell to an impoverished African country today, but China, India, Russia, etc. can absorb enormous levels of American output; e.g. power plants, computers, the Internet, aircraft, cell phones, movies, better foods, advanced machinery, and all types of technology.

Along the way, two billion people can shift from living on \$2 per day to \$20, \$200, and beyond. Failure to bring the bulk of the world's population into the middle class and staying competitive by moving up the value chain would be a stunning failure on the part of governments, leaders, and citizens of the world's most advanced countries.

On the other hand, following the policies laid out in this book will set governments, corporations, and individuals on the right path to competing in the 21st century. The world is changing rapidly and in the end, it's up to the entirety of Western society to react proactively to the opportunities and challenges afforded by globalization and the off-shoring of white-collar jobs. The world's economies are rapidly integrating, to the point where every component of every economy and society must adjust. The world is a fickle and fast-moving place, where nothing can be taken for granted and for which there can never be enough education, preparation, flexibility, and hard work.

Index

1 Lochhead, Carolyn. "Tech bosses defend overseas hiring Intel, HP chiefs warn that U.S. needs to improve education system." San Francisco Chronicle 8 Jan. 2004: A1. http://www.sfgate.com/cgi-bin/article.cgi?file=/c/a/2004/01/08/MNGDI45PV01.DTL

2 Wilson, Woodrow. "The Fourteen Points." Cong.Rec. 8 Jan. 1918. The World War I Document Archive, Brigham Young University Library. http://www.lib.byu.edu/~rdh/wwi/1918/14points.html

3 Lochhead, Carolyn. "Tech bosses defend overseas hiring Intel, HP chiefs warn that U.S. needs to improve education system." San Francisco Chronicle 8 Jan. 2004: A1. http://www.sfgate.com/cgi-bin/article.cgi?file=/c/a/2004/01/08/MNGDI45PV01.DTL

4 Democratic Peace Clock Website. http://www.hawaii.edu/powerkills/dp.clock.htm

5 Bardhan, Ashok D. and Kroll, Cynthia A. "The New Wave of Outsourcing." Fisher Center Research Reports, Fisher Center for Real Estate and Urban Economics, University of California, Berkeley 2003, 1103.
http://repositories.cdlib.org/cgi/viewcontent.cgi?article=1025&context=iber/fcreue

6 Schumer, Charles and Roberts, Paul C. "Second Thoughts on Free Trade." New York Times 6 Jan. 2004, late ed.: A23. http://www.nytimes.com/2004/01/06/opinion/06SCHU.html

7 Mieszkowski, Katherine. "How India is Saving Capitalism." Salon 1 April 2004.
http://www.salon.com/tech/feature/2004/04/01/collabnet/index_np.html

8 Peters, Tom. "'Off-Shoring' Manifesto/Rant: Twenty Hard Truths about Inevitabilities, Pitfalls, and Matchless Opportunities." Tom Peters Company 16 Mar. 2004.
http://www.tompeters.com/toms_world/obs_entries.php?note=000650&year=2004

9 Edwards, Ben. American Business Editor for The Economist, panel member for "The New Job Migration: Offshore Outsourcing." Meeting for the World Affairs Council of Northern California, San Francisco CA. 14 April 2004. http://itsyourworld.org/program.php?page=879#

10 Tansey, Bernadette. "Testing the offshore waters: Biotech firms experiment with moving work overseas." San Francisco Chronicle 18 April 2004: J-1. http://sfgate.com/cgi-bin/article.cgi?file=/chronicle/archive/2004/04/18/BUGAI66E7I1.DTL&type=printable

11 Wessel, David. "Outsourcing Creates Jobs and Widens the Wage Gap." The Wall Street Journal Online 13 April 2004. http://online.wsj.com/article/0,,SB108086082229572178-email,00.html
http://www.careerjournaleurope.com/myc/survive/20040413-wessel.html

12 Moore, John. "Welcome to McDonald's, may WE take your order?." Brand Autopsy Marketing Practice Blog Site, 18 July 2004. http://brandautopsy.typepad.com/brandautopsy/2004/07/welcome_to_mcdo.html

13 Herbert, Bob. "Who's Getting the New Jobs?" New York Times 23 July 2004, late ed.: A23. http://www.nytimes.com/2004/07/23/opinion/23herb.html

14 Konrad, Rachel. "Offshoring jobs could drain public coffers, critics warn." Associated Press 8 April 2004. http://sfgate.com/cgi-bin/article.cgi?file=/news/archive/2004/04/08/financial0316EDT0012.DTL

15 McCarthy, John C. "Near-"Term Growth Of Offshoring Accelerating" Forrester Research 14 May 2004. http://www.forrester.com/Research/Document/Excerpt/0,7211,34426,00.html

16 U.S. Department of Labor, Bureau of Labor Statistics. "Displaced Workers Summary: Worker Displacement, 2001-03" News Release, 30 July 2004: USDL 04-1381. http://www.bls.gov/news.release/disp.nr0.htm

17 Hwang, Suein. "New Group Swells Bankruptcy Court: The Middle-Aged." The Wall Street Journal 6 Aug. 2004. http://online.wsj.com/article/0,,SB109175077276084596-email,00.html

18 Beckman, D. David. "IBM Plans to Accelerate Offshore Outsourcing." Wash Tech News 22 July 2003. http://www.techsunite.org/news/techind/030722_ibm.cfm

19 Bernstein, Jared and Fungard, Yulia. Economic Policy Institute: Washington D.C. "Unemployment level of college grads surpasses that of high school dropouts." Economic Snapshots 17 March 2004. http://www.epinet.org/content.cfm/webfeatures_snapshots_archive_03172004

20 Fields, Jason. U.S. Census Bureau: Washington D.C. "America's Families and Living Arrangements: 2003." Current Population Reports Nov. 2004:20-553. http://www.census.gov/prod/2004pubs/p20-553.pdf

21 Schroeder, Michael. "Unions and States Aspire to Block Job Outsourcing." Wall Street Journal Online 12 June 2003. http://www.careerjournal.com/salaryhiring/hotissues/20030612-schroeder.html

22 World Bank Office, Beijing China. "China Quarterly Update." Feb.2005. http://www.worldbank.org.cn/English/Content/cqu-en.pdf

The World Bank Group. "India Data Profile." World Development Indicators Database Aug.2005. http://devdata.worldbank.org/external/CPProfile.asp?SelectedCountry=IND&CCODE=IND&CNAME=India&PTYPE=CP

23 Hookway, James. "An American Subculture Takes Hold in the Phillipines." The Wall Street Journal Online 20 Oct. 2003. http://www.careerjournalasia.com/hrcenter/articles/20031021-hookway.html

24 Program on International Policy Attitudes (PIPA), Washington D.C. Polls on International Trade 1999 and 2003. http://www.pipa.org

25 DiCarlo, Lisa. "Readers Comment on the Most Significant Trend." Forbes 23 Dec. 2003. http://www.forbes.com/2003/12/23/cx_ld_1223pollresults.html

26 McCarthy, John C. "Near-"Term Growth Of Offshoring Accelerating" Forrester Research 14 May 2004. http://www.forrester.com/Research/Document/Excerpt/0,7211,34426,00.html

27 Rollins, Kevin. "Dell Inc., On The Record: Kevin Collins." San Francisco Chronicle 18 July 2004:J-1. http://www.sfgate.com/cgi-bin/article.cgi?f=/c/a/2004/07/18/BUGQM7LCD31.DTL

28 International Monetary Fund, Washington D.C. "Global Trade Liberalization and the Developing Countries." Issues Brief Nov. 2001. http://www.imf.org/external/np/exr/ib/2001/110801.htm

29 Friedman, Thomas. "War of Ideas, Part 6." New York Times 25 Jan. 2004, late ed.:15. http://query.nytimes.com/gst/abstract.html?res=FB0D13FA345D0C768EDDA80894DC404482

30 McCarthy, John C. "Near-"Term Growth Of Offshoring Accelerating" Forrester Research 14 May 2004. http://www.forrester.com/Research/Document/Excerpt/0,7211,34426,00.html

31 Intel Corp., Chandler AZ, U.S. "Everything Matters: Global Citizen Report 2003." May 2004. http://www.intel.com/intel/finance/gcr03/intel_gcr_2003.pdf

32 McCormack, Richard. "Engineers Fear Offshore Outsourcing is Contributing to High Jobless Rates." Manufacturing & Technology News 4 Nov. 2003: 10 (20). http://www.manufacturingnews.com/news/03/1104/art1.html

33 Brookes, Bethan and Madden, Peter. Christian Aid, London U.K. "The Globe-Trotting Sports Shoe." Christian Aid News Nov. 1995. http://www.saigon.com/~nike/christian-aid.htm

34 CCNG Intl., Grapevine, TX U.S. "Delta Call Center on Bubble?" CCNG News 7 Oct. 2004. http://www.ccng.com/newsletter/newsletter_view.asp?newsid=356&Regionid=5

35 Slaughter, Matthew J. "Insourcing Jobs, Making the Global Economy Work for America." Organization for International Investment, Washington D.C. Oct. 2004. http://www.ofii.org/insourcing/insourcing_study.pdf

36 Organisation for Economic Co-operation and Development, Paris FR. "China Ahead in Direct Foreign Investment" OECD Observer Aug. 2003:n237.

http://www.oecdobserver.org/news/fullstory.php/aid/1037/China_ahead_in_foreign_direct_investment.html

37 Rabushka, Alvin. Hoover Institution, Stanford, CA U.S. "Nothing New about Outsourcing." Hoover Institution Weekly Essays 28 Apr. 2004. http://www-hoover.stanford.edu/pubaffairs/we/2004/rabushka04.html

38 Zachary, G. Pascal. "Searching for a dial tone in Africa." The New York Times 5 July 2003. http://www.nytimes.com/2003/07/05/business/worldbusiness/05VOIC.html?pagewanted=print&position=

39 Kripalani, Manjeet and Engardio, Pete. "The Rise of India," Business Week 8 December 2003 http://www.businessweek.com/magazine/content/03_49/b3861001_mz001.htm

40 Kirkpatrick, David. "The Net Makes It All Easier – Including Exporting U.S. Jobs." Fortune 12 May 2003. http://www.fortune.com/fortune/fastforward/0,15704,450755,00.html

41 Uchitelle, Louis. "A Statistic That's Missing: Jobs That Moved Overseas." New York Times 5 Oct. 2003, late ed.:1-24. http://query.nytimes.com/gst/abstract.html?res=F40F10F839580C768CDDA90994DB404482

42 Gilbert, Alorie. "Oracle Opens Beijing R&D Center." CNET News 29 Oct. 2003. http://news.com.com/2100-1008-5099011.html?tag=nefd_hed

43 Proctor & Gamble. "R&D's Formula for Success." P&G Website 2006. http://www.pg.com/science/rd_formula_success.jhtml;jsessionid=1XVQ0UKDWYHERQFIAJ1S0HWAVABHMLKG

44 Tong-Young, Kim. "HP to open research center in South Korea." CNET News 13 Oct. 2004. http://news.com.com/HP+to+open+research+center+in+South+Korea/2100-7337_3-5406895.html?tag=nefd.top

45 Iyengar, Sridar. "Cross-border partnering in Asia: Globalization challenges for high-tech industries." 30 Sep. 2004 http://asia.stanford.edu/events/fall04/

46 Weidenbaum, Murray. "Outsourcing and American Jobs." 24 Jun 2004. http://wc.wustl.edu/Breakfast_Programs_Transcripts/Weidenbaum_Outsourcing.pdf

47 National Center for Education Statistics. U.S. Dept. of Education, Washington D.C. "Bachelor's, master's, and doctor's degrees conferred by degree-granting institutions, by sex of student and field of study: 2000-01" Digest of Education Statistics 2002, Table 255. http://nces.ed.gov/programs/digest/d02/dt255.asp see original source above

http://spacsun.rice.edu/~neal/pdfs/moore.pdf Science and Engineering Indicators 2002; National Science Foundation; Table 2-18.

48 Brecher, Jeremy and Costello, Tim. The North American Alliance for Fair Employment (NAFFE), Boston MA. "Outsource This? American Workers, the Jobs Deficit, and the Fair Globalization Solution." April 2004: p.25. http://www.fairjobs.org/fairjobs/reports/

49 Dossani, Rafiq and Kenney, Martin. Asia-Pacific Research Center, Stanford University, Stanford CA U.S. "Went for Cost, Stayed for Quality?: Moving the Back Office to India" Nov. 2003. http://iis-db.stanford.edu/pubs/20337/dossani_kenney_09_2003.pdf

50 A.T. Kearney. "Business Process Offshoring: Offshore Leadership Survey for Automotive Industry Executives." Online Survey Results, Sept. 2003. http://www.atkearney.com/shared_res/pdf/Auto_BPO_Survey_Insights_S.pdf

51 Adcock, Kim A. "2003 Vohs Award Winner: Initiative to Improve Mammogram Interpretation." The Permanente Journal Spring 2004:8(2). http://xnet.kp.org/permanentejournal/spring04/vohswin.html

52 U.S. Department of Labor, Bureau of Labor Statistics. "Business Employment Dynamics Summary" News Release, 16 Aug. 2005: USDL 05-1562. http://www.bls.gov/news.release/cewbd.nr0.htm

53 Dudley, Brier. "India parlays education, timing into tech boom." The Seattle Times 22 Apr. 2005. http://seattletimes.nwsource.com/html/businesstechnology/2002000235_india09.html

54 Beutel, Constance and Barnstable, Susan. Personal Conversation. 30 Sep 2003.

55 Broad, William. "U.S. Is Losing Its Dominance In the Sciences." 3 May 2004. http://select.nytimes.com/search/restricted/article?res=FB0F16FB38590C708CDDAC0894DC4044 82

56 Badger, T.A. "White-collar blues: Workers weigh unionizing as off-shoring spreads to desk, lab jobs." Associated Press 8 June 2004. http://www.post-gazette.com/pg/04160/328465.stm

57 Cooper, James C. "The Pride of Efficiency." Business Week 22 March 2004. http://www.businessweek.com/magazine/content/04_12/b3875603.htm

58 Elber, Lynn. "TV's 'The Simpsons' Goes Global." 5 Aug 2001. http://www.snpp.com/other/articles/goesglobal.html

59 Mehlman, Bruce. Assistant Secretary for Technology Policy, Department of Commerce, "Offshore Outsourcing and the Future of American Competitiveness." http://infopolicy.org/pdf/mehlman.pdf

60 Bardhan, Ashok D. and Kroll, Cynthia A. "The New Wave of Outsourcing." Fisher Center Research Reports, Fisher Center for Real Estate and Urban Economics, University of California, Berkeley 2003, 1103. http://repositories.cdlib.org/cgi/viewcontent.cgi?article=1025&context=iber/fcreue

61 Chawla, Raj K. "The changing profile of dual-earning families." Perspectives on Labor and Income Summer 1992:4(2). http://www.statcan.ca/english/studies/75-001/archive/1992/pear1992004002s2a02.pdf

62 National Association of Software and Service Companies, India. "NASSCOM-McKinsey Report 2002." NASSCOM Research Report: http://www.nasscom.org/artdisplay.asp?Art_id=1225

63 Atkinson, Rob. VP and Director, Technology and New Economy Project, Progressive Policy Institute, Washington D.C. "Offshoring: What Should Government Do?" PowerPoint presentation 15 Dec. 2003. http://infopolicy.org/ppt/atkinson.pps

64 Slashdot Website. http://www.slashdot.com

65 Hire American Citizens website. http://www.hireamericancitizens.org

66 McCarthy, John C. "Near-"Term Growth Of Offshoring Accelerating" Forrester Research 14 May 2004. http://www.forrester.com/Research/Document/Excerpt/0,7211,34426,00.html

67 Mieszkowski, Katherine. "How India is Saving Capitolism." Salon 1 Apr. 2004. http://www.salon.com/tech/feature/2004/04/01/collabnet/index.html

68 Balfour, Frederick. "The Way, Way Back Office." Business Week 3 Feb. 2003. http://www.businessweek.com/magazine/content/03_05/b3818011.htm

69 Kably, Lubna. "Tax offshoring gets US thumbs-up." The Economic Times 16 Dec. 2003. http://economictimes.indiatimes.com/articleshow/359117.cms

70 Gentle, Chris. "The Cusp of a Revolution: How offshoring will transform the financial services industry." Deloitte Research, 2003. Deloitte Consulting Group, London U.K. http://www.deloitte.com/dtt/cda/doc/content/CuspRev%20DRf.pdf

71 Monastersky, Richard. "Is There a Science Crisis? Maybe Not." The Chronicle of Higher Education 9 July 2004. http://chronicle.com/free/v50/i44/44a01001.htm

72 Lazarus, David. "Crucial PG&E design information goes to Thailand." San Francisco Chronicle 5 Nov. 2003: B-1. http://sfgate.com/cgi-bin/article.cgi?f=/c/a/2003/11/05/BUGV72QC5P1.DTL

73 Coster, Helen. "Legal services are moving offshore -- will India's lawyers help reshape the U.S. legal market?" 1 Nov 2004. http://www.lawwave.com/bnews.htm

74 Fried, Jennifer. "Outsourcing Reaches Corporate Counsel." The Recorder 25 Aug. 2004. http://www.law.com/jsp/cc/pubarticleCC.jsp?id=1090180413835

75 Aman, C. "Going Off the Clock," Mar 2003 http://www.reser.net/download/Bryson_etc.pdf

76 Fried, Jennifer. "Outsourcing Reaches Corporate Counsel." The Recorder 25 Aug. 2004. http://www.law.com/jsp/cc/pubarticleCC.jsp?id=1090180413835

77 Solomon, Jay. "India's New Coup In Outsourcing: Inpatient Care." The Wall Street Journal 26 April 2004: A-1. http://online.wsj.com/article/0,,SB108293099927892916-email,00.html

78 Solomon, Jay. "India's New Coup In Outsourcing: Inpatient Care." The Wall Street Journal 26 April 2004: A-1. http://online.wsj.com/article/0,,SB108293099927892916-email,00.html

79 United Nations Conference on trade and Development (UNCTAD), Geneva, Switzerland. "FDI to Asia Booms, Fuelled by Hong Kong." UNCTAD Press Release 18 Sept. 2001: Box 1. http://www.unctad.org/Templates/webflyer.asp?docid=2524&intItemID=2022&lang=1

80 Dept. of Health and Human Services, Food and Drug Administration, Washington D.C. "Human Subject Protection; Foreign Clinical Studies Not Conducted Under an Investigational New Drug Application." [Docket No. 2004N-0018] Federal Register 10 June 2004:69(112), pp. 32467-32475. http://wais.access.gpo.gov

81 "US outsourcing prayers to India." 15 Jun 2004 http://sify.com/news/othernews/fullstory.php?id=13498514

82 Mehlman, Bruce P. "Offshore Outsourcing and the Future of American Competitiveness." Assistant Secretary for Technology Policy, U.S. Dept. of Commerce, Presentation 2003. http://infopolicy.org/pdf/mehlman.pdf

83 Institute for the Study of Labor, Germany. "IZA – Facts & Figures." IZA Impressum 2003: http://www.iza.org/index_html?lang=en&mainframe=http%3A//www.iza.org/en/webcontent/charts &topSelect=charts

84 Castillo, Monica D. Bureau of Labor Statistics, Washington D.C. "Persons outside the labor force who want a job." Monthly Labor Review July 1998. http://www.bls.gov/opub/mlr/1998/07/art3full.pdf

85 "EU cuts 2005 growth estimates." EU Business Ltd. 27 Oct. 2004. http://www.eubusiness.com/topics/Finance/forecasts.2004-10-27

86 Jing, Fu. "Policy makers weigh milder 2005 targets." China Daily News 8 Dec. 2004. http://www.chinadaily.com.cn/english/doc/2004-12/08/content_398475.htm

87 Economic Policy Institute, Wasington D.C. "Income." Facts & Figures: State of Working America 2004/2005, EPI Feb 2005. http://www.epinet.org/books/swa2004/news/swafacts_income.pdf

88 Landler, Mark. "International Business; France and Germany Dogged by Joblessness." New York Times 1 Apr. 2005: C4. http://query.nytimes.com/gst/abstract.html?res=F3091FFA3B5B0C728CDDAD0894DD404482&incamp=archive:search

89 Shinal, John and Kirby, Carrie. "Trying to cope when a job goes overseas; Workers left devastated as companies rush offshore." San Francisco Chronicle 7 March 2004: A-14. http://www.sfgate.com/cgi-bin/article.cgi?f=/c/a/2004/03/07/MNGRT5G2GL1.DTL

90 Arlington County Commuter Services, Arlington County Department of Environmental Services, Transportation Division. Arlington, VA U.S. "ACCS Service Environment; Arlington Profile." Commuter Assistance Program at http://www.commuterpage.com/ACCS/capserv.htm

91 Ptacek, Liz and Buss, Nicholas, PNC Real Estate Finance. Bach, Robert, Grubb and Ellis. "Myth or Reality: No worse, no better, no hope? Catching up with the office market." September 2003. http://www.grubb-ellis.com/research/WhitePapers/MythorReality.pdf

92 "New Survey Shows Americans Deeply Divided Over Off-Shoring By U.S. Companies, But ELA Poll Reveals Strong Preference For Government Penalties; Non-Union Workers Look To Unions For Help." U.S. Newswire 7 June 2004. http://releases.usnewswire.com/GetRelease.asp?id=103-06072004

93 Gilmor, Dan. "Now is time to face facts, make needed investment." San Jose Mercury News 14 Mar 2004

94 Badger, T.A. "White-collar blues: Workers weigh unionizing as off-shoring spreads to desk, lab jobs." The Associated Press 8 June 2004. http://www.post-gazette.com/pg/04160/328465.stm

95 Website http://www.hireamericancitizens.org

96 Kletzer, Lori G., Institute for International Economics, Washington D.C. "A Prescription to Relieve Worker Anxiety." Policy Brief 01-2 March 2001. http://www.iie.com/publications/pb/pb01-2.htm

97 PTI, New York. "Indiana lawmakers oppose anti-outsourcing bill." Press Trust of India 2 Dec. 2003. http://economictimes.indiatimes.com/articleshow/335111.cms

98 Hollings, Ernest F. "Protectionism Happens to be Congress's Job." Washington Post 21 March 2004: B-3. http://hollings.senate.gov/~hollings/opinion/2004321442.html

99 Oates, James. "German chancellor attacks 'unpatriotic' offshoring." The Register 23 March 2004. http://www.theregister.co.uk/2004/03/23/german_chancellor_attacks_unpatriotic_offshoring/

100 Cox, Michael W. and Alm, Richard. "The Great Job Machine." New York Times 7 Nov. 2003: A-27. http://www.nytimes.com/2003/11/07/opinion/07COXX.html

101 Kirkegaard, Jacob F. Institute for International Economics, Washington D.C. "Outsourcing – Stains on the White Collar?" Feb. 2004.
http://www.iie.com/publications/papers/kirkegaard0204.pdf

102 Kudrolli, Shakeel and Narayanan, Anoop. Majmudar & Co., Bombay India. "A changing IP Environment." http://www.buildingipvalue.com/05_AP/316_319.htm

103 Bush, Pres. George W. "President Talks Jobs/Trade at Women's Entrepreneurship Forum" Speech by the President at the Women's Entrepreneurship in the 21st Century Forum, Cleveland Convention Center, Cleveland, Ohio 10 March 2004.
http://www.whitehouse.gov/news/releases/2004/03/20040310-4.html

104 Schroeder, Michael and Rebello, Joseph. "U.S. Survey Finds Few Jobs Moving to Offshore Homes." The Wall Street Journal 11 June 2004.
http://online.wsj.com/article/0,,SB108688437416433828,00.html?mod=home_whats_news_us

105 Sanders, Bernie. "Anti-Offshoring Bill Lacks Silicon Valley Support." Business Journal 4 March 2004. http://bernie.house.gov/documents/articles/20040304115312.asp

106 Farrell, Diana. "Who Wins in Offshoring." International Herald Tribune 7 Feb. 2004.
http://www.mckinseyquarterly.com/article_page.aspx?ar=1363&L2=7&L3=10

107 Mieszkowski, Katherine. "How India is Saving Capitolism." Salon 1 Apr. 2004.
http://www.salon.com/tech/feature/2004/04/01/collabnet/index_np.html

108 World Trade Organization, Geneva Switzerland. "International Trade Statistics 2004."
http://www.wto.org/english/res_e/statis_e/its2004_e/its04_bysubject_e.htm

109 International Data Corp. http://www.dailytimes.com.pk/default.asp?page=story_20-10-2003_pg6_1

110 Reuters. "IBM looks to China in Mainframe Push." CNET News 7 Oct. 2004.
http://news.com.com/IBM+looks+to+China+in+mainframe+push/2100-7339_3-5401083.html?tag=st.ref.goo

111 Staff. "IBM to train 40,000 IT students in Asia." ZDNet Asia 6 Sept. 2004.
http://asia.cnet.com/news/systems/0,39037054,39192570,00.htm

112 Armstrong, David. "Bay Bridge to Beijing." San Francisco Chronicle 25 July 2004. http://sfgate.com/cgi-bin/article.cgi?file=/c/a/2004/07/25/BEIJING.TMP&type=printable

113 "The Internet Economy Indicators." Online database: http://www.internetindicators.com/features.html "India's Trade with U.S.: U.S. Trade with India (2005)." Source: U.S. Census Bureau 2005. http://www.indiaonestop.com/tradepartners/us/indo_us_trade.html

USCBC, U.S.-China Business Council, Washington D.C. "Understanding the U.S.-China Balance of Trade." http://www.uschina.org/statistics/2004balanceoftrade.html

114 Parker, Robert C. "Evolutionary Manufacturing Discussion Group: Success Story #2." Rocky Mountain Institute, Snowmass, CO U.S. Sept. 2002. http://www.rmi.org/sitepages/pid656.php

115 Organization for International Investment, Washington D.C. "The Facts About Insourcing Jobs to America." Online FAQ datasheet: http://www.ofii.org/facts_figures/

116 Pink, Daniel H. "The New Face of the Silicon Age: How India became the capitol of the computing revolution." Wired News Feb. 2004: 12(2). http://www.wired.com/wired/archive/12.02/india_pr.html

117 Wolfensohn, James D. President, World Bank Group. "Eradicating Poverty For Stability And Peace." Speech for Governors of the World Bank and International Monetary Fund, Annual Meeting, 3 Oct. 2004. http://web.worldbank.org/WBSITE/EXTERNAL/NEWS/0,,contentMDK:20264454~menuPK:34457~pagePK:34370~piPK:34424~theSitePK:4607,00.html

118 Wales, Jane. President & CEO, World Affairs Council of Northern California, San Francisco CA. "It's Your World." KQED Radio Show Sept. 2004.

119 Kristof, Nicholas D. "The Tiananmen Victory." The New York Times 2 June 2004: A-19. http://www.nytimes.com/2004/06/02/opinion/02KRIS.html

120 Porter, Eduardo. "Send jobs to India? Some find it's Not Always Best." The New York Times 28 Apr. 2004:A-1. http://select.nytimes.com/gst/abstract.html?res=FA0E1FF7355E0C7B8EDDAD0894DC404482

121 Porter, Eduardo. "Send jobs to India? Some find it's Not Always Best." The New York Times 28 Apr. 2004:A-1. http://select.nytimes.com/gst/abstract.html?res=FA0E1FF7355E0C7B8EDDAD0894DC404482

122 Trimble, Dan. Managing Director, The Convere Group, San Francisco CA. Personal communication.

123 Dossani, Rafiq and Kenney, Martin. Asia-Pacific Research Center, Stanford University, Stanford CA U.S. "Went for Cost, Stayed for Quality?: Moving the Back Office to India" Nov. 2003. http://iis-db.stanford.edu/pubs/20337/dossani_kenney_09_2003.pdf

124 "Information Technology CEO's call for renewed focus on U.S. growth and competitiveness." Press Release - Computer Systems Policy Project 7 Jan. 2004. http://www.bobpearlman.org/Strategies/Offshoring/ChooseToCompetePressRelease.htm

125 Moore, Geoffrey. Personal communications. 8 Jan 2004

126 Kanellos, Michael and Spooner, John G. "Barret Weighs In." CNET News 1 June 2004. http://news.com.com/Barrett+weighs+in/2008-1001_3-5222863.html?tag=nefd.lede

127 Lochhead, Carolyn. "Tech bosses defend overseas hiring: Intel, HP chiefs warn that U.S. needs to improve education system." San Fransisco Chronicle 8 Jan. 2004: A-1. http://www.sfgate.com/cgi-bin/article.cgi?file=/c/a/2004/01/08/MNGDI45PV01.DTL

128 "Intel's chief sounds ominous warning about U.S. software industry." Associated Press 13 Oct. 2003. http://www.smh.com.au/articles/2003/10/13/1065917314223.html?from=storyrhs&oneclick=true

129 "Intel's chief sounds ominous warning about U.S. software industry." Associated Press 13 Oct. 2003. http://www.smh.com.au/articles/2003/10/13/1065917314223.html?from=storyrhs&oneclick=true

130 Lohr, Steve. "NEW ECONOMY; Debate Over Exporting Jobs Raises Questions on policies." The New York Times 23 Feb. 2004: C-1. http://query.nytimes.com/gst/abstract.html?res=F10911FD3D580C708EDDAB0894DC404482

131 Karp, Jonathan. "Raytheon Engineers Fly High With Low-Tech Gear; Giving the "Whirl" a Whirl." Wall Street Journal 8 Sept. 2004: A-1. http://www.raytheon.com/feature/bike_shop/

132 Headd, Brian and Krafft, Rebecca. U.S. Small Business Administration, Washington D.C. "Small Business Economic Indicators for 2003." National Technical Information Service, Springfield VA, Aug. 2004. http://www.sba.gov/advo/stats/sbei03.pdf

133 Audretsch, David B. and Thurik, A. Roy. "Capitalism and democracy in the 21st Century: from the managed to the entrepreneurial economy." Journal of Evolutionary Economics Jan 2000: 10(1-2) pp. 17-34. http://www.springerlink.com/openurl.asp?genre=article&issn=0936-9937&volume=10&issue=1&spage=17

134 Headd, Brian. U.S. Small Business Administration, Washington D.C. "Redefining Business Success: Distinguishing Between Closure and Failure." Small Business Economics 2003: 21 pp. 51-61. http://www.sba.gov/advo/stats/bh_sbe03.pdf

135 Audretsch, David B. and Thurik, A. Roy. "What's new about the new economy? Sources of growth in the managed and entrepreneurial economies." The Istitute for Development Strategies, Indiana University Jan. 2001. www.spea.indiana.edu/ids/pdfholder/ISSN-01-1.pdf - Good on many economic items

136 Petron, Maureen. National Association for the Self Employed, Washington D.C. "Senate Health-Care Bill For Self-Employed Is "Major Step Forward" For Nation's Smallest Businesses." NASE Press Release 19 May 2004. http://news.nase.org/nase_about/pressrelease.asp?PRID=82

137 Jacoby, Jeff. "GM's healthcare dilemma." The Boston Globe 16 June 2005. http://www.boston.com/news/globe/editorial_opinion/oped/articles/2005/06/16/gms_healthcare_dilemma/

138 United States Patent and Trademark Office, Washington D.C. "Fiscal Year 2000 USPTO Annual Report." http://www.uspto.gov/web/offices/com/annual/2000/index.html

139 Nemiroff, George. "Space Ship One Designer talks about flight's future." The Desert Sun 21 Dec. 2004. http://www.thedesertsun.com/news/stories2004/local/20041220215558.shtml

140 Port, Otis. "Space Ship One's Heady Flight Path." Business Week 1 Oct. 2004. http://www.businessweek.com/technology/content/oct2004/tc2004101_6291_tc119.htm

141 Thursby, Jerry G. and Thursby, Marie C. "University Licensing under Bayh-Dole: What are the Issues and Evidence?" MIT Opensource Database May 2003. http://opensource.mit.edu/papers/Thursby.pdf

142 Thursby, Jerry G. and Thursby, Marie C. "University Licensing under Bayh-Dole: What are the Issues and Evidence?" MIT Opensource Database May 2003. http://opensource.mit.edu/papers/Thursby.pdf

143 Hopkins, Jim. "Google shows how schools turn research into big bucks." USA Today 13 May 2004. http://www.usatoday.com/money/industries/technology/2004-05-13-stanford_x.htm

144 Office of Technology Licensing, Stanford University, CA. Presentation and personal communication. http://otl.Stanford.edu

145 Wysocki Jr., Bernard. "College Try: Columbia's Pursuit of Patent Riches Angers Companies." The Wall Street Journal 21 Dec. 2004.

http://online.wsj.com/article/0,,SB110358988812705478,00.html?mod=home%5Fpage%5Fone%5Fus

146 Thursby, Jerry G. and Thursby, Marie C. "University Licensing under Bayh-Dole: What are the Issues and Evidence?" MIT Opensource Database May 2003. http://opensource.mit.edu/papers/Thursby.pdf

147 "Higher Education Retail Market Facts and Figures 2005" Almanac 2004-2005, Chronicle of Higher Education 27 Aug. 2004. http://www.nacs.org/public/research/higher_ed_retail.asp

148 Eagar, Thomas. "Role of Technology in Manufacturing Competitiveness." Testimony given at a hearing before Subcommittee on Environment, Technology, and Standards Hearing on Manufacturing R&D: How Can the Federal Government Help? 108th Congress - 1st Session, Washington D.C. 5 June 2003. http://www.house.gov/science/hearings/ets03/jun05/eagar.htm

149 Begley, Sharon. "Research Push: Anxious for Cures, Grant Givers Turn More Demanding." The Wall Street Journal 29 Sept. 2004. http://online.wsj.com/article/0,,SB109639542832130226,00.html?mod=home%5Fpage%5Fone%5Fus

150 Thursby, Jerry G. and Thursby, Marie C. "University Licensing under Bayh-Dole: What are the Issues and Evidence?" MIT Opensource Database May 2003. http://opensource.mit.edu/papers/Thursby.pdf

151 Timmerman, Lunke. "A Canadian Way to Make Connections." Seattle Times 11 Oct. 2004. http://www.larta.org/lavox/articlelinks/2004/041011_canadian.asp

152 Timmerman, Lunke. "A Canadian Way to Make Connections." Seattle Times 11 Oct. 2004. http://www.larta.org/lavox/articlelinks/2004/041011_canadian.asp

153 Murphy, L.M. and Edwards, P.L. "Bridging the Valley of Death: Transitioning from Public to Private Sector Financing." National Renewable Energy Laboratory, Golden CO, U.S. May 2003. http://www.nrel.gov/docs/gen/fy03/34036.pdf

154 Advanced Technology Program "How ATP Works." National Institute of Standards and Technology, Gaithersburg, MD U.S. http://www.atp.nist.gov/atp/overview.htm

155 Technology Ventures Corp., California, New Mexico, Nevada, U.S. http://www.techventures.org/NewMenuTechVentures/TVCHome/about.htm

156 Democratic Leadership Council & Progressive Policy Institute, Washington D.C. http://www.ppionline.org

157 Hodge, Scott A., Moody, J. Scott, Warcholik, Wendy P. "The Rising Cost of Complying with the Federal Income Tax." Tax Foundation Special Report No. 138, 10 Jan 2006.

158 Friedman, Milton. "Where Carter is going wrong: size up." U.S. News and World Report 7 March 1977: cover story.

159 National Center for Policy Analysis, Washington D.C. "The Luxury Tax." Online database: http://www.ncpa.org/ea/eama92/eama92k.htm

160 Crane, Edward H. and Edwards, Chris. "Tax Cuts on Savings are the Rx for Strong Growth." CATO Institute, Washington D.C. Investors Business Daily 4 Oct. 2002. http://www.catoinstitute.org/research/articles/crane-edwards-021004.html

161 World Trade Organization, Geneva Switzerland. "International Trade Statistics 2004." http://www.wto.org/english/res_e/statis_e/its2004_e/its04_bysubject_e.htm

162 House of Representatives Small Business Committee, Washington D.C. "Lowering the cost of doing business in the United States: How to keep our companies here." Hearing before 108th Congress, 20 Nov 2003. http://www.house.gov/smbiz/hearings/108th/2003/031120/

163 "Manufacturing R&D: How can the federal government help?" Hearing before the Subcommittee on Environment, Technology and Standards, Committee on Science, U.S. House of Representatives 108th Congress 5 Jun 2003. http://commdocs.house.gov/committees/science/hsy87544.000/hsy87544_0.htm

164 "Draper Fisher Jurveston On the Record: Tim Draper." San Francisco Chronicle 13 March 2005: B-1. http://sfgate.com/cgi-bin/article.cgi?f=/c/a/2005/03/13/BUGQQBND5L1.DTL

165 Dossani, Rafiq. "Chinese and Indian Engineers and their Networks in Silicon Valley." Asia Pacific Research Center, Stanford University. Stanford, CA. March 2002. http://www.infopolicy.org/pdf/Dossani.pdf

166 Kamins, Ted. Hewlett Packard. Personal Interview. 17 May 2004

167 Bruce Mehlman Mehlman, Bruce P. "Offshore Outsourcing and the Future of American Competitiveness." Assistant Secretary for Technology Policy, U.S. Dept. of Commerce, Presentation 2003. http://infopolicy.org/pdf/mehlman.pdf

168 "The 2003 Index of Silicon Valley." Published by Joint Venture: Silicon Valley Network, San Jose CA www.jointventure.org

169 Bronson, Po. Speech, San Francisco, CA. 7 May 2000. http://literati.net/Bronson/

170 Schneiderman, Ron. "Outsourcing: How Safe is Your Job?" Electronic Design 10 May 2004. http://www.elecdesign.com/Articles/Index.cfm?ArticleID=7993&pg=3

171 “Fueling the High Tech Workforce with Math and Science Education.” Hearing Charter, U.S. House of Representatives Committee on Science. 23 Jan. 2004. http://www.house.gov/science/hearings/full04/jan23/charter.htm

172 Democratic Leadership Council & Progressive Policy Institute, Washington D.C. http://www.ppionline.org

173 U.S. Dept. of Labor, Washington D.C. “Career Management Account Demonstration Project Evaluation.” Final Report Dec. 1998, prepared by Public Policy Associates, Lansing MI and Corp. for a Skilled Workforce, Ann Arbor MI. http://www.publicpolicy.com/reports/CMAReport.pdf

174 Employment and Social Services Policy Studies Division, National Governor’s Assoc. “Worker Displacement Continues Even in Good Economic Times.” StateLine 8 Sept. 1998. www.nga.org/cda/files/090898WORKER.pdf

175 “Clues to the Cure For Unemployment Begin to Emerge: One-Stop Career Centers And Cash Incentives Yield Successful Job Searches.” The Wall Street Journal 13 Oct. 2003. http://www.kctcs.net/todaysnews/2003/20031014.html

176 “Clues to the Cure For Unemployment Begin to Emerge: One-Stop Career Centers And Cash Incentives Yield Successful Job Searches.” The Wall Street Journal 13 Oct. 2003. http://www.kctcs.net/todaysnews/2003/20031014.html

177 Kletzer, lori G. and Litan, Robert E. “A Prescription to Relieve Worker Anxiety.” U.S. Economics Policy Brief #73, March 2001. http://www.brookings.edu/comm/policybriefs/pb73.htm

178 Roth, Mark. “Wage Insurance: a way to ease outsourcing angst? Pittsburg Post-Gazette 24 March 2004. http://www.post-gazette.com/pg/04084/290519.stm

179 U.S. DOL BLS 1999 could it be one of the reports listed here? http://www.bls.gov/opub/ils/opbilshm.htm

180 Foreign Policy Assoc., survey conducted by Zogby International. 22 Sept. 2004. http://www.zogby.com/news/ReadNews.dbm?ID=870

181 Rice, Condoleeza, Secretary of State. Speech: Press Release in Nomination of Karen P. Hughes and Dina Powell, Ben Franklin Room, Washington D.C. 14 March 2005. http://www.scoop.co.nz/stories/WO0503/S00246.htm

182 Walt, Stephen M. “Two Cheers for Clinton’s Foreign Policy.” Foreign Affairs March/April 2000. http://www.foreignaffairs.org/20000301faessay28/stephen-m-walt/two-cheers-for-clinton-s-foreign-policy.html

183 Walt, Stephen M. "Two Cheers for Clinton's Foreign Policy." Foreign Affairs March/April 2000. http://www.foreignaffairs.org/20000301faessay28/stephen-m-walt/two-cheers-for-clinton-s-foreign-policy.html

184 Center for Applied Linguistics, Washington D.C. "Foreign Language Instruction in the United States: A National Survey of Elementary and Secondary Schools." National K-12 Foreign Language Survey Results 1997. http://www.cal.org/pubs/results.html

185 EuroEducation.net "Sweden" Education System Profile http://www.euroeducation.net/prof1/swedco.htm

186 .S. Dept. of State, Washington D.C. "Passport Statistics: U.S. Passports Issued Per Calendar Year (1974-1995)." Online Datasheet: http://travel.state.gov/passport/other_stats.html

187 U.S. Census Bureau, "School Enrollment: 2000 Census Brief." Aug 2003 http://www.census.gov/prod/2003pubs/c2kbr-26.pdf

188 Winter, Greg. "Colleges Tell Students the Overseas Party's Over." The New York Times 23 Aug. 2004. http://www.nytimes.com/2004/08/23/education/23college.html

189 Armstrong, David. "HOMELANDS: VIETNAM New world city Poised on the brink of the future, Ho Chi Minh City is one of Asia's most exciting destinations." San Francisco Chronicle 24 April 2005. http://sfgate.com/cgi-bin/article.cgi?f=/c/a/2005/04/24/TRGE3CCFRP1.DTL

190 "61% Americans fear job-loss due to outsourcing." Rediff.com India Limited 17 March 2004. http://inhome.rediff.com/money/2004/mar/17bpo1.htm

191 Democratic Leadership Council & Progressive Policy Institute, Washington D.C. http://www.ppionline.org

192 Democratic Leadership Council & Progressive Policy Institute, Washington D.C. http://www.ppionline.org

193 Peters, Tom. "'Off-Shoring' Manifesto/Rant: Twenty Hard Truths about Inevitabilities, Pitfalls, and Matchless Opportunities." Tom Peters Company 16 Mar. 2004. http://www.tompeters.com/toms_world/obs_entries.php?note=000650&year=2004

194 U.S. Dept. of Labor, Bureau of Labor Statistics, Washington D.C. "Tomorrow's Jobs." 2 June 2004. http://www.bls.gov/oco/oco2003.htm

195 Friedman, Thomas. "Losing Our Edge?" New York Times 22 April 2004. http://209.157.64.200/focus/f-news/1134073/posts

196 Lochhead, Carolyn. "Tech bosses defend overseas hiring Intel, HP chiefs warn that U.S. needs to improve education system." San Francisco Chronicle 8 Jan. 2004: A-1. http://www.sfgate.com/cgi-bin/article.cgi?file=/c/a/2004/01/08/MNGDI45PV01.DTL

197 LAPCO Paintball Products, San Diego, CA U.S. http://www.lapcopaintball.com/paintcheck.html

198 Gilbertson, Dawn. "Laid off workers flock to motorcycle training school." Arizona Republic 28 Sept. 2003. http://www.billingsgazette.com/index.php?id=1&display=rednews/2003/09/28/build/business/50-cycletraining.inc

199 Staff. "What's Total Been Up To?" Total Performance News Page, Issue #5, 2003. http://www.tperformance.com/enews/e-news.cfm?issue=03-05-03.cfm

200 Abate, Tom. "The new workplace: Job reports can't track those who dropped off radar." San Francisco Chronicle 26 Aug. 2004: C-1. http://www.sfgate.com/cgi-bin/article.cgi?file=/chronicle/archive/2004/08/26/BUGII8E8VI1.DTL&type=business

201 Gates, William, Keynote, National Education Summit on High Schools, 26 Feb. 2005

http://www.gatesfoundation.org/MediaCenter/Speeches/BillgSpeeches/BGSpeechNGA-050226.htm

www.ingramcontent.com/pod-product-compliance
Lightning Source LLC
Chambersburg PA
CBHW031147270326
41931CB00006B/169

* 9 7 8 1 5 8 9 3 9 9 1 3 6 *